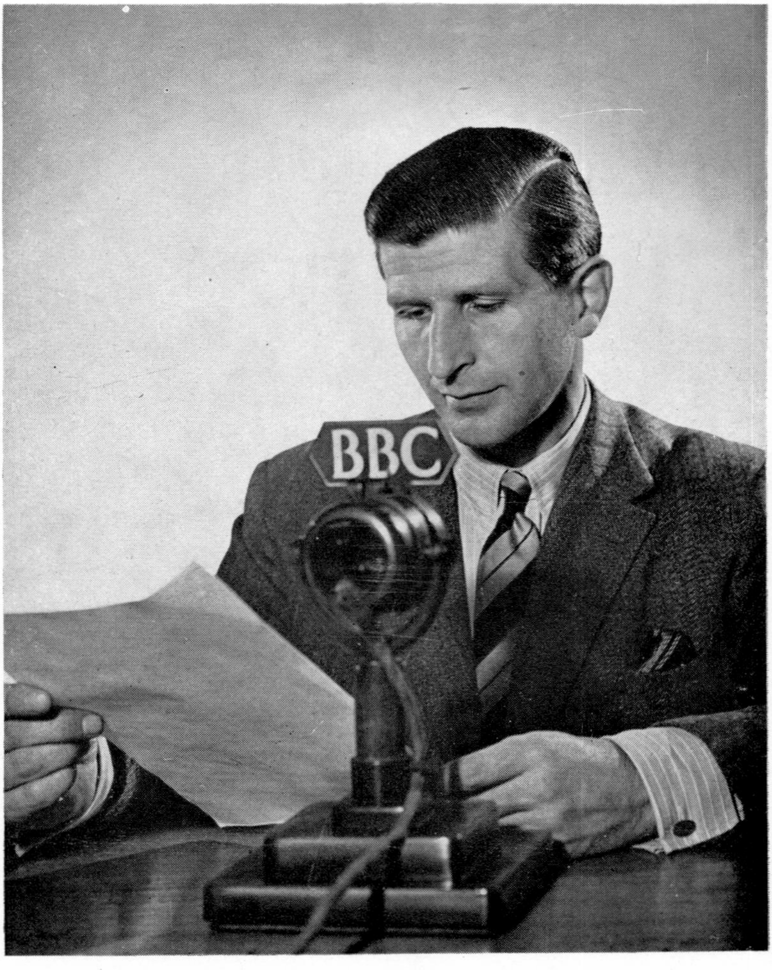

ALVAR LIDELL

SPEECH OF OUR TIME

Edited by
CLIVE SANSOM

Hinrichsen Edition Ltd.
25 Museum Street, London, W.C.1

Printed by
Claridge, Lewis & Jordan Ltd.
68-70 Wardour Street, London, W.1

INTRODUCTION

THIS is, we believe, the first attempt that has been made at a comprehensive survey of speech in this country. It considers the vast opportunities opened up by recent mechanical inventions, the position of speech in education and modern life, and in the arts of poetry and drama. Every article has been written by an expert in that particular department.

The publishers would welcome criticisms and suggestions so that, if a second edition is called for, mistakes or omissions may be corrected and further relevant subjects discussed. They would point out, however, that the authors have been left entirely free to express their own opinions, and that their views are not necessarily those of the editor or the publishers.

Owing to frequent changes and the further complication of a purchase-tax, all prices of gramophone records are omitted. Moreover, in the present state of the trade, book prices cannot be guaranteed, and books and records referred to may no longer be available.

Finally, the editor and the publishers would like to thank all contributors, and the many friends and advisors, whose generous help has made this survey possible.

CONTENTS

Contents continued

The history of speech is also the history of human understanding.

ALAN GARDINER.

Words are our subtillest and delicatest outward creatures, being composed of thoughts and breath.

JOHN DONNE.

Remember that you are a human being with a soul and the divine gift of speech : that your native language is the language of Shakespeare and Milton and the Bible; and don't sit there crooning like a bilious pigeon.

PROFESSOR HIGGINS in 'Pygmalion.'

Speech Survey

By CLIVE SANSOM

AFTER four hundred years' subservience to print, speech is coming into its own again. A change is taking place in society, which we, living in the middle of the revolution, can scarcely realise. But it is important that we should realise it, for it is as great as any that has taken place within human knowledge. Next to the development of speech itself, there have been two landmarks in linguistic history previous to our own time—the invention of writing, and the invention of printing, two methods of recording speech in a visual medium. Writing extended the audience, so that the words of Buddha, Socrates or Christ persisted beyond the lives of their hearers or their hearers' hearers, and persisted more accurately than they could have done by mere word of mouth; it made possible the *accumulation* of truth. The audience was still further enlarged by the printing-machine, for there was now no limit to the number of copies of each book, and only illiteracy separated the individual from the source of knowledge. From then onwards the printed word acquired a status far higher than the spoken word. Everyone could speak—after a fashion; not everyone could write. So that literacy became synonymous with power. Schools and universities gave their whole attention to writing and reading, ignoring the speech from which these had both derived.

In the last century, when universal literacy was the chief aim of compulsory education in this country, the supremacy of print was at its height. Reading and writing were more than keys to learning; they represented social and financial advancement, perhaps the difference between poverty and security. And then, when universal literacy (or semi-literacy) had just been achieved, there came the third invention which cut at the very roots of this supremacy—the speech-machine. The effects of the telephone, gramophone, radio and talking-film are as tremendous and far-reaching as those of the printing-press, and they are taking place all around us at this moment. For speech no longer requires a visual medium for either communication or permanence. It can come direct from speaker to listener, across space and out of time. It will take an historian to appreciate the significance of this in terms of human development, but two things at least are clear. First, that the written word can no longer claim a supremacy over the spoken word; indeed it may find it increasingly difficult to hold its own. Secondly, leaving aside work of real literary importance, the efficient speaker is becoming a more valuable asset to the community than the efficient writer. "Vocal literacy" will very soon assume the importance that visual literacy has enjoyed during the last four hundred years.

While all this has been going on, the supremacy of the written word has been challenged from other directions. Improved transport and greater opportunities for travel have been destroying the barriers of distance, and making direct communication more necessary. Phoneticians have been increasing our awareness of speech—how different people use it, and how the same person uses it under different conditions. Psychologists have been removing some of the complex coatings of our minds, revealing the relationship which exists between speech and thought, between speech and emotion, between speech and image, between speech and action; and showing us the central position held by speech in the development or retardation of the individual. Speech therapists have been developing a scientific treatment of those defects of speech which are the result of inner disharmony, and, basing their work on that of the phoneticians, psychologists, and even anthropologists, they are treating the patient and his defect at the same time. And lastly there have been those engaged in the actual work of speech training, who have helped to destroy the odium in which elocution was held for a long period, when it was too often treated as an artificial accomplishment removed from reality and daily life. All these considerations have made it certain that, in the world of the immediate future, speech will be more important than ever before. The ability to express one's thoughts and feelings clearly, fluently and intelligibly in speech, and to discuss with others, will be an essential need.

SPEECH EDUCATION

But what are we doing to equip ourselves and our children to live in such a world? Very little, it must be admitted. The Universities, which to some extent still set a pattern for education, concentrate on the written word. Nowhere does the criticism that the Universities are out of touch with modern life seem more justified than in their attitude to the spoken language. The position in the teachers' training colleges is rather better. Several have lecturers in speech, others consider the subject under their general "English" course. But in some it is still neglected, and in the majority "Speech" comes after handicrafts in order of importance, being fitted in wherever the other subjects permit. Yet speech is a key-subject. In whatever part of school work the student is interested, speech is his means of communicating it to his pupils. If the chief means of communication is faulty, how can he succeed in interesting and informing his class? In the schools themselves, the position varies from complete omission to something approaching perfection, everything depending on the interest of the head teacher or the enthusiasm of a staff-member. Where there is genuine interest and understanding, the standard of speech can be surprising high; where there is none, the result is only too obvious. The whole question of Speech Education is covered in a series of ten articles in this book, but future needs might be summarised as follows:

Universities

(1) A Department of Speech in every university, well-staffed, adequately housed. and thoroughly equipped for research on every side of the spoken language

(2) Compulsory attendance at speech lectures by all Arts students.

(3) Candidates for an English degree to satisfy the examiners in oral as well as written tests.

Training Colleges

(1) Adequate training for the students' themselves—in voice production, to improve ease of expression and carrying-power (apart from vocal strain, the psychological effect on children of harsh, strident voices has yet to be explored); in oral expression, so that they can "put over" their thoughts and explanations, simply and clearly; in speech and articulation, including an acceptable pronunciation.

(2) An oral test as part of the end-of-course examination, the result to be included on the Principal's report.

(3) Lectures on phonetics and the theory of speech, together with the discussion of practical methods of helping speech development in the school.

Schools

(1) Encouragement in the right use of speech from the Infant class to school leaving.

(2) An English curriculum more evenly balanced between the spoken and written sides of the language.

(3) Far more opportunities for using speech—verse speaking, choral speaking, talks, discussions, drama, puppetry, school parliaments, etc.

(4) The School Certificate or Matriculation examination to include an oral test in English.

(5) A speech clinic, or qualified speech therapist, under every educational authority, for the treatment of stammering and other nervous speech disorders.

Every child, whatever his school or parentage, should leave school expressing his thoughts and feelings intelligibly, and able to use a type of speech that will not limit him to any one class or district.

STANDARD ENGLISH

This last suggestion always raises a great deal of controversy. Most educationists have done their best to ignore it, and governmental committees have been generously vague about it in their reports. But it is a subject which must be faced sooner or later. We underestimate the part played by speech in social life. Our reactions to a speaker's quality of voice or type of pronunciation, to news-readers or political speakers, the associations and prejudices called up by a certain tone of voice — these and a hundred other aspects of the same problem might be worth studying by "Mass Observers" with some phonetic training. But one thing is clear from the start. "Accent," in a community where wide discrepancies in clothing, income and housing are quickly disappearing, remains the great class barrier, at least as formidable as the colour bar in the United States. And we shall be a democracy only in name so long as this barrier exists.

The question needs to be considered reasonably and dispassionately. What, for instance, is meant by "standard English"? Certainly not a standardised or robot speech. Speech could not be standardised, even if we wished, because the speakers who use it are as individual as their finger-prints. Speech is a matter of thought and emotion, not merely of sounds, so that what is known loosely as "standard English" would no more standardise our speech than a uniform spelling has standardised our style of writing. (Charles Morgan and Ernest Hemingway spell words with a uniformity that would have appalled the Elizabethans, but their styles are as individual as those of Shakespeare and Jonson). Nor, as Lloyd James said, can "standard English" be exactly measured, like a standard yard or a standard pint. But it is capable of this negative definition : the type of speech "that can be heard from Land's End to John O'Groat's without producing active discontent."

The opponents of this type of English complain that it will kill the dialects. Yet dialects were endangered long before the question of "standard English" arose. A language follows the life and character of its speakers. While they are separated into rural communities, the spoken language will retain its divisions; when the country is unified, the language will tend to follow suit. Dialects have survived largely because groups of people have lived in isolation from one another. Now that central government, transport, working conditions and broadcasting are bringing people closer together, dialects must gradually disappear. Already their edges are becoming blurred.

In many ways this tendency is to be regretted. Dialects contain innumerable words that we shall be the poorer for losing. They are rich in colourful phrases and they lend themselves to vigorous speech. Often they are the best means of communication between people of a similar class in the same environment, though they immediately lose their value outside that environment. So long as dialects exist, we should respect them, encouraging children in dialect districts to use their native speech as well as "standard English." But we cannot arrest the change without arresting the social changes which have given rise to it; nor are we entitled to deplore the growth of a "common dialect" unless we are prepared to abandon it ourselves. Before attacking "standard English," we might ask ourselves this question : "Are we willing for our own sons and daughters to leave school using *only* a dialect"? If the answer is "No," then have we a right to advocate it in the education of other men's children? Is it compatible with a democracy that large numbers of children are never taught to master a type of speech that will free them from the ties of class, occupation and district? It seems as if biligualism alone will prevent the complete extinction of dialects on the one hand, and the limitation of children's opportunities on the other.

Through bilingualism, too, "standard English" may gain from the dialects. Too often it is spoken without vitality. Indeed, the great danger in speech training is that we shall teach merely "correct" or "refined" pronunciation, forgetting the purpose of speech in a clutter of sounds. Or, almost as harmfully, we may concentrate on speech as an expression of ideas and facts. Really expressive speech springs from the heart and the imagination as well as from the intellect, and speech education will prove unsuccessful if the educational system of which it is a part pays too little attention to these elements. Perhaps that is the chief reason for the loss of spontaneity and originality that takes place in the average child's speech when he leaves the Infant school and enters the Junior. His mind is more educated, but the education of his imagination and sensibility does not receive the same attention. His spirit is often cramped, his appreciation blunted, his mind held down by the dead weight of Facts. The life and freedom of his speech withers, because its roots are no longer watered. Ultimately. more depends on the individual teacher's attitude than on curriculum or equipment. Education. including speech education, must open doors and windows. Or to quote Sir Richard Livingstone's essay on "Plato and Modern Education": "No one should study a subject without becoming conscious of something great, something momentous in it. The small rock-pools of the seashore have a life and beauty and interest of their own, but they owe their freshness and purity to the tides of a vast ocean far beyond our sight and ken."

WORLD ENGLISH

A similar problem may confront us in the world at large. For it seems as if a world standard—a compromise between the existing standards of English-speaking people—will become necessary before long. Already, in talking-films, some kind of compromise is often reached; there is a type of English which "can be heard without producing active discontent" in New York, Toronto, London, Sydney, Wellington and Cape Town. The Mayfair accents of the first British films have been toned down (though not always enough); so has the "tough guy" speech of American films. But there is a danger that what might be called "national dialects" may divide English and, consequently, the speakers of English. "Spoken English must never be allowed to disintegrate into a series of mutually unintelligible dialects; the forces of disintegration, fed by local prejudices. parochial patriotisms, and petty nationalisms, are a menace not only to the unity of the language, but to the unity of the English-speaking peoples. . . . It is possible that all these new speaking machines, telephone, gramophone, radio, film and blattnerphone, have come in time to save the situation."[1] Still, it is a question that calls for thorough consideration and there might well be a permanent committee of experts from the United States, Britain and the Dominions to discuss it.

All this concerns the nations which already use English. But it has also to be remembered that English is now the leading competitor for the position of a world auxiliary language. Even to-day, first out of 1,500 languages spoken in the world, English is the speech of between 150 and 180 million people. Only two things are likely to prevent its acceptance as the world's secondary language—certain grammatical difficulties that have not yet been ironed out of an otherwise simple language, and its spelling. As Sir Richard Paget points out, "The genius of the English-speaking people—the inventors of English—was swift and practical. It made wonderful changes in a very short period, by which the language became immeasurably simplified and more direct and expressive. Unfortunately, the initial effort of our rude forefathers has not been kept up. Literature, and above all the invention of printing, stepped in, and, like the Gorgon's Head before the court of Polydectes, turned all who saw it to stone. There have been hardly any essential improvements in English since the time of Caxton, while in the matter of spelling we have gone measurably backwards."[2] The possibility, which he envisages, for example, of "he do" for "he does" may offend our grammatical susceptibilities, but only if we are prepared to regard English as a language in which progress has been permanently arrested. If considered rationally, this change represents a logical step in its development, in its natural movement towards ever greater consistency and simplicity.

Our spelling is a more immediate obstacle for the foreign learner. Spoken English and written English have become almost separate languages, and the task of acquiring them is twice as long and as complicated as it need be, both for the foreigner and for our own children. English may not become the world auxilary language so long as we insist on tieing twentieth-century speech to a sixteenth-century spelling. There are, of course, innumerable difficulties in the way of spelling reform, or the use of additional symbols in the alphabet, but difficulties no less great have been met and overcome in other countries. In Turkey, for instance, Mustapha Kemal, seeing that the complicated Arabic script, which was incapable of representing Turkish speech-sounds, made general education impossible, adopted the Latin alphabet, invented a more or less phonetic system of spelling, and sent the whole nation to school with himself as headmaster.[3] Similarly in China the classical style of writing which had little in common

1. A. Lloyd James, *The Broadcast Word*
2. *Human Speech*
3. Dr. Bernard Lewis, *Turkey To-day*

with the speech of the time is being replaced by a style founded on the spoken language, with the result that a new literature is being created and millions of people, formerly illiterate, are finding education within their reach.[4] A similar gap exists between speech and writing in India. It is said that 90 per cent. of the population of that country is illiterate, largely because of the difficulty of mastering the written forms of the different languages—where there may be as many as 400 different characters in a single alphabet! If India were to follow Turkey in adopting a series of phonetic alphabets, simply and accurately recording her languages, there is no knowing what the effect might be on India's future.

These digressions show that the conflict between written and spoken language is a fairly general one in the modern world, and suggest that orthology is of great social significance. If the English-speaking nations were to adopt a simplified system of spelling that could be said to approximate roughly to our speech, the impetus to English would be tremendous. It might even justify Professor James's prophecy that English would be a universal language in two centuries. We need to keep open minds on these matters of linguistic change; or English, instead of developing into a world language, may join Latin as a dead one. To quote Sir Richard Paget again, "I believe firmly that the improvement of language is one of the great outstanding needs of the human mind—that it will give to human thought an increase of power such as the substitution of Arabic for Roman numerals gave to arithmetic, or the development of mathematics has given to science, and that we should not allow conservatism or indolent dislike of change to prejudice our minds. . . . It is high time that we began to study systematically how the English-speaking peoples can obtain the greatest benefit from their heritage of a common language. We have a splendid foundation to build on."

BIBLIOGRAPHY

Our Spoken Language. A. Lloyd James (Nelson, 3s.)
The Broadcast Word. A. Lloyd James (Kegan Paul, 8s. 6d.)
Human Speech. Richard Paget (Kegan Paul, 28s.)
Speech. J. R. Firth (Benn : out of print)
The Tongues of Men. J. R. Firth (Watts, 2s. 6d.)
The Miraculous Birth of Language. Richard Wilson (Guild Books, 1s.)
Language. Leonard Bloomfield (Allen & Unwin, 12s. 6d.)
The Loom of Language. Frederick Bodmer (Allen & Unwin, 15s.)
The Gift of Tongues. Margaret Schlauch (Allen & Unwin, 12s. 6d.)
Language: Its Nature, Development and Origin. Otto Jespersen (Allen & Unwin, 16s.)

4. Hsiao Ch'en, *Etching of a Tormented Age*

The Growth of the English Language. H. Wyld (Murray, 5s. 6d.)

The Growth and Structure of the English Language. Otto Jespersen (Basil Blackwell, 6s.)

Mankind, Nation and Individual From a Linguistic Point of View. Otto Jespersen. (Allen & Unwin, 8s. 6d.)

Language as a Social and Political Factor in Europe. Stanley Rundle. (Faber, 12s. 6d.)

Peoples Speaking to Peoples. L. White and R. D. Leigh (Cambridge University Press, 8s. 6d.)

English in the Future. J. H. Jagger (Nelson, 3s.)

SCIENCE AND SPEECH

Science and Speech

By DENNIS FRY

THERE is no scientific subject about which the layman feels himself so well qualified to speak as that of speech itself. Suggest to the man in the street that in point of fact he does not know how he speaks and you will meet with either blank incomprehension or a plain contradiction. Should you go so far as to suggest that his pronunciation is in some particular different from another person's, he will take this either as an insult or a compliment, but certainly not as an item of scientific information.

Fortunately, the certainty that we know all about speech is not shared by those whose business is the scientific investigation of the subject; rather is the opposite the case. Communication by speech is so complicated a process that until recent years it did not form the subject of any very systematic research. When we speak, we set up a train of events which take place in several different worlds, each with its own laws and each demanding different techniques of research. The interchange of ideas by means of speech requires the temporary establishment of a communication chain which appears in its simplest form when speaker and listener are within sight and earshot of each other :

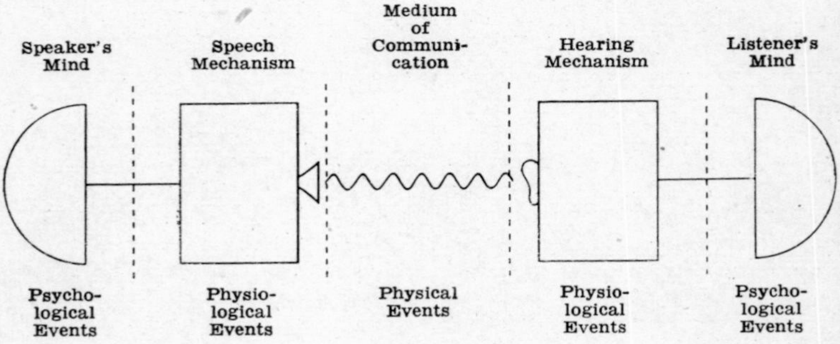

This simple diagram shows the territory which has to be explored; it is evident that the study of speech may take the form of psychological, physiological or physical research.

In practice, obviously, the three spheres will not be conveniently separated from each other; there will be a complicated interpenetration of the three worlds, with the physiological phenomena involving us all the time in physical problems, the psychological entailing the consideration of physiological effects, and so on. It is necessary, therefore, to do what is done in all scientific research, that is to limit deliberately and artificially the scope of the investigation to the observation of some particular type of event. Owing to the fundamentally psychological nature of the activity in speech, the purely physiological or physical information obtained in this way is not ultimately a great deal of use unless its relation to the psychological can be established.

Another fact about speech which adds to the difficulty of investigation is the rapidity with which events succeed each other on all three planes. There never exists for any length of time a "steady state" of affairs, and so observation of events is very difficult. We have, in fact, to make use of two different research techniques. One method is to develop means of recording events to such an extent that they can follow the continual changes which make up speech, at least well enough to avoid giving us a completely wrong view of what happens. The other is to obtain very short cross-sections of the flow of events and to establish what is happening at the particular instant when the cross-section is taken. It will be evident that these two methods are complementary; if we compare an ultra-rapid film taken at 1,000 frames a second with a snapshot taken with a short time-exposure, we see that the first is only an extension of the second method.

It is in the physical world that by far the greatest advances have been made in the scientific study of speech. This is inevitable in view of the importance which the transmission of speech has assumed in the twentieth century. Since the early days of the line telephone, constant efforts have been made to improve the quality of electrically transmitted speech, and the coming of broadcasting gave further impetus to this kind of research.

In the diagram above, the chief realm of physical study is shown to be the medium of communication between the speaker and the listener. In the case of direct communication, this medium is the air, and the subject of physical research the rapid fluctuations in air pressure which give rise to the sensation of sound. When apparatus for transmitting speech is inserted into the medium, the problem is complicated by the process of converting air pressures into varying mechanical and electrical pressures or light intensities. It is worth noting that no matter what electrical or mechanical links are inserted into the chain, the speech event involves (with certain rare exceptions) varying air pressures at the speaker's mouth and the listener's ear.

Research into the physical characteristics of speech is concerned primarily with the wave-form, frequency content and intensity of speech sounds. In recent years, the extensive use of the cathode-ray oscillograph for a time focussed attention upon the wave-form of sounds. Oscillograms of speech were studied and some workers were able to recognize by inspection the type of wave-form which belonged to a given type of sound quality. It was soon realized, however, that analysis of the curves would be imracticable—it is a long and tedious process—and further, that the solutions obtained would not, in many cases, represent the actual physical events, since a Fourier analysis gives all the components as terms in a harmonic series.

The determining of the frequency content of speech sounds by means of electrical analysis has yielded much more valuable results. It has long been held that the recognition of speech sound qualities at the psychological level depends, at the physical level, on the presence of a few specific frequencies or frequency bands in the whole frequency complex of the sound. Before any electrical analysis had been done, Paget was able to determine, by ear alone, the frequency regions which were important in his pronunciation of English vowels. Electrical analysis has since demonstrated the accuracy of Paget's analysis by ear. This electrical method has been used also to determine the frequency bands which are important in the various consonant sounds of the language. As a result of measurements made by combining the technique of electrical filtering with that of articulation testing (see a later paragraph) it is now possible to forecast approximately the efficiency of a transmission system from a knowledge of its frequency characteristic.

The examination of the overall intensity of speech sounds was an inevitable corollary of the study of frequency content and wave-form and has been necessitated, from a practical point of view, by the need for avoiding distortion and overloading in channels used for speech transmission. It is now common practice to express in physical units (decibels) the differences in power between speech sounds, and the information which is expressed in this way is in constant use by the communication engineer; he knows, for example, that a system which will deliver the sound *ee* of "sheep" to the ear at a comfortable level may well introduce distortion of the sound *aw* in "saw" from the same speaker, or that a channel which can transmit a realistic *sh* as in "shop" may leave *f* and *th* as in "fin" and "thin" either inaudible or indistinguishable the one from the other.

The physical picture of speech may be said to be reasonably complete. We know a great deal about the frequencies which go to make up particular sounds, about the relative intensities of these frequencies, about the overall intensity of the sounds and also something about their wave-form. But those who are interested in the physical composition of speech have been very much alive to the interdependence of the three worlds represented in our diagram and have recognized the need for some psychological criterion as to the physical efficiency of a communication system, if one may put it rather paradoxically. The method known as "articulation testing" is an attempt to meet this need. It consists in passing a large number of sentences, words, syllables or sounds over a given circuit and measuring the proportion of these units which is correctly received by a listener. Since the purpose of a communication system is the exchange of ideas between a speaker and a listener, it is obvious that some such method must finally be resorted to in assessing the quality of the system. A detailed account of the various types of articulation tests in use, and of the techniques employed, is to be found in the literature of the subject. One field in which more extensive use of this method might be made is that of building acoustics. It should be possible by means of experimental work to translate into articulation values the physical expression of the acoustic characteristics of a room. Data collected in this way would no doubt be of great value to architects and to all those interested in the design of rooms with desirable acoustic properties.

Turning now to physiological research in speech, this work is concerned with the action of the various parts of the speech mechanism which consists, in its simplest terms, of an air reservoir —the lungs; a reed system—the vocal cords; and variable resonators—the upper throat and mouth. The respiratory movements have been studied by registering graphically the movements of the thoracic and abdominal muscles during speech. These experiments have shown considerable individual variation in the movements made. Everyone makes a certain amount of both thoracic and abdominal movement, but the ratio of the one to the other varies a great deal; in general the ratio of abdominal to thoracic movement tends to be greater in men than in women. No one has yet been able to demonstrate that a preponderance of either thoracic or abdominal movement has any marked influence on the speech quality produced, and indeed there is no evidence to show that any particular aspect of respiration is important from this point of view.

The methods of studying the vocal cords include examination of the cord action in a laryngoscope, usually with the aid of some stroboscopic device, or through a periscope so small that the mouth can close over the shaft and make the normal speech movements with as little disturbance as possible. There has also been some very successful cine-photography of the vocal cords reflected in a laryngeal mirror. In addition to these attempts to see the larynx at work, models have been made to simulate the action of the cords and so examine the possibilities of movement.

Here once again it has to be recorded that no very conclusive information is available. It is fairly well established that the cords vibrate up and down, as well as in and out. and that the neighbouring parts are all involved in the movements made during phonation. The relative phase of the two cords whilst in vibration has not been determined. With the aid of films of the larynx, it has been shown that the ear detects no striking abnormality in sounds produced with only one of the cords moving. The mechanism of pitch-change is another subject which has given rise to many experiments. It is known that the length of the vocal cords is adjusted to change the frequency of the cord tone, but the mechanism by means of which this adjustment is carried out is not yet fully understood. Observations have shown that the movement of the cartilages as a whole may play a considerable part in the action of pitch-change.

Oral movements, and particularly the action of the tongue and soft palate, have long been recognised as most important for the production of speech sounds, but it is only in recent years that much experimental evidence has been collected on the manner in which these movements are made. Improvements in the technique of X-ray photography have made possible reliable radiographs taken with short time-exposures, whilst the development of X-ray cine-photography has made available the first pictures of the tongue in movement. These new tools have not yet been used for any systematic research into the oral movements in speech. Up to the present they have served only to throw into relief certain general facts which were known but not sufficiently appreciated before. The moving X-ray film has shown, for example, that the tongue moves bodily when we speak and acts as a solid plug or plunger of variable shape. It has shown that the movement of the whole tongue is much more important than the movement of any particular part of it in producing differences of sound quality. Again, it has demonstrated the extreme mobility of the soft palate which is seen to be continuously active during speech.

These facts have been strikingly confirmed by the first direct moving pictures of the tongue in action which have recently been made. This work of filming the tongue movements includes some high-speed cine-photography in which 1,000 pictures a second were taken. With such a frequent exposure there is a good chance that the tongue will be photographed at the limit of its movement in any given direction, whereas with the ordinary film rate of 24 frames a second there is a probability that some essential movements will be missed or at least not followed to their limit. A good deal of important information about the tongue movements may be forthcoming as a result of this latest work.

The psychological study of speech has been stimulated almost exclusively by the need for the diagnosis and treatment of pathological conditions, and it cannot be said that the study of normal speech has reached a very advanced stage. Experimental psychology has investigated numerous aspects of auditory perception, but has not yet dealt specifically with the perception of speech and its relation to language. It is true that all work in linguistics is an effort to explore the psychological sphere and its connections with the physiological and physical worlds, but all the work of the various schools of phonetics and phonology, immensely valuable though it is, has not yet succeeded in establishing linguistics as a fully fledged science.

The development of speech in young children is one of the more approachable subjects for examination from the psychological point of view and there exist some excellent detailed studies in this field. From the study of abnormal speech we have gained most of the available information about the functioning of the speech centres in the brain and about the psychological basis of many speech disorders. It is indeed one of the advances of recent years that disturbances like stammering are now treated by psychological methods since they are recognized as having a psychological cause. An interesting light was cast on the connection between the psychological and the physiological speech mechanisms, some years ago, when it was demonstrated that hysterical disturbances could not reproduce the evidence of physiological mal-functioning which was present in even the early stages of genuine pathological conditions. It was found that oscillograms of speech from the second type of patient showed certain well-defined abnormalities which were never present in oscillograms of speech by the hysterical patient.

It would require more space than is available here to give an adequate account of the work which has been done in speech pathology and speech therapy. It can only be recorded that the importance of these subjects is being more and more widely recognized, and this may be expected to give a decided stimulus to research in the psychological and physiological fields.

If this short article has left the impression that the scientific picture of speech is as yet nothing more than a sketch, this is certainly no less than the truth; if it should chance to inspire an attempt to fill in even one detail in that sketch it will have more than succeeded in its purpose. We can probably agree to leave the man in the street in his omniscience, recognizing no mysteries in one of the most complex of human activities.

BIBLIOGRAPHY

No specific references to the literature of the subject have been made in the text, but in the bibliography publications are listed in the order in which their subject-matter is referred to in this article :—

Speech and Hearing. Harvey Fletcher (Macmillan : out of print.)

"Speech recording and analysis with the cathode-ray oscillograph." R. Curry, *Journal of Physiology,* Vol. 83, p. 45, 1935.

Vowel Resonances. Richard Paget (International Phonetic Association, 1s. 6d.)

"Articulation Testing Methods." H. Fletcher and J. C. Steinberg. *Bell Telephone System Technical Publications,* Vol. 8, p. 806, 1929.

Various articles on respiration, *Studies in Experimental Phonetics.* Vol. 27, 1936 (University of Iowa)

"The Mechanism of Speech." G. Oscar Russell. *Journal of the Acoustical Society of America,* Vol. I, p. 83, 1929.

"The Nature of the Glottal Closure for Phonation." R. West. *Quarterly Journal of Speech,* Vol. 21, p. 455, 1935.

"The Mechanism of Laryngeal Pitch." L. H. Strong. *Anatomical Record,* Vol. 63, p. 13, 1935.

The Mechanism of the Human Voice. R. Curry (Churchill, 10s. 6d.)

"Vowel Positions as shown by X-ray." C. E. Parmenter and S. N. Trevino. *Quarterly Journal of Speech,* U.S.A., Vol. 18, p. 331, 1932.

"Synchronised X-ray, oscillograph, sound and movie experiments" *Proceedings of the Third International Congress of Phonetics,* 1935. (Cambridge University Press, £1.)

"The Movements of the Tongue in Speech." J. Yule Bogue and Dennis Fry. *Endeavour,* July, 1944. (Imperial Chemical Industries, 5s.)
The Language and Thought of the Child. J. Piaget (Kegan Paul, 15s.)
Infant Speech. M. M. Lewis. (Kegan Paul, 15s.)
Speech Disorders. S. M. Stinchfield. (Appleton-Century, 21s.)

Speech in Broadcasting

By GORDON McCONNEL

GOOD broadcasting voices are legion; good broadcasters few. The so-called "golden" voice cannot be self-sufficing in radio. Musicians are to a considerable extent dependent upon the high quality of musical instruments for the successful transmission of artistry; a radio talker can achieve world-wide fame with only mediocre vocal equipment. In the brief history of British radio a number of outstanding broadcasting personalities have thrust themselves through the technical processes of the medium, emerging from listeners' receivers intact. How many of these voices could be described as "golden" or musical?—Max Beerbohm, "Dick" Sheppard, John Hilton, J. B. Priestley, Walford Davies, "Mr." Middleton, and, from across the Atlantic, Raymond Gram Swing. All of these have used the microphone effectively. At least two of them have been handicapped by inefficient vocal organs. None of their voices, disembodied, could have scored full marks at an announcer audition, or test, nor would any one of them have been equally effective had their scripts been interchanged. Those speakers have been individually successful when they spoke in the language of their own thoughts, formulated in a lucid idiom, and delivered with a technique that established a personal relationship between broadcaster and listener.

So far as radio talks are concerned, therefore, speech quality appears to be of secondary importance, provided that the pronunciation and phraseology be comprehensible to the audience comprising the broadcaster's target. For technical reasons two physical qualifications are essential. The vocal power must be sufficiently strong to set the broadcasting machinery in motion, and muscular breath control must be adequate for the maintenance of a steady level of sound intensity. The musical pitch of a voice does not necessarily affect a talker's broadcasting value, provided that self-expression be achieved. For average transmission conditions and loud-speaker or headphone reception, baritone quality is more acceptable than the tenor or *basso profundo* registers, and. in the case of women's voices, *mezzo* pitch is preferable to high soprano or true contralto.

Hitherto we have only considered broadcast speech as delivered by laymen, creators and interpreters of programme material who are not members of the broadcasting profession. What of the news-reader and announcer? In this profession voice quality is of greater importance; but even here the "golden" voice is only valuable when it is associated with the requisite kind and degree of intelligence.

A B.B.C. Home Service news-reader is employed by the Corporation to broadcast news and information in a manner comprehensible to, and acceptable to, the widest possible listener coverage *within the British Isles;* and to interpret officially censored and formulated material without any suggestion of personal bias or self-dramatisation.

What constitutes the ideal B.B.C. announcer? Somebody who could read news bulletins regularly day after day to the entire satisfaction of all classes, creeds and communities in the English-speaking world; and who could also act as "presenter," or narrator, in any type of programme from vaudeville to grand opera. This ideal broadcaster only exists in the imaginations of captious critics.

Efficient news-reading, or "news-casting," depends upon an active brain that can assimilate the exact meaning of a bulletin instantaneously, on first sight; a retentive memory for the approved pronunciation of an extensive vocabulary including a long, and ever-growing list of foreign words; clear-cut articulation; a natural feeling for speech rhythm and phrasing. The voice should radiate an impression of authoritative self-confidence, and the dignity of public service—without any trace of bureaucratic arrogance. Is it surprising that many are called to announcer auditions, but few chosen?

Programme material conditions the announcer's output; and nowadays a very wide range of B.B.C. programmes is produced for home consumption. The Corporation also beams many services in the English language to specific audiences overseas. So far as existing conditions permit, the announcers and news-readers in these services have one characteristic in common, although their styles and pronunciations vary: each individual broadcaster has been selected in accordance with the known requirements of his or her own particular audience.

The radio dramatic artist comes into yet another specialised category, and here voice quality is of fundamental importance. By voice alone these players have to broadcast convincing sound pictures of authors' characters. Radio producers to some extent resemble orchestral conductors in that they have to think, plan and direct in terms of sound and all its dramatic possibilities. The casts should consist of players who have been trained to use their vocal organs as instruments of self-expression. For a radio player good voice production is essential, but stage technique should not be imported into radio drama. In a theatre the audience in static, watching and hearing the players from varying distances and angles. A *sotto voce* aside must be loud enough to reach the back of the gallery. In radio the audience is also static physically; but with only one of the senses, the sense of hearing, in action listeners' imaginations are free to soar into whatever realms the producer decides to lead them, playing silent parts in radio productions, invisible eaves-droppers hearing and visualizing the development of plots or ideas, capable of reading the very thoughts of the characters. Hamlet need not voice his soliloquy with gallery-reaching intensity. Hushed tones, whispers even, can be heard by a listener apparently from a range of two or three feet.

This still new technique is not easy for a stage artist to acquire, but once mastered it enables a player to broadcast subtleties of interpretation that could not be attempted on the stage. Owing to technical limitations the requisite emotional range should be conveyed more by variations of vocal colour than by extensive modifications of sound intensity or loudness.

Broadcasters in all three of the categories mentioned, "laymen," talkers, announcers and radio artists, require specialised "conditioning" or training or production. Unfortunately most people labour under the impression that good broadcasting merely consists in "being natural." Broadcasting is a most unnatural operation, and misuse of a microphone can nullify the efforts of writers, producers and speakers. Good microphone technique can be, and is, continually being taught by members of the B.B.C. staff; but the best in radio is innate, something that can be developed but not created.

After twenty-one years of practical studio experience I do not feel inclined to dogmatize about microphone technique, which must depend upon the relationship between broadcaster and listener. In the hour of Nazi domination Hitler's hysterical oratory was good radio; so are the Radio Doctor's intimate, informal chats.

Here is a maxim for all potential broadcasters: "It is not your vocal mechanism, but your manner of speaking that determines your broadcasting value."

BIBLIOGRAPHY

The Broadcast Word. A. Lloyd James (Kegan Paul. 7s. 6d.)

Radio Speech. Sheridan P. Lawton, U.S.A.

Effective Radio Speaking. William Hoffman and Ralph Rogers. (McGraw Hill, N.Y.)

Principles of Effective Radio Speaking. R. C. Borden (Modern Eloquence Corp., New York.)

Speech Signals in Wireless Telephony. A. Lloyd James (Pitman, 3s. 6d.)

"The Microphone Voice." Clarissa Graves. *Good Speech,* Jan., 1938.

"Speech and the B.B.C." Summary of Lecture of Christopher Salmon. Speech Fellowship, *News Letter,* Jan. 1945.

"Phonetics and Broadcasting in Britain." A. Lloyd James. (Third International Phonetics Congress of Phonetic Sciences, Ghent, 1938.)

"The Relation of Phonetics to Broadcasting." A. Lloyd James. *Proceedings of Second International Congress of Phonetic Sciences*, 1935. (Cambridge, £1.)

"You're On the Air." Lionel Gamlin. (Chapman & Hall, 7s. 6d.)

"The Voice of Britain." Discussion on Announcers' Speech. *The Listener*, March 2nd, 1939.

Radio Pronunciations. J. D. Zimmerman. (Oxford, 8s. 6d.)

Broadcast English. Edited by A. Lloyd James (B.B.C. Publications Dept.).

1. "Certain Words of Doubtful Pronunciation." (Out of print.)
2. "Some English Place Names," 1s.
3. "Some Scottish Place Names," 3s.
4. "Some Welsh Place Names," 6d.
5. "Some Irish Place Names," 6d.
6. "Some Foreign Place Names," 1s.
7. "Pronunciation of British Family Names," 1s. 3d.

For addresses see page 211

Film Speech

By ROGER MANVELL

THE artificial reproduction and amplification of the human voice is one of the gifts more recently acquired by our civilisation. In the summer the windows of cinema projection rooms are opened above the street, and harsh resonant voices and rich blares of music pour down to the pavements below. They help us to realise that the film is an entertainment for the eyes rather than for the ears. So we go in to see what the sound is about.

A good dramatist is essentially a writer of good dialogue; he serves his characters and situations through the medium of words. However beautifully produced and set a play may be, the actors depend finally on the quality of the words they are given. But with a film the impact of sight registers first. Consider the conditions in a cinema : the eyes are hynotised into attention. In the silent period an elaborate technique of filmcraft was evolved which developed the possibilities of making this purely visual experience exciting and emotionally expressive.

When sound was added it intensified this visual experience. The film became more real. Nothing increased that sense of reality more than the human voice. The titles went : the fact that the film characters spoke only made us see them more vividly than in the days of their silence.

The expense of making and exhibiting the early sound films meant that the all-talking picture had to be boosted like a giant new toy. The craft of film-making was forgotten in a rush of talking, singing and sound effects. These films were often visually dull or merely vulgar, and time was needed to prove that sound was not everything in the cinema. The fluent dialogue and the effective speeches of the stage were not right for the film. With its realistic potentialities much more in the foreground, it demanded more casual, less artificial speech than the drama. And it needed much less of it. For the screen required movement and action, variety of viewpoint and picture-position.

The standard of film technique set in Britain has been largely created by America. There is no space here to argue the toss about this : it is a fact that approximately 80 per cent. of our screen time is American. For fifteen years American voices have made themselves familiar in this country, and the American idiom, doctored for foreign distribution, has coloured our own patterns of speech. Good American films normally exploit speed of exposition, sureness of characterisation, swift movement from episode to episode, and a rich development of effective situations, whether tough or sentimental. The American idiom leads straight into the wisecrack, the knowing come-back, the resilient phrasing which is so full of imagery that it is half-sides over into poetry. Good American films have all these qualities of speech, timed to the moment by directors and actors so that they will hit the dramatic highspot.

It is a mistake to think that the American idiom is invariably quick. Slickness gives ground before the slow utterance of Gary Cooper, James Stewart, Henry Fonda or Thomas Mitchell. But the secret of American slickness is its sincerity : it belongs to the voice and manner of American society.

As in radio, the film voice has to have qualities which gain in reproduction. These qualities need not be those associated with resonant beauty. A voice need not be golden to be good. Some voices are harsh or dissonant, and through these qualities gain in effectiveness of characterisation and dramatic suggestion, like the voices of Katherine Hepburn, Tallulah Bankhead, Humphrey Bogart and William Bendix. But whatever the vocal qualities of the actor or actresses. the dialogue must be sympathetic to the screen. Artificial though it is, for it serves the end of art, it must come across easily when it is spoken.

The best of the recent British films have developed a scripting technique equal to the brightest American work, though in the slower idiom of the British people. Humour takes the place of gags : reticent dialogue replaces the more usual over-written emotional toplines. The scripting of *San Demetrio London* and *The Way Ahead* never appeared to get in the actors' way as they built up the personalities they had to play. In documentary film equally realistic scripting gave conviction to such pictures as *Target for To-night, The Harvest Shall Come* and *Fires Were*

Started. Some British cinema patrons complain of the slowness of our films. It is curious how the technique and idiom of entertainment can become so denationalised that British people prefer their fellow-countrymen to talk like Americans.

The pre-war French picture at its best (*L'Atalante, Un Carnet de Bal, La Belle Equipe, La Grande Illusion, La Femme du Boulanger, Le Fin du Jour*) approached life very differently from the average American production. The American producer seems normally to look in a prospective film story first for strong dramatic or comic situations, next for the link-up of these situations to the stars he has at his disposal, and only last for points of detail in the personalities of the characters in the story. The French directors seem to reverse this process: characterisation and atmosphere dominate the story, and the actors are immersed in the spirit of the people they portray. The characters in these film stories can be remembered for years, just as it is possible to remember actual people one has met. In American films one remembers the situation, the star, the technique: not often the personality of the characters in the film.

The cinema allows for certain experiments in the relation of speech to situation. In the film of Eugene O'Neill's *Strange Interlude*, the ancient device of the aside was developed so that the characters were able to state their true thoughts while they spoke to each other behind the mask of polite intercourse. When they talked aloud, their lips moved: when they thought, their lips were still, though their faces reacted to the thoughts recorded by their voices on the sound track. This device has re-appeared in many films, in soliloquy, in flashbacks of memory. Poetry was spoken on the screen in the film version of Maxwell Anderson's *Winterset,* but it was spoken so that many people did not realise the rhythm of the poetry.

No film version of Shakespeare's plays has yet been satisfactory. His words are too frequently embroidered with the rich rhetoric and flamboyance of a vigorous declamatory stage tradition to suit the intimate realism of the close-up. Leslie Howard and Norma Shearer almost succeeded with the beautiful imagery of *Romeo and Juliet,* but they seemed always to be the distinguished actor and actress quoting Shakespeare.

The poetry of the screen is essentially the poetry of common speech, of the brief deeply-felt phrases of intense emotion. It is further the integration of such words with visual imagery, so that we realise more intensely the meaning of the outward manifestations of emotion in the actor's face and body. It is these moments which so frequently illuminated the great French films; the restraint of the dialogue left the powers of suggestion to the genius of the director and the actor.

We do not always see the person of the voice we hear. In the news reels the unseen commentator points or blunts the issue aided by appropriate music and sound effects. He demands our attention in such films as *The March of Time.* He speaks impersonally, or at worst facetiously, behind documentary and the so-called interest films. On rarer occasions he becomes part of the dramatic structure of the film, as in the feature *Citizen Kane* and the documentary *The World of Plenty.* The film allows us to watch the faces of our distinguished men and political leaders as they speak to us. It records their expressions as well as their voices : sometimes it records their absence of expression. What is important is that the faces and voices of their leaders can now become intimately known to the people whose affairs they control, and that contemporary events can be shown all over the world a few days after they have happened. The use of films for such record purposes is of the greatest significance : history can now speak directly to succeeding generations.

Next we must consider the question of dialect. The film, like the radio, is very much a national institution, and has increasing international pretensions. When the American voice first resonated through our cinemas British eyebrows arched like the backs of startled cats, but a little practice accustomed us to catch the words. American audiences still find the British standard voice colourless and the slightest dialect unintelligible. The film industry can ill afford to include among its actors people who speak a broad dialect which when recorded will be unintelligible to the relatively slow up-take of British audiences, and the long-hoped-for audiences of America. This means that actors who possess a specialised dialect have to modify its idiom and intonation. Words which are part of the rich dialects like Scots, Cockney, Lancashire and Tyneside have to be ruthlessly cut out. None the less, on a very broad basis, dialect has been introduced into our war films, like *San Demetrio London, Nine Men* and *The Way Ahead.* Comedians like Fyffe, Trinder and Holloway use modified dialect with great liveliness and humour : straight actors like Mervyn Johns and Bernard Miles use their dialect to achieve greater authenticity in their characterisation.

Even in documentary, dialect has made many films difficult to show. Some farming films recorded in south country dialects have been unintelligible to northern village audiences. The problem here has been once more to modify the dialect sufficiently to make it nationally intelligible without so emasculating it that it no longer sounds genuine. But one feels that a proper film record of the British dialects should be undertaken. Britain is peopled by a variety of different temperament-groups, and to see them speak is almost as important as to hear them.

So far, apart from the ever-present American film, the showing of foreign pictures in this country has been severely limited for box-office reasons. Yet some of the finest films ever made have been produced in France and Soviet Russia. When a foreign play is put on in Britain, it has to suffer two serious transmutations : translation and interpretation by a British producer and his actors. The film need not suffer these interventions. It can either be "dubbed," that is have a new sound track recorded in a different language with the dialogue specially spoken in synchronisation with the lip-movements of the original tongue, or it can be titled with a running translation printed at the base of the picture. The latter method is the best, because an absolute minimum of intervention stands between the audience and the foreign artists. We hear the intonations their speech, which are an important part of their acting quality and of the atmosphere of the film. The titles offer comparatively little distraction from the basically visual experience of the picture.

There should be an increased provincial showing of foreign films. They offer one of the few direct experiences the larger British public can hope to have of foreign art and life, with a possible gradual increase of our understanding of and tolerance for customs and temperaments different from our own. Soviet Russia, with a nationalised film industry, encourages the different racial groups within the Republics to make films in their own languages. After the war the film industries of Europe, disrupted and scattered by invasion and racial persecution, are reassembling to continue the work of producing films from the heart of their national life. We are beginning to hear French, Russian, German and Italian voices in our cinemas, as well as American and English. The film can become a power to promote international understanding. As an art it has won the heart of the vast peoples of the cinema-provided world. It remains for us to use it for this common end.

SELECTED BOOK LIST

The Film Till Now. Paul Rotha (Cape).
The Film in National Life. A. C. Cameron (Allen & Unwin).
Film Technique. V. I. Pudovkin (Newnes).
For Filmgoers Only. Edited by R. S. Lambert (Faber)
Film Acting. V. I. Pudovkin (Newnes).
Garbo and the Night Watchman. Alistair Cooke (Cape)
Footnotes to the Film. Edited by Charles Davy (Lovat Dickson.)
Movies for the Million. Gilbert Seldes (Batsford)
History of the Film. Bardeche and Brassilach (Allen & Unwin)
Documentary Film (Revised Edition). Paul Rotha (Faber).
The Film Answers Back. E. W. & M. M. Robson (Bodley Head)
The Cinema To-day. D. A. Spencer and H. D. Walyey (Oxford)
America at the Movies. Margaret Thorp (Yale Univ. Press.)
The Rise of the American Film. Lewis Jacobs (Harcourt Brace).
Film. Roger Manvell (Pelican Books, 1s.)

Also *Sight and Sound* and other periodicals of the British Film Institute, Great Russell Street, London, W.C.1.

Gramophone Records

WRITING and printing enabled men to record speech, very sketchily, in another medium. Then with the invention of the gramophone it became possible, for the first time, to record speech itself. In its early days these records, too, were imperfect; but continual experiment has produced methods which give an accurate reproduction of the original, conveying not only the easily definable qualities of speech, such as pronunciation and emphasis, but something of the personality of the speaker that lives in the tone and timbre of the voice.

Thanks to Alexander Graham Bell and others, the speaking and singing voices of men and women long dead can be preserved, and posterity can hear them as if they were contemporaries. But the gramophone is helping to register types of speech as well as speakers. Nothing has been attempted in this country on the scale of the Linguistic Survey of the United States, though our own styles of speech, in proportion to the size of country, are much more varied; but a beginning has been made with the dialect records of the British Drama League, described by Mr. Whitworth in the next article. There is scope here for a benevolent millionaire to finance a really comprehensive survey of English dialects, in gramophone or Blattnerphone recordings, which there is still time.

The gramophone, however, has more than interest or historical value. It is indispensible in the study of language. Records can never replace the teacher, who is needed to point out faults which the student is generally incapable of recognising in his own speech—subtle but essential differences in pronunciation, stress, intonation and rhythm—but they can supplement the teacher's work and save him a great deal of hard labour. They also give the student an opportunity of listening to different voices speaking the same language and, more important still, the voices of native speakers. The experiment of using records of children's voices in the teaching of children's classes is another experiment that should have far-reaching effects. A sentence spoken by an adult sounds very different in pitch and in range of intonation, from the same sentence spoken by a boy or girl. Children's work is sure to gain from hearing the style of speech used by those of their own age in other countries.

Another advantage of the gramophone is that the student can play the record in odd moments. Not only will he be able to devote a few minutes every day to the language, but it will turn his attention to the *spoken* language, which is the chief means of communication in any tongue, whereas a text-book tends to confine him to the written. The student can also concentrate, with the help of a "groove indicator" (H.M.V., 2s. 6d.) on those parts of the record which present special difficulties for him. So it is not surprising that Lloyd James said, "Learning a foreign language nowadays without a gramophone is like learning chemistry without a test-tube."

The gramophone is of considerably less value in the teaching of one's own language; there are so many examples of living speech around one. Records, however, have been used with some effect as demonstration-lectures for teachers living in rather remote parts of the country—notably the three experimental records made by H.M.V. of speech training and choral speaking in Infant, Junior and Senior classrooms (page 147). Examples of fine speaking are also useful in school work, and records of different dialects might help to break down the prejudices which most of us have in regard to the "accents" of counties outside our own.

But the chief educational value of the gramophone, in connection with the teaching of English, is likely to be the recording of the students' own voices. This is a subject which might well receive the consideration of educationists, especially those concerned with the training of teachers. In the United States every training college possesses a reliable recording apparatus. With play-back equipment, students' voices can be repeated immediately after speaking, and these records can be kept to show their progress from the beginning of their first year to the time they leave college. One of the most difficult things in the world is "to hear ourselves as others hear us." Few can listen accurately to other people's speech; with our own it is almost impossible unless we have had some systematic training. But a good play-back gramophone can take us outside ourselves and enable us to listen objectively. The teacher's work of pointing out errors or differences in speech is made easier and—very important where anything so intimate as speech is concerned—more impersonal. It is to be hoped that some such equipment as the Western-Electric "Mirrophone" will soon be available for use in English training colleges, and that the principals of these colleges will take advantage of it. The cost would be small compared to the present outlay on equipment for physical training and science, and it is no less necessary.

Details of speech records are given in the bibliographies to many of the articles in this book. Chief among them are:

	Page
Spoken English for Foreign Students	180
Learning Foreign Languages	189
Dialects	36
Spoken Poetry	136
Choral Speaking	147
Actors' Voices	154

These particulars are taken from the Editor's lists in *Good Speech* for July 1937 and *Spoken English* (Methuen), and also from the library of records in the possession of the Rev. H. Dagnall.

Addresses of leading gramophone companies producing speech records and apparatus are given on page 211.

BOOKS

How to Make Good Recordings (Audio Devices, 1600 Broadway, New York City, $1.25)

Recordings for School Use. J. R. Miles (World Books, New York, $1.25)

Audio-Visual Aids. McKown & Roberts (McCraw-Hill Co., New York, $3.00)

Recording Dialects

By GEOFFREY WHITWORTH

WHEN the British Drama League decided to undertake a survey of the principal dialect variants still spoken throughout the British Isles, I had little idea of the magnitude of the task which lay before us. Twenty-four variants were to be studied as examples of the speech current in twenty-four parts of the country, and these examples were to be placed on permanent record by means of the gramophone. In this and in other lands, as we soon discovered, dialect records are not unknown. Collections exist in phonetic institutes on the Continent and in America. The catalogues of the leading gramophone companies include items—mostly humorous—by singers and reciters of dialect, song and verse. But ours was certainly the first attempt to record the principal variants throughout the United Kingdom, and on a basis which was in some degree scientific.

As a matter of fact, the extent of the field to be covered precluded a strictly scientific line of approach. The confusion of tongues around the Tower of Babel must have been insignificant compared with that which has evolved since then. In Yorkshire alone the Yorkshire Dialect Society has envisaged the need of no fewer than 100 records if justice is to be done to the complicated network of dialect forms whereby throughout the Ridings one can almost distinguish the inhabitants of one hamlet from those of another by their way of speech. So we must acknowledge that the twenty-four records in our series touch but the fringe of the problem. Though we have provided a large-scale map which is serviceable enough as indicating the general lie of the landscape, the addition of many smaller-scale sections would be needed by any traveller who prefers the byways to the highways.

The recognition of these limitations did not, however, discourage us; for it must be remembered that the project had been undertaken by the Drama League not so much in the interests of research as to provide actors and stage producers with a trustworthy standard of reference when in doubt about the pronunciation or intonation required in performances of dialect plays.

Dramatists are not normally concerned with the precise degree of latitude or longitude on which their scenes take place. Audiences still less. For our particular purpose, then, a skeleton series would serve, and with four examples from Scotland, two from Wales, two from Ireland, and the remaining sixteen from England, our large-scale map might be regarded as fairly complete.

The omission of certain important dialects will no doubt be severely criticized. But there is nothing to prevent these gaps being filled later on should the occasion arise and the demand prove sufficient. And here it should be noted that even so much could never have been accomplished had it not been for the help so generously given by the committee responsible for the ordering of the series, by the speakers who offered their services free, and by those institutions and individuals who responded to our first appeal for subscriptions to guarantee the heavy initial expense involved in the manufacture of the records. For, strangely enough, the project did not appeal to the trade as a commercial proposition, and had therefore to be undertaken and carried out by private enterprise.

Having decided on the counties to be included in the series, the next problem which faced the committee was the choice of speakers. Originally we had planned to discover the rustic talking at his ease in the village "pub" or the factory hand at work on his job. Like the cameraman who photographs the bird on its nest, we would track our innocent victim to his haunts, and then, unseen and unsuspected, imprison through the microphone his native woodnotes wild. But, as we soon discovered, even if the expense had not been prohibitive, technical difficulties were. So we were forced to abandon the chase and content ourselves with conveying the speakers one by one to London, to the studios of the Columbia Graphophone Company, which had been commissioned for the actual work of recording. What may have been lost in sentimental verisimilitude would be more than gained in the perfection ensured by the facilities of expert reproduction. Moreover, we could now concentrate on finding practised speakers for the task—an essential condition if the records were to provide more than an unintelligible mush of sound or a hybrid imitation of "standard" English.

A Cockney speaker had been highly recommended as "the real thing." By birth and calling he certainly was. But at rehearsal he broke out into an almost perfect Oxford accent. It was only as we said good-bye that he forgot himself so far as to relapse into his own vernacular and show us what an excellent speaker had been lost to us by the veneer of "education" that he had been too self-conscious to lay aside. One of the best records was subsequently obtained from a Cockney of equally unassailable pedigree. Being an amateur actor in an East-End settlement dramatic society, he was able to enter into the spirit of the thing and to give us an authentic contribution.

Profiting by this experience, our speakers were now sought

without prejudice of class or position. The list includes a working bootmaker, a builder, a doctor, a farmer, and an actor. All were real natives of their respective counties and men, with few exceptions, who had lived all their lives there and had thus maintained a daily contact with the speakers of the soil. For the most part the items recorded are verses and local stories of the speaker's own choice, with extracts, when these were suitable, from Shakespeare, Robert Burns, William Barnes, Tennyson, Kipling, Synge, Shaw, and Mary Webb. Each record starts with the same "Standard Passage," which is thus common to all the records, and consists of a short monologue based on Skeat's *Phonetic Survey* (1884) comprising in the shortest possible space all the sounds in the phonetic alphabet. This "Standard Passage" suffers curious changes as it comes from the lips of the different speakers. It is fascinating to hear the identical subject matter in successive forms, as varied as those current, for instance, in Devon, Aberdeen, Norfolk and Eire.

Playing over the records, the listener will be at once convinced of a truth well known to those who have made a serious study of dialect in whatever language. With rare exceptions dialect variants are not, as is sometimes thought, degraded forms of a pure and pristine type. On the contrary, dialect conserves an earlier mode of speech that is rooted in the past and is itself the expression of some forgotten but historic racial settlement or invasion. Thus in the county of Somerset we find three distinct dialects spoken to-day, probably indistinguishable, or largely so, to a stranger but easily recognised by the initiated. The River Parret, which flows through the centre of the county to the sea at Bridgwater, was for many centuries the border between Saxon and Briton, and it is easy to understand that North Somerset is predominantly Saxon in origin, West Somerset predominantly British, and Mid Somerset a mixture of the two. These racial origins have left their traces in the local speech. Dialect is fossilized history.

There are of course, exceptions. What we now call "Standard English" is nothing else but a shadowy relic of that more racy and more coloured "Middle English" which was once spoken in the midland counties of England, but scarcely survives to-day as a spoken, much less as a literary, form. Seeking in Shakespeare's own county for an example of this central stock of English pure and undefiled we found no speaker worthy to provide an extract from his plays. We were driven to fall back on the neighbouring county of Oxfordshire, where a Banbury man rendered some lines by Autolycus from *The Winter's Tale*.

Most of the speakers were themselves greatly interested in the subject, and all those from the south were agreed in regarding the death of dialect as only a matter of time. Already dialect vocabulary has suffered a serious diminution. The old words are gradually being filtered out, and our elder speakers would tell of such and such a word or phrase, remembered from their boyhood, that was now obsolete. Pronunciation and intonation are a different matter and these may persist in individual areas long after the etymological idiosyncrasies of their dialect have faded away.

As we travel northwards, dialect resumes its hold. The influence of London is no longer paramount, and big cities like Manchester and Leeds can even assist in maintaining the local character of speech, though they tend to furnish new peculiarities of intonation which in some cases suggest a definite break from the family type. This may actually result from a physical deterioration in the vocal apparatus—as in London where, according to Miss Elsie Fogerty, Cockney speech is, in its more nasal forms, attributable to the permanent "cold in the head" of the slum dweller.

True dialect, however, is utterly alien, as I have already ventured to suggest, from any process of deterioration, and the ultimate test to apply is the ability of the dialect to provide a vehicle for first-rate works of literature. It is evident that a poem by Burns translated into the normal language of to-day would not be the same thing, any more than a translation from French or German can be accepted as identical with the original work. So long as human life in various parts of our country maintains essential differences, so long will dialect persist, and so long will it remain valuable. It is right and proper that the thoughts of a Scotsman or a Cornishman should be subtly distinct from the thoughts of a Londoner and these distinctions are articulated in the spoken word. The trend of modern existence seems to lie in the direction of standardization. This trend is promoted not only by our system of state education, but also by the activities of the British Broadcasting Corporation, and more than all by the ever increasing dislike which people feel for remaining long in the same place. A population which is always hurrying to and fro is likely to acquire a common way of speaking. More, self-interest demands that peculiarities of speech should be eliminated. It is only the aristocrat who can afford such survivals as "huntin'" and "shootin'."

All this may be regrettable, but the conscious effort to preserve dialect is probably as useless as the conscious attempt to revive, by artificial means, the Gaelic language in Ireland or in Scotland. It is true that from time to time certain groups or sections of society will always evince a liking for novel speech forms, and their affectations will be ardently imitated by those who desire to enter the group. The "Oxford accent" is a new dialect in embryo, and the same impulse is at work in the clipped inaudibilities of the bright young things. But on the whole there is little doubt that dialect as we have hitherto known it will pass away. Only such records as the Drama League has provided will be left as a monument to qualities of speech which to posterity, we believe, will remain at least as charming and as interesting as they seem to us to-day.

DIALECT RECORDS

The following are the records referred to in this article. They are intended primarily for actors taking part in English dialect plays, but they should be in the possession of anyone who is interested in dialects from any point of view. There are twelve double-sided records in all. They may be had for £4 10s. 0d. complete, or 7s. 6d. each, from the British Drama League, 9 Fitzroy Square, London, W.1:

1. Cornwall : Richard Noall.
   Devon : Abel Johns.
2. Somerset : J. A. Garston.
   Dorset : Walter Bawler.
3. Gloucestershire : T. Hannam-Clark.
   Oxfordshire : F. H. Grisewood.
4. Shropshire : Edward Benbow.
   Lancashire : L. Shaw.
5. Westmorland : John Mason.
   Northumberland : Rowland Lishman.
6. East Riding : F. Austin Hyde.
   West Riding : Joe Lunn.
7. Lincolnshire : Arthur Newstead.
   Norfolk : H. Fitch.
8. Cockney : George Cross.
   Sussex : R. W. White.
9. Scottish Border : John Laurie.
   Ayrshire : James Woodburn.
10. Fife : John Oliphant.
    Aberdeen : William Dalarno.
11. North Wales : W. J. Gruffydd.
    South Wales : D. Haydn Davies.
12. Ulster : Richard Mantell.
    Eire : Tony Quinn.

SOME BOOKS ON DIALECTS

English Dialects. Walter Skeat (Cambridge, 2s. 6d.)

English Dialect Dictionary. Joseph Wright. 6 vols. (Oxford, Out of print).

Etymological Dictionary of the English Language. Walter Skeat (Oxford. Out of print.)

English Pronunciation through the Centuries. H. C. K. Wyld, 3 records (Linguaphone, £1 2s. 6d. the set).

History of Modern Colloquial Speech. H. C. K. Wyld (Blackwell, 8s. 6d.)

Growth and Structure of the English Language. Otto Jespersen (Blackwell, 6s.)

American Dialect Dictionary. Edit. Harold Wentworth (T. Y. Crowell Co., U.S.A., $6.00.)

Publications of the English Dialect Society, Philological Society, and local dialect and folk-lore societies. (Enquire at the Central Office of the County Library.)

Speech in Modern Telephony

By A POST OFFICE ENGINEER

In the early days of telephony the main requirement was to obtain the maximum possible output of sound from the receiver with the minimum input of electrical power, and the maximum possible output of electrical power from the transmitter (or "microphone") when the user spoke into the mouthpiece in a normal voice.

In order to obtain this maximum sensitivity both the receiver and transmitter were made to have resonant moving systems. The frequencies which were then transmitted extended mainly over a narrow band of only about 600 to 1,800 cycles per second, although the speaking voice contains frequencies from about 80 to 10,000 cycles per second. It was found however, by trial, better to transmit a narrow band sufficiently loudly to be heard than to use less resonant apparatus which would give better quality speech but be inaudible over the longer lines.

The loss of power (attenuation) in the transmission line was found to be a minimum when heavy gauge overhead wires were used. The congestion caused by the rapidly growing numbers of overhead wires made it necessary to put them underground wherever possible. Unfortunately, however, the loss of power (or attenuation) is then much greater. For example, if wire weighing 100lb. per mile is placed in a cable it is only possible to use it over one quarter of the distance over which it could be used if placed overhead in the open.

The first big step towards an improvement in underground telephony was made by Pupin in his application of Oliver Heaviside's theory, who had shown that by adding inductance in series in the wire the effect of the capacity can be reduced. The inductance can be added in the form of coils of wire at intervals (Pupin's scheme) or by winding fine iron wire spirally over the copper conductor. These methods, known as coil and continuous loading respectively, have been considerably used.

In coil loading the coils are inserted at regular intervals along the line and reduce the attenuation at frequencies from very low up to some upper limit (known as the cut-off point). Above this limit the attenuation rises suddenly and nothing is transmitted. If the coils are placed too far apart the cut-off will occur at a low frequency.

Modern telephony can be said to have commenced with the invention of the thermionic valve. This enabled amplifiers to be placed in long distance lines to increase the distance over which speech can be transmitted and also made accurate measuring instruments possible. Before the advent of the thermionic valve trial and error methods only could be used to effect improvements. The valve made it possible to make acoustic measurements and has led to the development of telephone receivers with a response which is reasonably constant from 200 to 3,000 cycles per second. Transmitters have also been improved and give not only more output than the earlier ones but an output which is far more uniform with frequency.

Further development lies in the reduction of the remaining distortion present in the transmitter. This chiefly consists in the non-proportionality between the output and the intensity of the sound input, and the production of harmonics and of beat tones between the different frequencies present in the speech input. Progress in this direction is being made.

Tests have shown that 98 per cent of the intelligibility of speech is conveyed by the frequencies between 300 and 3,400 cycles per second and it has been agreed internationally that this band shall be transmitted. The use of amplifiers (known as "repeaters") at suitable intervals along a line together with light loading (*i.e.*, small coils placed at moderate intervals) or no loading, with equalisers (combination of coils and condensers) associated with the amplifiers has enabled this frequency band to be transmitted with negligible distortion to almost any distance over quite light underground conductors (usually weighing 20lb. per mile). Large numbers can hence be made up into one cable. Also as the wires are small and as amplifiers only transmit in one direction it has become the custom to use four wire circuits for long distances, one pair of wires carrying the speech in one direction and another pair in the other direction.

Using four wire circuits, it is possible to work the amplifiers so that there is almost no overall loss between the terminals of the long distance line. Good transmission can then be obtained between the telephones, even if wires weighing as little as 6½ or even 4lb. per mile are used in the cables from the local exchanges to the telephones.

The next step in line economy was the introduction of carrier working, by which the band of frequencies belonging to one channel was separated from another by being placed 4,000 cycles-per-second apart. The standard system in this country is a twelve-channel one; the channels being assembled at the sending end and sorted at the receiving end by means of filters, and the original audio frequency band restored.

By means of this system the complete twelve channel "group" is transmitted over one pair of wires (with amplifiers at intervals), the corresponding return path being a similar group on a second pair of wires.

Carrying this principle still further, a number of such groups can be further modulated and assembled into a super group, and a number of super groups simultaneously transmitted over a common cable. At present this system is in use on most of the main routes in this country, and up to 400 separate audio channels transmitted without mutual interference. Frequencies up to 3,000,000 cycles per second are involved, and in order to transmit them without loss, a special "coaxial" cable is used. This consists of a single wire held centrally by spacers in a tube about ½in. diameter. One tube is used in each direction with an amplifier about every 7 miles. For example, between London and Birmingham there are 19 4-stage amplifiers in each direction, or a total of 152 valves, all of which will be used by each pair of subscribers making a call. Special problems are involved in the design of these amplifiers, as they each have to handle the whole 400 simultaneous conversations without interference between them.

Research is going on in all countries to make it possible to span greater distances at lower cost. Many thousands of trained workers are engaged and the apparatus grows more complex, requiring greater skill and knowledge in its manufacture and maintenance, but the big increase in the number of conversations transmitted, keeps the cost per connection low.

From the subscriber's point of view, the important matter is to get the message from speaker to listener with the least effort at one end and the least misunderstanding at the other. To accomplish this, the following suggestions summarised from the Post Office pamphlet, *Speaking on the Telephone,* may prove useful:

> The first essential is to speak close to the mouthpiece and directly into it. If you move away from the mouthpiece, far more than a proportionate volume of sound will be lost without reaching the telephone. The instrument can only transmit the sounds which reach it. If you keep close to the telephone, there is little need to raise the voice, but you must speak clearly. In particular, sound your consonants distinctly. They are apt to be blurred in telephone transmission, and therefore need greater precision than in ordinary speech. A medium level of tone, at a low pitch rather than high, is the most serviceable. Speak with reasonable deliberation. Give the vowels their full ordinary value. Do not allow the voice to drop at the end of a sentence.

Talking Books

By J. DE LA MARE ROWLEY

FROM 1920 onwards, the Technical Research Committee of the National Institute for the Blind considered many different inventions for recording speech, with the object of finding some system whereby the blind—particularly those unable to master finger-reading—could "read" by listening to the spoken word. Several inventions were tested but were found either impracticable or too expensive, and research ultimately crystallized into two main lines of approach to the problem, the gramophone disc and the film strip. In 1934 the Technical Research Committee decided to set up an experimental studio in London, in order to study both these methods and a Sound Recording Committee was appointed, under the Chairmanship of Sir Ian Fraser, St. Dunstan's volunteering to bear half the costs of the experimental work. Both the gramophone and film methods were found technically practicable, but the cost of the latter was high owing to the absence of commercial demand, whereas the manufacture of gramophone records for reproducing music was already a considerable industry. The gramophone method had the further advantage that Talking Books of this type were already in use in the U.S.A., and it was obviously advantageous if books could be interchanged with the American Libraries.

The main technical difficulties encountered with the gramophone disc method were that disc revolving at the standard music speed of 78 r.p.m. could only reproduce a number of words equivalent to 5 or 6 minutes' reading time, and a whole book would therefore require a large number of discs, making it both expensive and cumbersome. The Sound Recording Committee, after much experiment, eventually produced a 12in. disc, cut at 200 grooves per inch, running at 24 r.p.m., and giving 25 minutes' reading time on each side. The use of such a record meant that the gramophone for playing it would need a motor capable of successful operation at this slow speed, and a specially lightweight pick-up to ensure that the fine grooves of the record were not damaged. Other problems, such as the finding of a suitable needle and the designing of the machine to make it easy of operation by the blind were successfully overcome, and the Gramophone Companies agreed to manufacture such special records for us.

In 1936 the Talking Book project in its present form was inaugurated by the Sound Recording Committee. The project was of necessity launched on a limited scale, having regard to possible wider developments of the film strip or other methods of recording. A limited number of machines were manufactured, the Committee's policy being to sell them to the blind at manufacturing cost only. A book selection sub-committee was then formed to advise on the most suitable books for recording, and numerous tests were made at the studio to select readers with the right type of voice and delivery. The Publishers' Association was also approached, with the result that authors, publishers, and the owners of copyright invariably grant a generous permission to record copyright works on payment of a nominal fee, provided the recordings are for the sole use of the blind. Lord Nuffield demonstrated his interest in the project by making a magnificent grant of £35,000 to assist its launching.

At the present time the Talking Books Library has issued about 1,800 machines. The majority of these are used by some 1,600 individual blind persons in their own homes, but many are installed in Blind Homes and Institutions. Many local Blind Societies have purchased machines which are lent to various blind persons in their respective areas. Machines are allotted on the basis of 60 per cent. for the needs of the civilian blind and 40 per cent for St. Dunstan's blinded ex-servicemen, both of this war and the last. Nearly 500 machines have also been supplied to Blind Institutions in the various Dominions and Colonies, who have formed Talking Book Libraries of their own, and copies of books are regularly exported to them.

The Central Library has now recorded 464 books, comprising fiction, biography, history, travel, etc. The aim of the Library is to provide amusement and recreation and not, in its present stage of development, to provide educational books or study courses. About half the titles were recorded in the Committee's own studio, and the other half are recordings made in the U.S.A., and purchased by the Committee for circulation in this country. Works of fiction are very popular and a smaller number of readers enjoy books on science, philosophy, etc., as well as plays. There is a well-sustained demand for detective stories. The Book Selection Committee's aim is to provide for all tastes as far as possible and to see that the books chosen are the best of their respective kinds. Certain books which present technical or phonetic difficulties are not suitable for recording, but apart from these exceptions no censorship or text-cutting is imposed on the blind reader as such.

From its inception, the Talking Book Library has been very popular with the blind, and large numbers of appreciative letters have been received testifying to readers' enjoyment of the service. Membership of the Library is free,* and the only expense incurred by its members, after the initial purchase of a machine, is the payment of postage when returning the book containers. By special concession from the Post Office the containers are carried at the Blind Literature Rate, whereby a maximum weight of 15lbs. may be sent through the post for 2½d. Outgoing postage on containers is borne by the Sound Recording Committee, who may also at their discretion assist individual cases of financial hardship towards the purchase of the machine. Three books at a time may be borrowed by members and the reading time allowed is one month. 23,572 books were circulated in 1943, representing the despatch and receipt of 35,128 containers, holding on an average about 12 records apiece. These figures exclude the despatches of Talking Books to the U.S.A., and the Colonies.

Unfortunately, the outbreak of war so soon after the inauguration of the project severely restricted further expansion, particularly in regard to the manufacture of machines, and there is now a considerable waiting list of blind persons anxious to purchase machines whose demands can at present only be met gradually and in rotation. Further difficulties encountered by us have been the shortage of components for servicing machines already issued, and unavoidable shipping delays in obtaining American Talking Books. Restrictions on record material limited the studio production to 25 new books a year, and rendered it difficult to replace worn or broken records quickly enough to

---

*Enquiries should be addressed to the Secretary-General, National Institute for the Blind, 224 Great Portland Street, London, W.1

keep the full number of books in constant circulation. On the whole, however, the Library has maintained its service very well and we look forward to future improvements and further expansion.

Phonetics

By CLIVE SANSOM[1]

"PHONETICS" does not mean merely "phonetic symbols." It means the study of the whole structure of speech—the formation of vowels and consonants, the length and stress of sounds, the intonation given to a string of sounds in conversation, and the characteristic rhythm of a language. All these are covered by the word "phonetics." Phonetic symbols are simply the means of recording, as accurately as it is possible to record anything as changeable and transitory as speech, in terms of writing.

It is important to get this meaning clear, because sometimes a foreign language is alleged to be taught "on the phonetic method" when the pupils learn the symbols only, no attempt being made either to explain the differences between the foreign sounds and our own, or to show how these differences are caused. But phonetic study is no less important in the teaching of our own language. Unless we understand the structure of spoken English, we are like surgeons operating without a knowledge of anatomy. Admittedly, anatomy is not enough, but it is a useful foundation—as the patient would be the first to admit. As Professor Lloyd James said at the International Congress of Phonetic Sciences in 1935 : "Phonetics provides the only safe and sure basis for the study of the spoken word, and it must become a compulsory discipline for those whose business it is to raise the study and teaching of the spoken language from the level of an empirical dogma to that of a rational and scientific body of knowledge."

Some people must have been rationally and scientifically interested in speech several thousands of years ago, for the order of the letters in the Sanskrit alphabet suggests that its inventors realised exactly how these sounds were formed. But the modern study may be said to date from 1569, when John Hart published *Orthographie*. Several other books followed, including the chapters on speech sounds in John Wallis's *De Grammatica Anglicona* (1653), but eighteenth century Englishmen were silent on the subject. Probably they were too busy talking to analyse their talk. It was not until 1848 that *The Essentials of Phonetics* was written by Alexander Ellis, to be followed by the works of Melville Bell, Henry Sweet and others, of which *The Sounds of English* and *A Primer of Spoken English* are perhaps the best known. In his preface to *Pygmalion,* Bernard Shaw describes

(1) The author is indebted to Professor Daniel Jones for supplying him with many of the facts included in this article..

these men as they appeared in the nineteenth century :—

When I became interested in the subject towards the end of the eighteen-seventies, the illustrious Alexander Melville Bell, the inventor of Visible Speech, had emigrated to Canada, where his son invented the telephone; but Alexander J. Ellis was still a

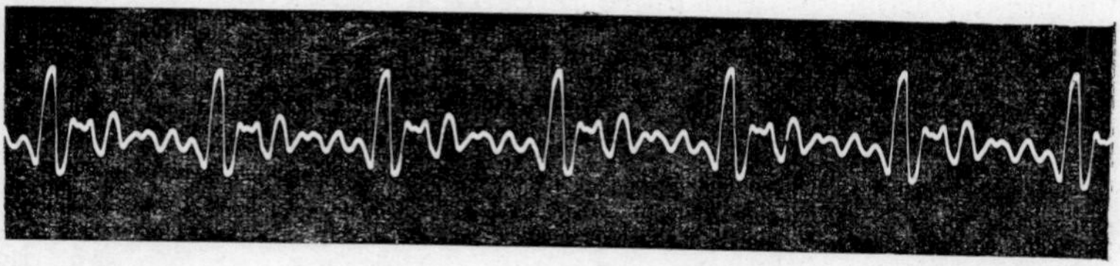

See page 17 **Kodak Ltd.**

The wave-form of a vowel of the type **ah** in "father." This picture was obtained by photographing the trace on the screen of a cathode-ray oscillograph when the vowel was spoken on a fundamental of 150 cycles per second.

London patriarch, with an impressive head always covered by a velvet skull cap, for which he would apologise to public meetings in a very courtly manner. He and Tito Pagliardini, another phonetic veteran, were men whom it was impossible to dislike. Henry Sweet, then a young man, lacked their sweetness of character; he was about as conciliatory to conventional mortals as Ibsen or Samuel Butler. His great ability as a phonetician (he was, I think, the best of them all at his job) would have entitled him to high official recognition, and perhaps enabled him to popularise his subject, but for his Satanic contempt for all academic dignitaries and persons in general who thought more of Greek than of phonetics.

Sweet, as Shaw later puts it, was "squeezed into something called a Readership of phonetics" at Oxford, but "he impressed himself professionally on Europe to an extent that made his comparative personal obscurity, and the failure of Oxford to do justice to his eminence, a puzzle to foreign specialists in his subject." For while this work was going on in England, similar movements had sprung up on the Continent. In Russia, there was Baudouin de Courtenay, a Pole living in St. Petersburg, whose work is still influential in Slavonic countries. It was he who conceived the idea of the "phoneme," a collection of sounds all closely enough related to be recognised as belonging to the same family—for example, the *k* in "keep" is not quite the same as the *k* in "come," but the two are sufficiently similar for the ear to accept them as members of the same group. In France and Germany there were Paul Passy and Wilhelm Viëtor, and a large number of their followers; in Denmark, Otto Jespersen, who died in 1942, and whose knowledge of the English language was so profound. In 1886, the International Phonetic Association was founded. (See page 64).

Back in England, the work of Daniel Jones was recognised by

the University of London in 1907, when he was appointed Lecturer in Phonetics at University College (page 128). His department soon became the chief centre of study in this country, and his influence has had a gradual but far-reaching effect on speech training in Britain and America, and on modern language teaching in general. Extensive researches have been made at University College—and more recently at the School of Oriental and African Studies by Professor Ida C. Ward, Mr. J. R. Firth and others—into the less familiar languages. Dr. Ward's *Introduction to the Ibo Language* and *The Phonetics and Tonal Structure of Efik* represent some of the results of this study. Working in Africa, phoneticians have often had a completely free field so far as orthography is concerned, being the first people to invent written alphabets for these languages. Some of the alphabets, built on the phonetic principle of "one sound, one symbol," have been adopted as the official manner of writing the languages of these territories.

Between 1910 and 1930 the study of phonetics made such progress that the need was felt for a regular international gathering of phoneticians, to discuss their work and share the results of their research—a conference which would not only bring together phoneticians of different nationalities, but also workers in different fields of study, such as phonology, experimental phonetics and psychology. The first International Congress of Phonetic Sciences was opened at Amsterdam in 1932 under the presidency of Professor J. van Ginneken. 136 members came to it, from 16 different countries. The second Congress, in London in 1935, was attended by 262 members from 29 countries. Opening this conference, Professor L. N. Filon, Vice-Chancellor of London University, spoke of the possible value of phonetics in international relations. "For such relations are based upon mutual personal acquaintance, and this can be effective only between those who really understand one another's speech. . . . I think it would be true to say that men nowadays are far more separated by difference of language than by differences of so-called race." At the third Congress, held in Ghent in 1938, there were 273 members, representing 18 academies and societies, 38 universities, and 32 different countries.

PHONETICS AND ENGLISH TEACHING

In our own country, the growth of interest in phonetics is due to a large extent to the late A. Lloyd James, first linguistic adviser to the B.B.C., whose broadcast talks to children and adults helped to popularise a subject that many people had regarded as dry and dull. A great debt is owed to him for acting as interpreter between the phonetician and that elusive and touchy person, the man in the street.

There are several reasons why phonetic study is of value in the teaching of English speech to English pupils. In the first place, it makes us analyse speech and our own attitude towards it. Most people listen to speech, if they genuinely listen at all, through a welter of prejudices and preconceptions. As Professor Daniel Jones has pointed out, the use of certain sounds may recall an unpleasant circumstance, or remind us of somebody we dislike, and we may unconsciously attribute ugliness to the sounds themselves. Take the Cockney "fice," for instance. "Many people think it ugly to pronounce 'face' as **fais.** But if you come to think of it, there is nothing intrinsically ugly about this syllable, or about my pronunciation of it; we use the vowel sound **ai** in 'nice,' 'twice,' and 'ice' without thinking it ugly, and the sound cannot become ugly simply because someone puts an *f* in front of it. In fact, I can imagine that if we were thinking of snow and ice skating, many people might consider the sound of the word 'ice' rather pretty. . . . The real reason why people who pronounce **ei** do not like the sound **ai** is that they connect the variation **ai** with Cockneys and slums and what they call 'vulgarity,' while they connect by a convention **ei** with gentility or elegance or culture." (2) And Professor Ida Ward suggests in her *Phonetics of English* that "the dialect of a distant part of the country may be thought 'quaint' and romantic, while that nearest is looked on as a debased form of English."

The study of phonetics helps us to sort out these prejudices from our genuine impressions and observations. It also encourages us to be more tolerant. The Southerner is inclined to think that the Northern pronunciation of 'laugh' as **laef** is wrong—or, if not wrong, at least 'lahfable.' The Northerner considers the Southerner's pronunciation of this word as 'ugly' or 'affected,' although he himself probably makes the identical sound in a word like 'psalm.' The Northerner, too, regards the Londoner's pronunciation of 'white' (**wait**) without the *h* sound, as a modern defect of speech, although Professor Wyld discovered that this has been a common recognised practice for at least five centuries. For it is another prejudice which dies hard, but which the study of phonetics is helping to kill, that "words should be pronounced as they are spelt." The reverse would be a more sensible suggestion, because speech came before writing, and written English is merely an attempt to record and perpetuate spoken English. It is futile to expect twentieth century speech—something living and developing—to conform to the spelling of Caxton's time.

The third advantage of phonetics is accuracy. It is surprising what statements learned and otherwise intelligent people are prepared to make about speech and pronunciation. In the *Sunday Times* a few years ago there was a lengthy correspondence in which some fifteen people offered fifteen different suggestions for making the Welsh *l*—the voiceless consonant that comes in

(2) Lecture at the British Psychological Society, 1934

'Llangollen.' Only one of these explanations was correct. One also hears constant complaints about speakers who 'drop their voices,' and they are advised to 'keep the voice up at the end of sentences.' Usually there is no appreciable drop in the *pitch* of the voice; the speaker has allowed the tone to decrease in volume, or the energy of breath or articulation to weaken. This kind of inaccuracy, which is bad enough in ordinary commentators, becomes positively dangerous in a teacher.

If, for example, we are to help the user of a local dialect to acquire 'standard English,' the knowledge of two things is essential—(a) exactly how each dialect sound is produced, and (b) exactly how each standard sound is produced. A great deal can be done in speech training by imitation (assuming that the teacher himself is a reliable model), but there are some difficulties which can only be overcome by accurate knowledge, and this is the knowledge which phonetics can supply.

It would be a mistake, however, to assume that the phonetician is trying to kill dialects, or setting out to define good and bad speech. The chief virtue of the phonetician is that he regards speech objectively, and keeps cool about pronunciation where other people often burn with indignation. He is interested in all types of speech, and does not try to label them 'right' or 'wrong,' 'beautiful' or 'ugly.' To him Scots, Dorset, 'Oxford' or 'Standard' English are all equally dialects—that is, variations of English belonging to certain districts or classes. As an individual he may have a preference for one of these varieties, but he recognises this as being the result of his personal make-up, education and environment, and he does not believe that an absolute value attaches to it simply because he uses it himself. His concern is to analyse speech as it is, in all its forms. It is the business of the teacher or the speech trainer to decide what type of pronunciation should be taught in the schools, using the body of information which the phonetician has collected for him.

SOME BOOKS ON PHONETICS

GENERAL

General Phonetics. G. Noël-Armfield (Heffer, 5s.)

The Elements of Phonetics. Wilhelm Viëtor (Dent, 3s. 6d.)

What is Phonetics? H. E. Palmer (Int. Phon. Assoc., 1s. 6d.)

The Phoneme. Daniel Jones (Heffer).

Proceedings of the International Congress of Phonetic Sciences, Amsterdam, 1932; London, 1935; Ghent, 1938.

Le Maître Phonétique. Edited by Daniel Jones. Organ of the International Phonetic Association.

Studies in Experimental Phonetics. (University of Iowa).

Articles in *Quarterly Journal of Speech* (U.S.A.)

ENGLISH PHONETICS

Outline of English Phonetics. Daniel Jones (Heffer, 12s. 6d.)
Phonetics of English. I. C. Ward (Heffer, 5s.)
English Phonetics. Walter Ripman (Dent, 3s.)
Our Spoken Language. A. Lloyd James (Nelson, 3s.)
Phonetics for Scottish Students. I. F. Williams (Jackson, Glasgow, 2s.)
English Pronouncing Dictionary. Daniel Jones (Dent, 7s. 6d.)
Pronunciation of English. Daniel Jones (Cambridge, 4s.)
Pronunciation of English in Scotland. W. Grant (Cambridge, out of print).
Handbook of English Intonation. Armstrong & Ward (Heffer, 5s.)
"Phonetics and its Relation to the Aesthetic Use of Speech." Barbara Storey. *Proceedings of the Second International Congress of Phonetic Sciences* (Cambridge, £1)
See also "English for Foreign Students," page 180, and "Charts, Diagrams and Models," page 195.

Psychologists and Speech

By T. H. PEAR

To many psychologists interested in speaking, the controversy, now rather outmoded, concerning the proper sphere of the psychologist, whether he should limit himself to the study of experience or behaviour, never seemed worthy of consideration. For while any sensible person would naturally do his best to ensure that as adequate a record as possible (by gramophone, film, cinema—natural rate, slow-motion and X-ray) should be made of any speech he wished to study, it would seem perverse not to enquire into the speaker's experience, while uttering or preparing to utter the sounds in question.

"Speech" and "language" are words with so many shades of meaning that they will be avoided here. This chapter is about speaking. The old tripartite division of "modes" of awareness (feeling, willing, knowing, or to use their technical equivalents, "affection," "conation," "cognition") is relevant. The functions of speaking are (a) to induce sympathetic emotion in others (b) to issue directions or commands (c) to impart or to ask for information. Usually when adults speak, all three aspects are discernible, but one is uppermost.

Appreciation of this fact implies that the student of speaking is often a social psychologist, even if he is known professionally under some other name. A. Lloyd James's *The Broadcast Word* contains much social psychology. Most people talk to themselves but seldom, and even those thinkers who, the cruder behaviourists claim do their work by "sub-vocal muttering," are usually thinking in a social relationship. Yet few books on social psychology yet contain any detailed accounts of ways of speaking.

The now popular study of the meanings of words often seems to neglect the important distinction between oral and scriptorial communication (14). In English, for example, intonation and speech-melody are often the chief bases upon which the real meaning of a communicated phrase rests. The vocal skill necessary to produce these—even the state of mind to appreciate them—are not easily acquired by the "foreigner" (though great individual differences exist). This raises the doubt whether certain interviews; for example, those with a psychotherapeutic aim, can be efficiently carried on without a very intimate understanding both by "empathy" and sympathy, of the sounds emitted by the speaker as well as of his gestures, posture and facial expression. Testers of "verbality" usually avoid this complication of their problem. Yet knowledge of the different preferences of examinees for the written examination or the "viva" should make clear the importance of these considerations. Moreover, ability to express oneself orally on controversial matters without antagonising the person or persons spoken to—an important factor in any democracy which needs many thousands of interlocking committees—may have little to do with ability to write a persuasive essay.

The affective aspect of speaking has so far been little studied, except by teachers of elocution or dramatic art. Yet the friendliness or enmity produced by ways of speaking are important factors in the relations between different countries using the same language (e.g. England, as contrasted with the rest of Great Britain, the U.S.A., the Dominions and Colonies) and between different social strata of the same country (cf. almost any English play, especially on the radio, where speech-differences are a goldmine to the producer). It is not only inhabitants of the U.S.A. who are repelled by what seem to them "cissy" or "patronising" accents from the English.

In England itself, ways of speaking which are regarded by the inhabitants of one county as expressing blunt friendliness may seem aggressive and truculent to incomers (also English) from another, and the quiet under-statement characterising one social class may be interpreted as cold-blooded lack of enthusiasm by members of a different one.

Underlying most controversies about "ruling" class and "upper" class manners; the educational advantages of the public schools; the way in which the social hierarchy is mirrored in certain ways of speaking which characterise members of the Forces, there are many factors, to discuss which needs not only the phonetic knowledge of Professor Higgins in *Pygmalion,* but much more social insight than, for good theatre-reasons, Mr. Bernard Shaw allowed him to possess.

In this country discussions about speaking almost inevitably gravitate towards the problems of "Standard English" and dialect. Too often the distinction between geographical and social dialects is omitted—sometimes consciously. At speech-day, prize distributors often urge the pupils (of non-public schools) to stick to their beautiful, historically-interesting, flexible, local dialects while the speaker himself betrays his birthplace in no single syllable. The bitterest opponents of standard English are often themselves play-producers, or academic students of "dialect." Since the latter are sometimes polygot, their plea that nobody in England ought to speak two varieties of the language (even, say, one for addressing millions by radio, the other for making jokes or love) seems rather weak. Moreover, it is difficult to counter the thrust that geographical dialects are laughed at, even if affectionately, by people who do not, or do not now, speak them. "A Cockney Romeo or a Devonshire Hamlet would be laughed off the stage," said a recent radio-speaker. Furthermore, the ways of talking which label classes "lower" than the hearer's own are often actively disliked. If in England a man is being interviewed for a post which will necessitate his speaking in public, he will find "low-class" Scottish less of a handicap than "low-class" Cockney.

Obviously speaking has its cosmetic aspects and it is as old-fashioned to object to them as to the results of other attempts (when successful) at self-beautification.

The psychologist cannot stop short at the study of monologue, since most people speak with the intention of producing an answer. The subject of conversation has not been examined in detail as yet (9) (13), though interesting discussions of the interview, a conversation brought about deliberately, are available (1). A problem for democrats to study, as objectively and with as little prejudice as possible, is how far the privileged or richer social strata have, by means of their greater leisure, opportunities for bodily and mental travel, intellectual exploration and the sense of social security due to their assured position, developed an art of conversation denied to the poorer, harder-working strata. How far the ancient social and cultural developments inside the universities of "Oxbridge" have tended to foster an art of conversation and discussion (not to be confused with undergraduate's stylised debating) superior to that which characterises the "Redbrick" universities is another interesting question, discussion of which requires unusual coolness and recent knowledge of both types of institution.

Most people would admit the desirability of a method of speaking which shall (especially on the radio) produce the maximum of understanding, both cognitive and affective, between the inhabitants of all English-speaking countries, and those understanding English in all other countries. There is, for example, recent evidence that when the speech of Greer Garson, Ronald Colman and Herbert Marshall was modified, more emphasis being given to vowels, this "mid-Atlantic English" was liked by Americans. Many leading speakers, offered the chance of addressing millions about a matter of importance, might be willing to try to effect such changes.

This, however, is related to one of the newest and most interesting problems of social psychology and ethnology; that of "culture pattern" (2, 8, 20) (the pattern into which the dominant sentiments, ideas and values of a culture are woven). The high standard of living in the U.S.A. has inevitably facilitated many deliberate alterations in the outward and visible signs of personality. Speaking is an obvious sign of personality, as experiments have shown (15) with results more striking in England than elsewhere. This fact is easily explained, since our social layering is largely a matter of vocation. In England, up to 1939, many members of the professions and "services" spoke in ways which allowed a shrewd guess at their job, apart from the vocal signs of the social stratum from which the recruits were drawn. Many comfortably-off Americans, however, while intensely face-conscious, are not at all voice-conscious; this assertion many of them make about themselves, while others may believe special consideration of speech to be undemocratic. Here a distinction must be made between manner and matter, for articulate citizenship is implied in all democracy.

BOOKS REFERRED TO IN THIS ARTICLE

1. *The Study of Society*. Edited by F. C. Bartlett. Chapters bv S. Clement Brown, S. F. Nadel and A. Rodger (Kegan Paul, 14s.)
2. *Patterns of Culture*. Ruth Benedict (Harrap)
3. *The English People*. D. W. Brogan (Hamish Hamilton, 10s. 6d.)
4. *The Psychology of Speech*. Jon Eisendon (Harrap, 8s. 6d.)
5. *The Tyranny of Words*. Stuart Chase (Methuen, 7s. 6d.)
6. *The Art of Interrogation*. E. R. Hamilton (Kegan Paul, 8s. 6d.)
7. *Infant Speech*. M. M. Lewis (Kegan Paul, 15s.)
8. *The American Character*. Margaret Mead (Penguin, 1s.)
9. *The Psychology of the Interview*. R. C. Oldfield (Methuen)
10. *The Meaning of Meaning*. C. K. Ogden and I. A. Richards (Kegan Paul, 21s.)
11. *Psyche*. Published annually by the Orthological Institute (10s.)
12. *The Psychology of Effective Speaking*. T. H. Pear (Kegan Paul, out of print)
13. *The Psychology of Conversation*. T. H. Pear (Nelson, 3s.)
14. "Are Linguistic Tests Adequate." T. H. Pear. *British Journal of Psychology*, 1934, XXV
15. *Voice and Personality*. T. H. Pear (Chapman & Hall)
16. "Psychological Effects of a Good Speaking Voice." T. H. Pear. *New Era*, December 1935.
17. "Modern Psychological Problems of Speaking." T. H. Pear. *Speech*, October 1935
18. *Speech in Childhood*. Seth & Guthrie (Oxford, 10s. 6d.)
19. *Good Talk*. E. Wingfield-Stratford (Lovat Dickson, 6s.)

SPEECH SOCIETIES

The Speech Fellowship

By GERTRUDE KERBY (*Hon. Secretary*)

THE Fellowship was founded by Marjorie Gullan and the present writer in 1927. Perhaps the names of its patrons will best indicate the range of its interests : P. B. Ballard, M.A., D. Litt., F. S. Boas, M.A., LL.D., Gordon Bottomley, LL.D., D.Litt., Sir Cyril Burt, M.A., D.Sc., Walter da la Mare, Edith Evans, Eleanor Farjeon, Susan Isaacs, M.A., D.Sc., Daniel Jones, M.A., W. Kingdon Ward, F.C.S.T., M. M. Lewis, M.A., Ph.D., Gilbert Murray, M.A., LL.D., Allardyce Nicoll, E. V. Rieu, A. Maude Royden, C.H., D.D., George Sampson, M.A., Mary Somerville, M.A., Marjorie Tait, Ida C. Ward, D.Litt., and W. E. Williams, C.B.E., B.A.

The aims of the Fellowship have been summarised as follows :

(1) To encourage the study of speech from every angle and for every purpose—social, educational, curative and artistic.

(2) To act as a link between all interested in the spoken language—teachers, lecturers, public speakers, youth club workers, phoneticians, speech therapists, verse speakers and others who, though not actively concerned with speech, realize its vital importance in the community.

(3) To develop speech education so that every child, whatever his school or parentage, is helped to speak effectively, to express his thoughts and feelings, and to communicate his ideas, besides taking his rightful share in the heritage of the English language.

(4) To assist human relationships by stressing the value of speech in the making of personal contacts, the helping of understanding, and the sharing of knowledge and experience.

In pursuing these aims, the Speech Fellowship organised lectures, conferences and teachers' refresher courses in all parts of Britain. In 1932, when the need was felt for regular day and evening classes, two of its most active members—Marjorie Gullan and Clarissa Graves—opened the Speech Institute at 56 Gordon Square, London, which was taken over by the Fellowship two years later. Here, until the outbreak of war, classes were held in speech training, voice production, phonetics, oral expression, public speaking, Bible reading, verse speaking, choral speaking, play production, mime and drama, the psychology of speech, and spoken English for foreigners.

In addition, there were special classes for school teachers in speech training and poetry speaking for children, rhythmic movement, acted ballads, reading aloud, and the use of puppets in speech education. Frequent demonstrations were held at the Polytechnic Cinema, Regent Street, and the Conway Hall. Lectures were arranged with local authorities, and vacation courses held during the Christmas, Easter and Summer holidays at the Speech Institute or University College. Every year from 1927 onwards the London Speech Festival was organised, in which as many as 1,200 children from elementary and secondary schools took part. The entry-fees were merely nominal, in order to allow children to enter from the poorest districts. We always felt, in spite of the loss incurred each year, that this was one of the most rewarding parts of our work.

At the same time, special service work was carried on in various fields, including teaching courses for the National Union of Girls' Clubs, the National Union of Townswomen's Guilds, classes for club leaders, and conversation classes for Czech refugees.

War and evacuation stopped the practical part of the work to a large extent, but it has now been revived again with evening and vacation courses for teachers, and classes for public speakers. Important work not immediately cocnerned with teacher-training was continued right through the war period. But the Fellowship, as its title suggests, also aims at helping to establish a sense of fellowship between people through the medium of speech —and not merely between people, but between nations as well. It regards the language-link between the United States, the Dominions and ourselves as one of the utmost importance. Before the war, lecturers travelled in all parts of North America, attending conferences and lecture courses, giving recitals, and taking part in vacation schools at the leading Universities. Summer schools were arranged in London for overseas visitors, and the membership has now spread to every part of the English-speaking world.

The Fellowship also acts as a centre for the interchange of views. Information and advice is given, free of charge, to members. *Good Speech,* a magazine published quarterly before the war, kept members in touch with each other and with new ideas, methods and developments. It attracted contributors well known in every field of speech work. At present its place is taken by a two-monthly *News Letter,* of some 3,000 words, giving information about talks, books and people, quotations from articles, and reports of meetings.

Saturday afternoon meetings are held, once a month, at our headquarters in Fitzroy Square for the discussion of a variety of subjects. Those in recent months have included "Speech in Education," "Help for the Inarticulate," "Contemporary Poetry," "Speech and the B.B.C.," "New Trends in the Training of Speech," "Basic English," "Links Between Song and Speech," "Youth Organisations," "The Dangers of Speech Training," and "Speech and Citizenship." Besides these, recitals of poetry are arranged, and the Fellowship co-operated with the Save-the-Children Fund for a series of readings by well-known writers from their own work.

There is a library of reliable books, open to members daily from 10 a.m. to 1 p.m., or by appointment. Books may also be borrowed by post for 2d. a week, plus postage, and new publications bought through the Fellowship's book department.

Anyone interested in speech may apply for membership. The minimum subscription is 10s. a year (2 dollars to American members) which covers the receipt of the News Letter, and the use of the library and information service. An application form and specimen copy of the News Letter may be had from the Secretary, The Speech Fellowship, 9 Fitzroy Square, London, W.1.

The Incorporated Association of Teachers of Speech and Drama

By GEOFFREY CRUMP

(Hon. Secretary)

THE original Association of Teachers of Speech Training was founded in the first decade of the century for teachers trained at the Central School of Speech Training and Dramatic Art, and for the first twenty-five years it was maintained by them; but in 1934 it was re-organised under the name of the Association of Teachers of Speech and Drama, with membership open to all teachers with high qualifications. The first Annual General Meeting of this new Association was held in January, 1935. Miss Fogerty of the Central School and Mr. Acton-Bond of the Royal Academy of Music were joint Presidents, Miss M. Gulick was Hon. Secretary, Miss J. Van Thal was Hon. Treasurer, and the Council included Sir (then Mr.) Kenneth Barnes, Mr. J. Compton, Miss Gwynneth Thurburn, Miss Marjorie Gullan, Mr. Walter Ripman and Dr. Boome. The new Association took over from the Association of Teachers of Speech Training funds, library and periodical; revision courses and competitions for members' pupils were all well established. The A.T.S.D. formed a Remedial Section, which remained attached to the parent body until, in 1943, it formed an Association of its own, which is now merged into the College of Speech Therapists. In November, 1938, the joint Presidents, Miss Fogerty and Mr. Acton-Bond, resigned, and the office of President was abolished. Mr. J. Compton was elected Chairman, and remains in that office to-day. In 1943 Miss Gulick was succeeded as Hon. Secretary by Mr. Geoffrey Crump. The Association now has 350 members.

The new A.T.S.D. which came into being in 1934 was no longer merely a society of teachers, but an organisation for the purpose of emphasising the importance of speech in education in every possible way. As the Association was now a body of national importance, steps were taken to secure its incorporation; but it was several years before the preliminaries were completed, and the Association was not finally incorporated until May, 1944. The Memorandum of Association defines the main objects of the I.A.T.S.D. as being to promote the advancement of the knowledge, study, and practice of speech and dramatic art in every form, and for this purpose to organise conferences, courses, competitions, etc., and to publish literature for the benefit of members and others. During the years following its institution, refresher courses and conferences were frequently held, and a competition for pupils of members took place every year; these were highly successful, but had to be largely discontinued during the war. They were chiefly confined to members : but under the new Articles of Association the responsibilities of the Association have become wider, and open courses of instruction, competitions and examinations are now being organised as extensively as possible.

The first thing the A.T.S.D. set itself to do was to secure better recognition of Speech Training in schools, and to bring about the inclusion of a speech test in the School Certificate Examination. Considerable progress was made in this direction, and the proposal was sympathetically received by several examining bodies. Negotiations for trying out an oral test were actually in progress in 1939, but practical difficulties prevented its actual institution; and now, owing to the probability of a complete revision of the public examination system, this is not a reform for which the Association are pressing as pre-eminently important. In view of the new Education Act, and the vast increase in schools and the number of teachers to be trained, it is only through the teacher that improvement in speech can come; and it is on the training of teachers that the Association feel it important to concentrate. A memorandum on the subject was submitted to the Norwood Committee. In April, 1944, a conference of representatives of Teachers' Associations was called by the A.T.S.D. This was very well attended, and remarkable sympathy was shown for the reforms proposed. In August, 1944, a deputation appointed by this Conference was received at the Ministry of Education, and the following were among the points put forward :

i. The Ministry should impress upon schools and upon the public generally the importance of Speech Training, and suggest means for making it more effective. The recognition of oral work in schools should be equal to that paid to written work.

ii. Short courses for present teachers should be arranged, and Speech Training should be a part of the training of all future teachers.

iii. The question of speech tests in examinations should be explored.

iv. A three years' course at a recognised training institution should be recognised as equivalent to a degree course.

The I.A.T.S.D. considers it of urgent importance that all teachers should know enough of Speech Training to safeguard their own vocal health, and to combat slovenly speech in their pupils : also that all specialist teachers should be properly trained and qualified. Membership of the Association is confined to such specialist teachers. It is clear, however, that it will be some time before fully qualified teachers of speech can be appointed to all schools, and the I.A.T.S.D. has accordingly instituted a Certificate of Proficiency for Speech Training in Schools, examinations for which are held twice a year.

The attitude of the I.A.T.S.D. to Speech Training is summarised in the following extract from a *Memorandum on the Teaching of Spoken English* recently published by the Association :

> *What "Speech Training" is NOT.* It is not an attempt to lay a veneer of uniform culture on the many varieties of English speech. It is not a training for the stage or platform only. It is not a mere technical accomplishment, aimed principally at the speaking of verse, and unrelated to the lives that ordinary men and women have to live.
>
> *What "Speech Training" IS.* It is an essential part of the education of every child, and must include training in the oral expression of ideas (in ordinary conversation and committee as well as in public), in addition to the correct oral interpretation of printed language (both by reading and from memory). It must also include such instruction as is necessary for a clear and intelligible pronunciation of the language, and the proper use of the voice.

Enquiries may be addressed as follows :

Hon. Secretary : Geoffrey Crump, Oakhurst, Steep, Petersfield, Hampshire.

Hon. Secretary for Northern England : Miss B. Barton, Oak Mount, Oak Park, Sheffield, 10.

Hon. Secretary for Scotland : K. Morrison, 5 Garscombe Terrace, Edinburgh.

L.A.M.D.A. Teachers' Association

By W. JENKYN THOMAS

THE Public Examinations of the London Academy of Music and Dramatic Art have been held for the last fifty-five years. Contacts have been maintained between the teachers at the various centres by correspondence, by the visits of examiners, and by conferences and refresher courses in London. The need was felt, however, for a definite organisation which would speak for them collectively, and enable them to co-operate with other institutions and persons having similar ideals and interests. Consequently, in May, 1941, the L.A.M.D.A. Teachers' Association was formed.

Membership is limited to teachers who enter candidates for the L.A.M.D.A. examinations and are also graduates, licentiates, or associates of the following institutions, or hold one of their recognised teaching certificates: Central School of Speech Training, Guildhall School of Music and Drama, London Academy of Music and Dramatic Art, Royal Academy of Music, Royal College of Music, Trinity College of Music, and the Universities, and a strictly limited number of persons in respect of outstanding work in connection with speech, drama, literature or education. There are already some 600 members.

Naturally, an association of this kind, consisting of highly skilled and highly qualified teachers, was bound to have a considerable influence, and no time was wasted in setting to work. One of the most urgent problems to be considered was the place of speech in education. Sweeping post-war plans were being contemplated, and in the Association's view it was imperative that the authorities should recognise the importance of speech in the school and in the life of the pupil after leaving school. A petition was prepared and signed by teachers, speech specialists, and the principals of Universities and some of the largest schools and colleges in the country, and on June 29th, 1943, this was personally presented to Mr. Butler, President of the Board of Education. The deputation, which was led by the Rt. Hon. Lord Brabazon of Tara, M.C., P.C., consisted of Miss Laura G. Branson, Vice-President of the National Association of Head Teachers; the Rt. Rev. Dr. J. G. Vance, M.A., Ph.D., Headmaster of the Cardinal Vaughan School, and Canon of Westminster; R. W. Moore, Headmaster of Harrow; Wilfrid Foulis, Governing Director of the London Academy of Music and Dramatic Art; and the present writer, a member of the Middlesex Education Committee, who represented the English Association.

The President and members of his staff heard, with evident interest, the views and suggestions put forward by the deputation, and asked the L.A.M.D.A. Teachers' Association to send in a written memorandum. This was done, and it is clear that the results of the deputation have been definitely beneficial to the cause in question, and the friendly interest of the Minister suggests that the project was well worth while.

Another constructive piece of work which the Association has undertaken is the printing of a Register of Teachers, which lists its members under the alphabetical order of their names and under their various teaching districts, so that parents and the principals of schools and colleges are able to see at a glance the name and address of fully qualified teachers in their area. This Register has been very widely circulated and has already been instrumental in securing for its members a number of excellent posts.

Besides this, the Association, in conjunction with the Academy, has arranged for authorities on speech to write articles in booklet form which it has circularised not only to its members but to all the leading speech-specialists in Britain. The following have so far appeared. Those marked with an asterisk are out of print; the others are obtainable by non-members for 6d.:

**Elocution Examinations.* Comments and suggestions arising from a survey of examiners' reports.

**Books on Speech.* A survey for students.

Choral Speaking. Suggestions for its practice and study. By Clive Sansom.

Spoken English, as taught to our Polish Allies. By Helen Thomson, M.A., L.G.S.M. (Eloc.)

Speech in Schools: An address prepared for the Heads of Elementary Schools. Anonymous.

Speech Tunes, and their importance in teaching. By Rodney Bennett, M.A.

Speaking Lyric Verse. By Clive Sansom.

In the short space of five years, therefore, the Association has done some really valuable practical work for teachers of speech and drama, and for the cause which all its members have at heart—the improvement of standards of speech. Membership is open to all those satisfying the conditions mentioned on the preceding page, and application forms may be obtained from the L.A.M.D.A. Teachers' Association, Tower House, Cromwell Road, London, S.W.5. At present there is no subscription, but members are asked to pay one shilling towards postage costs.

English Association

THE English Association was founded in 1906 with the following aims:—

(1) To unite and introduce to one another those who are interested in English Language and Literature, whether as writers, teachers, artists, actors, or administrators; and to act as a link between groups engaged in specialised English work.

(2) To uphold the standards of English writing and speech; to contribute to English letters, scholarship, and research; to discuss methods of English teaching; and to encourage especially the work of younger members.

(3) To spread as widely as possible the knowledge and enjoyment of English Literature.

(4) To put these aims into practice by providing lectures, readings, discussions, social functions, a magazine and other publications; and to organise occasional visits to dramatic performances and places of literary interest.

The first number of its magazine, *English,* contained an article by the late Professor Lloyd James on "The Spoken Word," and since then it has printed several articles on speech training and reviews of important books on the subject. *The Year's Work in English Studies,* compiled annually by the Association, gives particulars of books published during the past twelve months on spoken and written English. The Association has also issued more than a hundred pamphlets on language and literature, including *The Scottish Dialects* by W. Grant; *Colloquial Language of the Commonwealth and Restoration* by Margaret Williamson; *The Claim of Our Mother Tongue* by Edward Lyttleton; and *Poetry and Contemporary Speech* by Lascelles Abercrombie.

Enquiries should be addressed to the Secretary, English Association, 3 Cromwell Road, London, S.W.7

British Drama League

THE position of speech training at the end of the last century was lacking in coherence and scientific basis. The theatre, and a group of "Readers," of whom Brandram was the greatest, maintained an artificial and exaggerated standard of vocal tone. The idea was to attain audibility by a certain approach to the incantation of song. The same idea was apparent in the ill-trained and unmusical "intoning" of the Liturgy.

Against this, a group of players had formed itself who, above all other things, strove to be "natural." But there was no logical method of notation which marked clearly the standard of educated speech—the selection, as opposed to the formation, of spoken sounds. The phoneticians, working from the basis of phonetic spelling in shorthand, first clearly noted what it was that people actually *did* say. Professor Daniel Jones and Walter Ripman used this method for the acquisition of foreign languages, though they paid more attention to pronunciation than to inflexional variety.

The position of the Drama League as a public body with a membership open to all gave it a strong influence in this matter. Its leaders were not distinguished by the assertive idiosyncrasies of delivery which marked the speech of the "star" actor, and the careful mimicry of his tricks which the star amateur rejoiced in. It must be remembered that such a teacher as Herman Vezin trained his students by means of the opening scenes of *Julius Cæsar*. Standing on the hearth-rug of his little studio he forcibly uttered a sentence:—

"Hence! Home! ye idle creatures. Get ye Home!"

The pupil—standing on the doormat—reiterated the line with utmost mimicry of voice inflection, vowel-quality, force and variety. When a listener would have felt it impossible to distinguish between the two renderings, the pupil was regarded as deserving top marks.

The great work accomplished by the Drama League was to help in a task which William Poel had already almost accomplished. The removal of the barrier which divided the educated student from the trained actor, who knew how, but not *why*, he should get his effects. The League blended discussion, lecturing and public performance in its meetings and Summer Schools. It educated audiences, not to lower the electric power of dramatic inspiration, but to acquire a control of expression which reflected the author's intention, and the actor's power of expressing character and variety by means of a perfectly trained instrument. Everywhere men of real appreciative force began to demand a range of intelligent expression, derived from true technique—the technique of the musician, who does not play Bach or Mozart as he plays Chopin or Franz Liszt.

The great revival in true verse-speaking which coincided with the work of the Georgian Poets, and the use of Greek and religious plays with their fundamental dependence on the spoken word, helped the new movement. Sir Lewis Casson, one of Poel's earliest disciples, was the earliest interpreter of the newer methods and one of the first supporters of the League, which also has had from the beginning the untold advantage of the advice and support of one of its Council members, the late Elsie Fogerty, C.B.E., then Principal of the Central School of Speech Training and Dramatic Art.

Besides this general policy in regard to speech training, mention should be made of the series of 24 gramophone records of the principal dialect variants current throughout England, Scotland, Wales and Ireland, which was issued in 1936. Each begins with the same "standard passage," a short monologue based on Skeats' *Phonetic Survey,* 1884, which comprises in the shortest possible space all the sounds in the phonetic alphabet. This was followed by small items in poetry and prose, indigenous to each region represented, and spoken by a native thereof. The sale of these records has been continuous since their first publication, and in addition to their general interest, their utility to students, actors and stage producers need not be stressed. (See page 36).

MEMBERSHIP

Individual membership of the League may be acquired by the payment of an annual subscription of £1 5s. 0d. At the same subscription any organised Society or group of not less than ten persons may become affiliated to the Drama League, and as an affiliated Society shall acquire and exercise all the privileges afforded by the League. Subscriptions count as from January 1st or July 1st, whichever date is nearer to the first application for membership. Life membership (for individuals only) can be acquired by a single payment of twelve guineas.

The Library of over 50,000 volumes is available to all members of the League and affiliated societies who may borrow under their subscription three books at a time without extra charge, and complete acting or reading-sets of any published play for a fee of 2/6 for one week, 3/6 for three weeks, or 5/- for six weeks, postage extra.

Other privileges of membership include the free receipt of the League's quarterly journal, *Drama,* the right to consult the Information Bureau on any matter connected with the stage, advice on the running of Drama Festivals, the right to a free criticism of an original m.s. play, postal course in play-writing, etc., etc. Experts are available by arrangement to advise on, or help with, the initiation of every kind of dramatic activity, professional or amateur. Special attention is given to the requirements of H.M. Forces as well as schools, rural groups, and youth clubs. In certain circumstances these last may affiliate to the League at half the normal fee.

Further particulars may be obtained from the Director, Mr. Geoffrey Whitworth, British Drama League, 9 Fitzroy Square, London, W.1.

The Poetry Society

By GALLOWAY KYLE (*Director*)

WHAT has for above a third of a century been known as the Poetry Society grew out of a discussion in the correspondence columns of the old *Daily News* on the apparent neglect or poor methods of reading and speaking poetry. Art and interpretation were submerged by inferior, stereotyped elocutionary technique. Hence the formation of a society intended to promote and develop better methods, to raise the standard of elocution as the not-to-be despised preparation for the vocal interpretation of poetry, and thereby to secure more intelligent and widespread appreciation of poetry, which, adopting de Quincey's dictum, we believed primarily to be written for sound rather than sight reading, and the most likely way to realise effectively that clearer, deeper sense of poetry and the strength and joy to be drawn from it, which Matthew Arnold passed on to us as our objective, a very desirable and definite purpose, amplified in Lady Margaret Sackville's first presidential address.

The concrete unassailable background thus constituted was strongly buttressed and dignified by the active collaboration of Sir Johnstone Forbes-Robertson and Sir Frank Benson, the two leading masters of diction and vocal artistry at that time, who approved the policy of the Society, and under whose guidance the design and rules of the Society's examinations in diction and verse-speaking were drawn up. They acted as the first examiners for the Society, the first of its members who wished to give public readings—it had been found that members' enthusiasm frequently over-ran their abilities, and that a love of poetry did not confer the gift of satisfactory voices and pleasing reading—and then developed into more general tests for young people, a remarkable unanticipated demand arising from schools and teachers of elocution for examinations in "verse-speaking."

We coined the phrase, but it should have been "poetry" speaking, as the Society's primary concern was the use and appreciation of poetry. The auditions spread rapidly under the influence of Sir Johnstone, who became President of The Poetry Society, and acted as an examiner and adjudicator over seventeen years, confining himself in later years to the Gold Medal examination, the final of a progressive series of auditions in three divisions, Junior, Senior and Adult, for the certificate, the bronze medal and the silver medal for verse-speaking, grading the candidates' pleasant ascent of Parnassus.

Later examiners derived their experience and authority from the original eminent couple, whose advice, policy and rulings still animate and guide the Society's work in this fruitful field. An incalculable influence has been exercised on youth. Firm, resolute, flexible speech has been applied to the intelligent, individual production of fine poems—an artistic accomplishment soundly based, constituting a valuable contribution to real education and the assured cultivation of personality, with hitherto unrecognised physical, mental and even spiritual advantages. I have seen the transformation of ordinary young people under the influence of poetry, the physical as well as the mental reaction, the production of an outward and visible sign of an inward and spiritual grace, giving and finding life in the spoken word, seizing and expressing the immortality inherent in great poetry and in this way sharing in that immortality by assisting in perpetuating the poet's immortality—a marvellous transfiguration that intensifies one's faith in and enjoyment of poetry, a vital realisation of fundamental education in which it is a privilege and a joy to participate. I may go to a school or general audition feeling dull and harassed, but invariably I come away with buoyant heart, stimulated by what I have heard. Some of the candidates may be feeble and pedestrian, with vocal and facial immobility, impervious to the music of the words and the beauty of the thought, dully or glibly repeated, and under the nervous tension of the test falling back into elementary errors and weaknesses, indefinite finals, slurred line endings, clipped vowels, jerky phrasing, prepositional emphases, neglect of metre, loss of rhythm, and that fatal sinking feeling that is the bane of more experienced speakers than children in their 'teens. But for all the feebleness there is more than compensation provided by the rarer candidates with clarity of enunciation, cadenced inflexions, smooth, compact, rhythmical phrasing, sustained continuity, clean definition and a vital quality that gives life to the words and phrases, braces the body and brings a glow to the eyes and beautifies the feature—an artistic, eurhythmical performance that is more than cleverness and superior to intelligence. Such instances of special distinction occur daily. They are not produced by strenuous effort, they are free from objectivity, exhibitionism, artificiality: their strength is based on quiet confidence and serenity.

I need not enlarge on the significance and value of this approach to poetry, developed and deepened by so many years of practical experiment and test in collaboration with a devoted body of ever-advancing teachers throughout the country. It is simple, not elaborate and not highly technical, a matter of sense and sensibility. Its influence has been apparent on the present generation; it will affect more profoundly the next. Its scope and application are illimitable and too little realised yet. When the report of the Norwood Committee to the Ministry of Education complained of the deplorable state of English in secondary schools, I wrote to our old friend and supporter, the ex-Head of Harrow, pointing out how I knew of secondary schools, and of one in particular, where a knowledge of English had been extended, deepened, made lucid, by the adoption of our auditions and the training incidental thereto. Sir Cyril replied, "Thank you for your letter, with which I am in sympathy. The work of the Poetry Society is one of the ways by which better standards may be reached. But it does not help for the School Certificate and so many schools cannot be bothered. I agree that your work should be more widely known and I hope that in the discussions which will rage as the result of our outspoken report your work will be mentioned and will come to the fore."

Membership of the Poetry Society is open to all who are interested in the speaking or study of poetry. The minimum subscription of 10/- entitles each member to the receipt of *The Poetry Review,* published every two months, and attendance at the weekly poetry readings in London. All enquiries should be addressed to the Secretary, Poetry Society, 33 Portman Square, London, W.1.

Society for Pure English

THE Society for Pure English was founded in 1913 by Dr. Robert Bridges, with Henry Bradley, Sir Walter Raleigh and Mr. Logan Pearsall Smith as members of the Committee, and at that time obtained the support of many names of influence and authority in English literature. The object of the Society was then stated in these words: "The reason for the existence of the Society is the duty of the English-speaking peoples to make their language adequate and efficient and worthy of its increasing and world-wide use; and this practical responsibility is so great as almost to overshadow that other vast responsibility, our obligation in honour to safeguard the splendour of our rich inheritance. The appeal of the Society is therefore to all branches of the English-speaking race; and its purpose is to further the best interest of the language by the promulgation of sound knowledge; so that our public opinion and common practice, which ultimately decide linguistic usage, may be guided by scientific, philological and historic facts."

The Society has published sixty "tracts," of which these deal especially with spoken English :—

2. *On English Homophones.* Robert Bridges.
4. *The Pronunciation of English Words Derived from the Latin.* John Sargeaunt.
22. *The Nature of Human Speech.* Sir Richard Paget.
26. *English Vowel-Sounds.* W. A. Aiken.
30. *American Pronunciation.* H. Kurath.
32. *The B.B.C.'s Recommendations for Pronouncing Doubtful Words.* Edited by Robert Bridges.
36. *Colloquial Language in Literature.* Lascelles Abercrombie.
37. *"Oxford" English.* R. W. Chapman.
39. *The Best English.* A claim for the superiority of Received Standard English. H. C. Wyld.

Most of these tracts are now obtainable only in volume form. Information and particulars of membership may be had from the Secretary, S.P.E., c/o Clarendon Press, High Street, Oxford. American enquiries should be sent to Mr. Henry S. Canby, Editor, *The Saturday Review of Literature,* 25 West 45th Street, New York City.

International Phonetics Association

THIS society, founded in 1886, is composed of persons interested in the science of phonetics, chiefly professors, teachers and students of languages. Its main object is to promote the scientific study of phonetics and the various practical applications of that science, and particularly to simplify the accurate teaching of modern languages. The Association believes that in pursuing this object it is contributing to the promotion of friendly relations between people of different nationalities.

The society consists of "ordinary" and "active" members. The annual subscription is 8/- for the former, and 12/- for the latter. New members are enrolled on the payment of an entrance fee of 4/-, in return for which they receive publications to the value of that amount.

The Association has devised a phonetic alphabet which may be used for the purpose of transcribing any language phonetically. This alphabet is very widely used, and there are several hundred published books in which it is employed. A detailed description of it, with examples showing its use in different languages, will be found in *The Principles of the International Phonetics Association* (6d.), and various other publications.

Examinations for a Certificate of Proficiency in Phonetics are conducted in English and French, by examiners appointed by the Council of the Association. The examination in English relates more especially to the phonetics of English, and that in French relates more especially to the phonetics of French. The English examination, conducted by Professor Daniel Jones, consists of English phonetic dictation, phonetic dictation in an unknown language or dictation of meaningless words (for testing the candidate's capacity to recognise sounds), transcriptions of a passage of English, reading aloud a passage of English in phonetic script, reading aloud a passage of English in current spelling, and answering questions on phonetic theory. Marks are also given for the candidate's ordinary speaking.

All members of the Association receive its official organ, *Le Maître Phonétique*. It is written in various languages, but printed in the international alphabet. The articles deal with all branches of phonetics and its applications, and give information respecting the progress made by the science in different parts of the world. The best methods of language teaching are also discussed, and special texts suitable for students are given in each number.

Applications for membership, and enquiries relating to examinations or the publications of the Association, should be addressed to its Secretary: Professor Daniel Jones, University College, Gower Street, London, W.C.1.

Elocution and Drama Diploma Teachers' Association

This association was founded by Mr. Acton Acton-Bond, with Mr. Wilton Cole and Mr. E. Guy Pertwee as joint chairmen, and is open to teachers holding any elocution diploma which is accepted by the Royal Society of Teachers. Distinguished teachers of not less than ten years' active experience in any part of the United Kingdom and the Dominions, and known to the Council, may be invited to join the Association.

An insurance scheme and benevolent fund are under consideration, and teachers are offered all the benefits of assistance and protection which only a corporate body can provide.

The subscription for membership is fixed at ten shillings per annum, due on the first of January. Further particulars may be obtained from the Hon. Secretary, Mr. Raymond Rayner, 9 Palace Mansions, Addison Bridge, London, W.14.

SPEECH EDUCATION

The Ministry of Education and the Local Education Authorities

By J. COMPTON

WHEN with the passing of the Education Act 1944 the Board of Education became the Ministry of Education it had nothing in the shape of a directive policy in speech education to hand over. There had been references to the problem of spoken English in Departmental Reports which revealed a growing concern with it, but they were essentially non-committal, and produced no evident practical results. *The Teaching of English in England,* 1921, had advocated (a) the scientific teaching in Preparatory Schools of the sounds of spoken English and (b) a knowledge and use of phonetics by the teacher, who should also be acquainted with the methods of voice-production. In *The Infant and Nursery School,* 1923, a recommendation was offered for the correction of "slovenly and inaccurate utterance by connecting it to the child's sense of rhythm," through tongue-twisters and simple poetry. *The Education of the Adolescent,* 1926, urged that "definite training should be given in distinct articulation and the proper use of the organs of speech" and considered that the elements of phonetics "might well become a valuable introduction to the study not only of a foreign language but of English." *The Primary School,* 1931, included a paragraph on "Speech and Speech Training" devoted chiefly to advocating the claims of oral composition and making some rather confused observations on dialect.

The Board had no responsibility for any of these publications, but adopted or summarised some of their suggestions for use in *The Handbook of Suggestions for Teachers.* The last edition of the *Handbook* was published in 1937 (a comparison of its treatment of speech and that in its forerunner, published in 1929, is interesting) and provides the last pronouncement of the Board of Education on this subject. The advice offered is in line with approved pedagogic practice. "Every teacher should know how the individual sounds are articulated." "Attention should be paid especially to united and final consonants." "The first essential of speech is clarity; the basis of clear speaking is precise articulation, which can only be secured by careful training." "Tone in speech can also be trained." "A short daily practice is necessary." "Teachers should encourage the children to speak their dialect freely and boldly in the Infant School and in the earlier stages of the Junior School, and then build upon that." What is said is all shrewd and helpful: but it lacks the cutting edge which a deep conviction of the importance and urgency of the matter would have given it.

Formal recognition of the gravity and range of the problem, and of the ineffectiveness of existing measures for dealing with it, did not come until the publication in 1943 of the report on *Curriculum and Examinations in Secondary Schools* by the committee presided over by Sir Cyril Norwood and hence usually known as the Norwood Report. "The evidence is such as to leave no doubt that we are here confronted with a serious failure of the Secondary Schools. The complaint briefly is that too many pupils show marked inability to present ideas clearly to themselves, to arrange them and to express them clearly on paper or in speech; they read without sure grasp of what they read, and they are too often at a loss in communicating what they wish to communicate in clear and simple sentences and in expressive and audible tone." "The third element in education which we postulate is training in English, that is, clear expression in English, both spoken and written, based on the logical arrangement of ideas." However, there is no specific recommendation. "We content ourselves with recording our belief that no school is doing its duty by the community which does not do everything in its power to bring its pupils to use such speech that everything they say can be easily apprehended in any part of the country."

The McNair Report of 1944 on *Teachers and Youth Leaders,* arriving at similar but reinforced conclusions, makes some cogent observations and important suggestions. "Language is the instrument through which teachers both teach and educate. Unless a teacher has at least a moderate competence in reading, writing, speaking and listening he is hampered at every turn. This competence is far from being acquired in the secondary schools." "Three things are involved: clear and, if possible, pleasant speech; the power to say and write what one means; and the capacity to direct one's understanding to what other people say and write. Children are sensitive to the quality of a teacher's voice, and even though they may not give it any conscious attention, it not only influences their own manner of speaking, it also directly affects a teacher's ability to manage children happily. There are few students who will not need some help in the use of their voices and advice about their manner of speech. There are some who will need definitely therapeutic training and for such it should be compulsorily prescribed."

"What we urge is that every student should be trained to acquire a sufficient mastery of his own language to enable him to use it as an effective instrument for his own education and for that of his future pupils; and in the matter of speech we make specific recommendations."

These recommendations are:—

"(a) that the Board of Education should require every training institution to pay attention to the speech of every student, and every area training authority to include in the assessment of a student's practical teaching ability to use the English language; and

(b) that the Board of Education should require every training institution to make arrangements for the detection of speech disabilities and for the provision of speech therapy and training where necessary."

The McNair Report is now receiving the consideration of the Minister. He will know that in one department of speech, that of Speech Therapy, progress can be reported. Since the outbreak of war the Ministry of Education revealed anxiety about the inadequacy of the provision made, taking the country as a whole, for children suffering from speech defects and the manifest need for many more Speech Clinics.* Accordingly they pressed Local Education Authorities to make new schemes or improved schemes in relation to Speech Therapy, and now there are not enough qualified speech therapists to fill all the appointments that would be made.

In relation to the speech of normal children we should note that the recommendations of the McNair Committee, if adopted, will affect only students in training. What of our present teachers, many of whom have through the years done valiant things despite immense handicaps, of which crowded classes, and the non-co-operation of parents are only the most obvious and usual? They need expert guidance and help, more and better equipment, and, perhaps more than anything else at the outset, an official plan which will show clear understanding of the nature of their task in this matter.

Such a plan can be produced only when the Ministry of Education have given a lead and sought the co-operation of the Local Education Authorities. The first stage in that co-operation should cover appropriate and well-organised Refresher and part-time courses for teachers, some to be organised by the Ministry and some, with the approval of the Ministry, by the Local Education Authorities themselves. Some Education Authorities may desire to appoint experts or peripatetic teachers to visit the schools giving help, advice and encouragement, and the Ministry should enable them to do so. The success of this kind of appointment in Aberdeen offers a good precedent.† Furthermore the Local Education Authorities should overhaul the relevant equipment in their schools and ensure that every school has a good wireless set and a good gramophone, and every secondary school a microphone and internal telephone. And it is time they accepted, for the benefit of their schools, some responsibility in local dramatic enterprises and made it their care to give an opportunity to every boy and girl to hear the

†page 81 *page 198

speech of our great dramatists finely spoken. For, as only one manifestation of the educational process is revealed in the classroom, so the problem of good speech is not, in the end, a curriculum problem, a problem to be solved by pedagogical methods alone, but a problem for the community. "Education must teach you your own language, its songs and its novels, the speech of the common people and the plays of the great dramatists, so that it will seem to every pupil the road to his sweetheart's door."

Speech in the Universities and in the Education of Teachers

By M. M. LEWIS

I. UNIVERSITIES

WHAT is the place of speech education in university education? Long tradition has made the written word the centre of all education; the ultimate test of a student's ability, the degree of his achievement, is measured by his power of expressing himself on paper. What need is there for any change in this tradition? The answer is that it is demanded by the place that the university holds in the society of our day.

Education is an instrument designed to serve social needs, so that the problems of education are always social problems. As a society changes the problems of education change with it. Today the fundamental change in the university is that it is more universal. In a planned society one function of the university must be to prepare for every profession, so that the university, drawing its students from the whole community, will in turn provide the leaders for the whole community. This means that at the university level, education in speech—always an intrinsic part of education in general—must be directed to provide every student with the skill in spoken language necessary for his work in society, and in particular to provide every teacher with the spoken language necessary for his work as a teacher.

A profession is that kind of work in which a man is directly and immediately occupied with his fellow-men. In every profession, therefore, the art of speech is a primary tool: the civil servant, the doctor, the lawyer, the priest and the teacher alike must have the power of entering into communication with those in their charge.

By the time he leaves the university every student must be a good speaker in the fullest sense—a person skilled in the art of spoken intercourse. To enter easily into relations with others, so that mutual confidence is at once established; to give instructions so that they will be both willingly and accurately carried out; to persuade as well as command; not least, to be able to listen; together all these varied skills make up a complex art. Today, in a world in which spoken language is perhaps the dominant means of communication, it is an art which education dare not neglect.

Leaving aside for the moment the special education of the teacher, what provision should be made in a university for the speech education of every other student? First of all it is clear that every student should be able to converse pleasantly and effectively in his mother tongue. Today a master of arts of a university may be quite uncivilised in his speech. An honours graduate in English need not be able to speak English. To make this impossible we need not only the guidance of students in the art of everyday speech, but some attention also to minor defects; the McNair Committee has already recommended the provision of speech therapy in every institution for the education of teachers.

But beyond this primary necessity of everyday speech we see around us the growing importance of more formal speech; the radio alone is giving the arts of discourse and discussion a place they have never held in any society since the days of the city-states of ancient Greece. The leaders of a society need to be able to speak to their fellow-citizens, and not only speak to them but speak with them. Discourse and discussion : the university student needs education in these. But—and the question must be asked—how many university teachers, even those whose chief instrument is the spoken language, are as distinguished in the practice of these arts of discourse and discussion as in their fields of study?

Further still : our universities today are recognising their wider responsibilities as centres of learning not only for the British Commonwealth but for the world. There is every likelihood that within a generation English will become a general auxiliary international language. The very least we can offer students from abroad is a fit education in spoken English.

It is evident then that a minimum essential in every university is a Department of Spoken Language devoted both to teaching and research. Already there is the important department, concerned however mainly with phonetics, in the University of London at University College; and the small department at University College, Nottingham. But the functions of such a department must be more widely conceived than is anywhere yet the case.

First, research. Here problems are plentiful. There are the medical and psychological problems of the pathology of speech, to the study of which two Englishmen have made outstanding contributions—Hughlings Jackson and Henry Head; and the study of deafness, so well established in the University of Manchester. There remains much more : such problems as the relation between speech defect and mental retardation; detailed questions of the development of speech from infancy; the psychology of spoken communication; the psychology of learning a second spoken language; the practical problems of learning and teaching speech.

In research of this kind a department of spoken language would naturally collaborate with a medical school, and with departments of physics, psychology and education.

As for its teaching, this should certainly not be confined to a group of specialist students within the department, but—and this is perhaps its most important function—its work should irradiate throughout the university institution of which it is a part. It should be a centre of instruction and guidance for all members of the university—not excluding the university teachers; taking a central place very much in the manner of a competent department of physical education. It should give special instruction in the linguistics of speech, including phonetics, to all students of languages, ancient and current; nothing can be more sterile than phonology without phonetics. The department should also be ready to deal with the minor defects of speech of any member of the university; and—where there is a medical school—this therapeutic service should be extended to include major defects also. And the department should play a central part in the education of all foreign students, so that they leave England enriched with experience of what since Elizabethan times Englishmen have been proud to praise—the spoken word.

II. TRAINING OF TEACHERS

In the education of the future teacher, education in speech must obviously play a very special part. The teacher next only to the mother is the guardian of the spoken word. By his example, by the specific instruction he gives in the art of speech, by the opportunities he provides in the classroom for the exercise and practice of this art, by his skilled detection of speech disabilities and co-operation with the therapist who treats them; in all these ways he may have a supreme influence upon the development of good speech in every child, and therefore upon the preservation and promotion of spoken language in our society.

There is, of course, nothing new in these demands upon the teacher: probably not a school in the country to-day is unmindful of its duty towards the cultivation of good speech. But what we are asking here is that teachers shall be fitly educated for their special task. This does not mean that every teacher need become a specialist in speech. In every school, perhaps, there should be at least one specialist, to act as a centre of speech education and an adviser to all other teachers who are interested enough to wish to help in this work. But all these other teachers need knowledge and skill if their co-operation is to be fruitful.

In the education of teachers, education in speech must therefore move along three lines. Every teacher, whatever he teaches, must be able to speak well in order to teach well: his professional education must therefore indispensably include his personal education as a speaker. And since most teachers will wish to take some part in the speech education of their pupils, they must have had the opportunity of making some study of the theory and practice of the cultivation of speech. Finally there will be some teachers who, as we have said, will need a more specialised preparation in order to be fitted to take over the general supervision of speech education in a school.

First, the personal speech education of the future teacher; this is a task to which every training college and department of education must address itself with even more energy than hitherto. Not every teacher needs the higher arts of speech—the speaking of verse, prose and the drama. These are arts which certainly must not be neglected in any school; but they can only take their rightful place if every teacher is already fully competent in a more fundamental art—everyday speech in the classroom, including as it must vivid narration, graphic description and lucid exposition. One could name a number of colleges where the education of future teachers in this fundamental art is being carried on with insight and skill, but always under the major handicap of poverty, the lack of means to provide all the necessary tutors and equipment. We may begin to believe that our society really means business in the education of our children when we see the finances of training colleges lifted above the level of bare subsistence.

If we succeed in equipping every teacher with the fundamental art of everyday speech we shall certainly have done a good deal. But this is only the beginning. Many teachers—perhaps the majority—while making no claim to be specialists in speech, would hold that the speech of children is always their concern. The education of such teachers must include something more than personal fitness in speech. They should know something of the development of speech in children, the psychology of speech and its relation to behaviour, the common speech disabilities, the practical methods of cultivating correct, effective and pleasing speech, and the arts of guiding children in the appreciation and production of beautiful speech. Few colleges, if any, are as yet equipped to give future teachers as wide a speech education as this

Finally there is the education of the specialist teacher. This obviously might be left to specialist colleges, but there is much to be said for the principle of educating all teachers in the same general colleges, whatever their future specific work in a school. Certainly every college for the education of teachers would gain much from the presence of both students and tutors giving special attention to speech—just as many colleges already benefit by the presence of specialists in music, art or handicraft.

The future specialist teacher of speech needs an education as full and as strenuous as that of the specialist in any other field. Only a few can hope to be equally skilled throughout the whole range of speech, and probably none can hope to combine preparation for teaching with the clinical experience necessary for therapeutic work. But every specialist teacher in a school must have some understanding of all aspects of the spoken word; speech as an expression of thought and personality, as an instrument of communication and as an interpretative art. The education of the specialist must needs be both theoretical and practical, and the mark of his proficiency a high degree of competence in both knowledge and skill.

The universities of this country have within the last century taken over step by step the responsibility of preparation for one profession after another. There are still many of them reluctant to accept the same responsibility for other professions, notably for the education of teachers. But ultimately they cannot escape this responsibility and with it their responsibility for the education of speakers of English in the arts of speaking English.

Primary and Secondary Schools

By RODNEY BENNETT

It is not easy to give an idea of the present state of speech work in schools, since, perhaps more than any other subject, speech training, with its inseparable partner, dramatic work, suffered from evacuation, shortage of teachers, and war-time conditions, which also made adequate observation impossible. But attendance at conferences and most of the few Refresher Courses which persisted during the war years suggests that this set-back will prove no more than temporary, and that speech will quickly regain its place in the curriculum now that schools have returned to normal.

Meanwhile it may be instructive to consider what that place in fact amounts to—what has really been achieved, and not achieved, since 1921, when that epoch-marking Stationery Office publication, *The Teaching of English in England,* made the famous and memorable statement which begins, "It is the first duty of the elementary school to give its pupils speech," and went on to make recommendations about classroom dramatic work which are still more valuable, since they are capable of neither misunderstanding nor limitation.

Between 1921 and to-day the only really new factor which has entered into the speech problem is that of wireless, which has now had time to reveal and define the extent and limitations of its influence. In the early days it was assumed, especially by devotees of dialect, that wireless would level speech to a uniformity in which dialects would inevitably vanish. Time has proved this argument to be almost precisely opposite to the fact. Wireless has had comparatively little effect upon speech beyond making people more conscious of it, at least in others—especially speech of kinds which they happen not to like. Far from eradicating dialects, it has increased general interest in and tolerance for them, and has tended, by providing contrast, to stimulate what may be called "pride of dialect" in many of those who use it.

In sum it would appear that, in so far as wireless is influential at all in the teaching of speech, it is in providing audible material for discussion and criticism—a use which may well be much further exploited, and the more valuably if criticism remains at least tolerant, if not positively friendly.

THE PRIMARY SCHOOL

Operative though the passage quoted from *The Teaching of English* has been with teachers, and with some education authorities, it would have been still more influential if, when removed from its large context, it had left less room for misconception. For example, although the whole book made it clear that the word "speech" should be taken in the large sense as well as in the more specific meaning of speech training, it was possible to read the word in the narrower sense only, and this had the effect of alarming many teachers. While recognising the importance of speech, not only as an educational but also as a social factor, they tended to regard its teaching as being beyond their capacity, as something to be attempted only by the specialist, in special periods. This fear has given place to a realisation that speech training is a whole-time activity, that for good or ill it is proceeding during the pupil's whole waking hours, in school and out, especially if his ear has been to some extent awakened; and that the chief qualifications are an acceptable manner of speech, genuine interest in the spoken word, and the ability to communicate that interest with more certainty than the visiting specialist can command, in brief and comparative rare periods, even if he or she is expert in the handling and disciplining of large classes.

The marked and happy decline of this wary attitude towards speech has been chiefly due to the increased availability of speech courses, and of publications dealing with the problems of the class procedure. At first these were mostly teachers' books, but later came various series of pupils' books. These were opposed by some specialists on the ground that the teaching of speech is essentially an oral activity. While this is, and must always be. obviously true, pupils' class books would seem to have justified themselves by providing the teacher with material for oral work, and by stressing the humour and quiddity of speech, and, above all, its inexhaustible human interest. This is all to the good, since it militates against certain pedantic tendencies which are descernible in speech training, not only in the primary school, the first being to isolate speech from its essential dailiness and humanity.

A similar tendency, more notable among women teachers than men, is to talk about "good" and "bad" speech, a practice which, however natural, is impolitic, since it tends to produce antagonism in the child and at home. It also shows a failure to differentiate between what is slovenly and what is merely unfashionable or non-standard, a failure which causes perplexity about the proper treatment of regional speech. It is fortunately noticeable that the tendency to decry dialect is giving way to the more sensible practice, which *The Teaching of English* advocates in connection with dramatic work, of cultivating and studying it, while recommending the acquisition of standard English as an interesting and expedient accomplishment—a point of view which children can understand if it is discreetly presented.

A similar confusion of thought is evident in the excessive concern shown by some teachers, again especially women, at the fact that many children fail to adhere to their acquired speech habits out of school. This is natural, since children, especially boys, are like adults in their fear of being "different"; neither is it an evidence of failure in teaching, since the ability to differentiate between two speech customs indicates at least the beginnings of that aural awareness which it is the first aim of speech work to awaken.

An anti-pedantic swing is indicated by the question whether special speech periods are essential. This is becoming decreasingly frequent with the realisation that, besides underlining the importance of speech and providing a nucleus for more general work, special periods actually save time as compared with casual correction, as well as avoiding the irritation and diffusion of interest which so often render that method useless if not worse.

It may be said that, so far, the most effective speech work has been done informally in the infant school, more formally in the junior school, and, again largely but not entirely informally, in classes devoted to backward and retarded children. In the three-month courses for teachers of such children which were held annually at Goldsmiths' College before the war, much attention was given to speech, especially in connection with drama and puppetry, since it was recognised that children are less aware of their retardation where speech is concerned, and are therefore more readily able to escape from it.

These two incentives to speech, dramatic work and puppetry, share the double advantage that they provide children with an understandable and appreciable purpose for acquiring efficient, varied and expressive speech, and that they link speech study with crafts and other activities, thus rescuing it from an air-tight seclusion. Dramatic work also has provided a solution to the difficulties of teaching solo reading, which had hitherto proved so formidable, especially in large classes, that some local authorities had ruled that, in spite of its acknowledged cultural value, it should be discontinued. It is quite commonly found that children who read badly in the normal way discover new ability in the course of dramatic reading, the reason being that dialogue promotes correlation between the printed word and real and vigorous speech of everyday life.

Another incentive which was gaining popularity before the war was the inter-class non-competitive speech festival within the school, which allowed children to show their prowess in solo and choral speech, team reading, acting, and even impromptu speaking and debate. Enough had been done to show that boys no less than girls so enjoyed these functions that they were eager to work hard for them in their own time—a fact which suggests large future possibilities.

SENIOR SCHOOLS

Here speech work has been, and remains, less general, less thorough, and less effective than in the younger departments. One reason for this is the prevalent belief that seniors, especially boys, who have reached the self-conscious age without speech study, can hardly be induced to undertake it, while those who have received junior speech training, especially if it has been of a less than captivating nature, regard its continuation as beneath their dignity—though why this does not also apply to other subjects is not stated. These difficulties, even when not purely imaginary, are more imaginary than real, and can easily be overcome by approach through impersonal humour, human interest, and dramatic work and its manual adjuncts, about which boys are at heart quite as enthusiastic as girls, in spite of greater initial diffidence.

Another deterrent to senior speech work is the antiquated notion that the spoken word is less important than the written, a fallacy which gains force from the comparative neglect of the spoken word in examinations. Indeed, it may be said that, at every stage except the infant and lower junior, speech work is seriously deterred by written examination, and by insufficient recognition of the two facts that free and enthusiastic speaking is the surest road to vital writing, and that it is precisely at the self-conscious stage that children most need the freedom which speech and action can alone confer.

THE SECONDARY SCHOOL

What has been said of the deficiencies of speech work in the senior elementary school applies with added force to the majority of secondary schools. It is symptomatic that the first conference to deal with speech in such schools did not take place until as late as the late 'thirties. With some notable exceptions, secondary education lags severely behind elementary in its approach to speech. This is partly due to a complacent assumption, unfortunately fostered by the phrase, "it is the first duty of the *elementary* school," that secondary school speech is all that it might be—an assumption which even the most sympathetic listening fails to confirm. Even if it were ever true that the large majority of secondary pupils came from homes in which cultured speech was the rule, the extension of the scholarship system has radically altered the situation. Finally, even if secondary school practice were in fact more acceptable than it is there would still be no justification for failing to associate speech with language and its deep and varied human interest.

Another reason for neglect is the imminence of the School Certificate examination and its equivalents, and the extraordinary fact that, in spite of agitation during at least twenty-five years, they still fail to give candidates an optional opportunity of showing oral proficiency in their own tongue, although they are encouraged to do so in any other living language which they may be offering. This anomaly is mirrored in the not uncommon secondary practice of treating English speech, like music, as an "extra"—of providing children with the best available coaching in the speaking of foreign languages, while regarding proficiency in their own as something which either does not matter, or must be separately paid for.

One would suggest various remedies for this Gilbertian state of affairs: (a) more official stress upon the importance of the spoken word in general education, and especially in the teaching of English; (b) more official stress upon the cultural and social value of that "good appearance and address" which dramatic work helps to produce; and (c) insistence upon the inclusion, in School Certificate and all examinations which qualify for Matriculation, of at least an optional examination of oral English.

Another reform, which would be vastly influential in raising the status of more than spoken English, would be to make acceptable speech a condition of employment for all teachers, irrespective of subject or grade, with the addition, for teachers of English, of evidence of practical acquaintance with at least the rudiments of speech training and classroom dramatic work.

Speech Education

SOME BOOKS AND RECORDS

GENERAL:

Language in School. M. M. Lewis. (Univ. of London Press, 6s.)
English for the English. George Sampson. (Cambridge, 3s. 6d.)
Spoken English: Its Practice in Schools and Training Colleges. (Methuen, 7s. 6d.)
Practical Speech Training for Schools. Rodney Bennett. (Univ. of London Press, 4s. 6d.)
Speech Training in the School. Marjorie Gullan. (Evans, 1s. 6d.)
Speech Education Supplement, *British Journal of Educational Psychology,* 1934. June, 1934.
Speech Number, *New Era,* July, 1941.

Memorandum on the Teaching of Spoken English. (Inc. Association of Teachers of Speech and Drama, 1944.)
Speech Fellowship *News Letter* (page 52).

PRIMARY :

Speech Training for Infants. Hilda King. (Nelson, 3s. 6d.)
First Steps in Speech Training. Rodney Bennett. (Evans, 1s. 6d.)
Infant Speech. A Study. M. M. Lewis. (Kegan Paul, 15s.)
Speech Training Records. Infant and Junior classes. Marjorie Gullan. 2 records. (H.M.V.)
Primary Teacher's Guide to Speech Training. Anne McAllister. (Univ. of London Press, 4s. 6d.)
Steps in Speech Training. Class readers. Anne McAllister. (Univ. of London Press. Books 1 and 2, 10d.; Book 3, 11d.; Book 4, 1s. 1d.; Book 5, 1s. 3d.)
Speech Training in the Primary School, 3 vols. Isabel Best. (Macmillan, 1s. 6d. each.)
Playway of Speech Training. Rodney Bennett. (Evans, 3s. 6d.)
Adventures in Words. First Series. Class readers. Rodney Bennett. (Univ. of London Press. Book 1, 6d.; Books 2-3, 7d.; Book 4, 8d.)
Speech Rhymes. Clive Sansom. 3 books. (A. & C. Black, 1s. each.)

SECONDARY :

Exercises to Our Spoken Language. A. Lloyd James. (Nelson, 1s. 6d.)
Speech Training Record. Senior Class. Marjorie Gullan. (H.M.V.)
Adventures in Words. Second Series. Class readers. Sansom & Bennett. 3 Books. (Univ. of London Press, 1s. each.)
Speech Training in the School. Marjorie Gullan. (Evans, 1s. 6d.)

ADULT :

A Tongue in Your Head. L. A. G. Strong (Pitman, 5s.)
Voice and Speech. Gwynneth Thurburn. (Nisbet, 6s. 6d.)
Speech Craft. Elsie Fogerty. (Dent, 4s.)
The Way to Good Speech. Barbara Storey. (Nelson, 3s. 6d.)
A Year's Course in Speech Training. Anne McAllister. (Univ. of London Press, 4s. 6d.)

See also the bibliography to "Phonetics" (page 46). "Spoken English" (page 180).

The Aberdeen Experiment

By CATHERINE HOLLINGWORTH

In September, 1941, I was appointed Teacher of Speech Training in the Schools under the Aberdeen Education Committee. The task that confronted me was a formidable one. The number of children in attendance at school was approximately 25,570, distributed as follows :—

25	Primary Schools	18,700
8	Junior Secondary Schools ...	4,050
3	Secondary Schools	2,400
2	Special Schools	260
2	Nursery Schools	160

I decided that, to begin with, my services would be used to greatest advantage if I were to concentrate on the Primary Schools, and work from the Infant departments upwards. In the first place, I visited all the Primary Schools in order to find out what precisely was being done to promote good speech, and no less important, to discover how teachers would react to efforts on my part to invest Speech Training with an importance comparable with that accorded to other subjects on the curriculum.

It was very gratifying to find that despite the insistent demands of a multiplicity of subjects, effective work was being done in the classroom, and many teachers were eager to improve their methods and to co-operate with me in every way.

As a first step, demonstration lessons were conducted in classes from infants up to the qualifying-class stage. On the invitation of infant mistresses, special lessons were given in a large number of schools with the teachers present. These were inspiring occasions; lively discussions took place, and advice was sought and given on many individual speech problems. In the Junior and Senior departments the children responded with great interest; and where the teacher displayed equal enthusiasm, there seemed to be a development of spontaneity, not only in speech, but in the children's reactions to the teaching of other subjects.

I did not attempt to keep a complete record of every speech disorder brought to my notice, because it was not possible for one person to undertake the normal work of speech training and act in the capacity of Speech Therapist at the same time. When defects were brought to my attention by teachers, I prescribed a list of suitable exercises to be done, either by the whole class, or in the case of serious defects, by the individual children concerned.

Saturday morning classes for Primary School teachers were held, and 190 teachers enrolled. Teaching methods were discussed and a demonstration lesson was given to a group of unselected children. One of these classes was run on the lines of a Brains Trust, consisting of Miss Jackson, Lecturer in Phonetics at the Training Centre; Miss Bailey of Westburn Road Special School; Miss Smith, Speech Therapist and Lecturer at the Training Centre; Miss Braithwaite, Speech Therapist for Dundee Education Committee, and myself. Speech difficulties were discussed and analysed, and methods of correction suggested.

By this time visits to schools were conforming to a regular time-table. As a rule, a visit was made every three weeks to Primary Schools. My next step was to contact the Junior Secondary Schools where the age of the boys and girls is 12 to 14 years. A programme including acted ballads, choral verse speaking and a scene from *Julius Cæsar* was undertaken by one school, and a performance given in the school hall at the end of the term. On the invitation of the Headmaster of another Junior Secondary School, I visited and gave weekly demonstration lessons to many classes of boys and girls. There was close co-operation with the teachers, who readily undertook to develop the work on broad and liberal lines; and at Christmas a performance of acting and verse-speaking was given to the rest of the school.

To enable teachers to help stammerers and children whose speech was undeveloped through some nervous affection, classes in muscular relaxation were given after school hours. Many teachers attended these and stated that they themselves derived much benefit from the instruction given.

At this point a refresher course was held for teachers; subjects studied included voice production, poetry speaking, choral verse speaking and dramatised ballads. The original intention was to conclude the course at Christmas; but at the request of the teachers it was continued for another term. At this time also, a Children's Theatre was run by way of an experiment during the last week of the Christmas term. In all about 180 children took active part in plays, dramatised folk-songs, choral verse-speaking, etc. Children and teachers from neighbouring schools were invited to each of the three performances. The items were prepared by class teachers under my supervision where desired.

My next venture brought me into Powis Community Centre, where the Warden and some of the members wished to form a speech class. My talk was illustrated by a class of children from one of the Primary Schools. They gave ample proof of what can be done to correct the common faults of slovenly articulation and ugly enunciation of vowels. This class has also been used for the same purpose in connection with Recreation Clubs.

A puppet theatre was made available to any teacher wishing to use it; and, at the invitation of Infant teachers, I have given demonstrations of puppetry in the Infant departments of the schools. This work has led to a discernable improvement in expression and self-confidence; and such is its value that many of the schools are now using their own puppet theatre and puppets.

By the end of the second year's work, regular visits were being made to the various departments of all Primary schools, and weekly visits to certain Junior Secondary schools, where special experimental work was undertaken with the co-operation of the class teacher.

Since I believe strongly that education should fit us for leisure as well as for work, by developing the cultural aspects of life, it has been and is my ardent wish to organise a Children's Theatre scheme. A report has previously been drawn up of the first experiment in this work.

In June, 1943, the second activity of this nature took place. The programme consisted of a part of *A Midsummer Night's Dream,* dramatised ballads, folk-songs and verse-speaking by pupils of Junior Secondary and Primary Schools.

During the period September to December, 1943, my work seemed to develop in all directions at once. Routine visits were made to schools, school concerts which included plays and acted ballads and verse-speaking were organised for the Christmas term; a third Children's Theatre was organised with a programme of plays, songs, etc., and was presented on four occasions to 2,000 school children. Almost 300 children took an active part, each item being a class activity. On this occasion, comment was made on the interest and excellent behaviour of the audiences of children.

The appointment of a Speech Therapist at this juncture was a great help, relieving me of the whole onus of the remedial side of speech work.

Visits of travelling companies such as the Scottish Children's Theatre, the Curtain Theatre directed by Miss Ann Casson, and the Viennese Glove Puppet Theatre, were also arranged. Performances attended by school children were given in various halls in the town.

In June, 1944, the appointment was made of an Assistant in the Speech Training section of the work. The two branches, Speech Training and Speech Therapy, were then linked together in a Department of Speech, or, to be more exact, a Department of Speech Training and Speech Therapy.

A most interesting experiment was carried out in June, 1944. A day of poetry speaking was arranged, with classes from 35 schools in the town; the ages of the children varied from 6 years to 16 years, and specially selected programmes included choral verse, activity-rhymes, dramatised ballads, mimes, puppetry, stories and scenes from plays. This was a "Festival" in the true sense of the word. Miss Gullan of the Speech Fellowship was our guest on this occasion; and encouraged and inspired us with her constructive and helpful comments. There was no competition; the atmosphere was happy and free, and the performance was a joy for pupils and teachers alike.

From the foregoing, it is evident that the scope of the work has developed so much and on such interesting lines largely because of the co-operation of the teaching staffs of the schools.

This work has for its aim the fostering in the child of a confidence in self-expression, no matter in what society he may find himself, and it will do much to develop courageous and confident citizens of the post-war world. It is therefore to be hoped that this democratic experiment will in some measure inspire other education authorities to consider an appointment of this kind.

The Visiting Teacher

By MARGARET ARNOTT

The position of the visiting specialist in any subject is difficult because (a) she has little opportunity of taking part in the corporate life of the school and (b) her subject tends to be regarded as exclusive to the privileged few and outside the general syllabus. This state of affairs is deplorable enough even for music and dancing, which should be part of every child's education, but for speech it is disastrous. For speech is not a "subject" to be taught in the confines of the classroom. It is part of human behaviour, and is as much bound up with every lesson as is "English" itself. Children love to keep their subjects in water-tight compartments: sentence construction learnt so laboriously in the English lesson is forgotten in the history essay; posture, practised with such care in the gymnasium, is left there with the apparatus. Anything which tends to encourage this lack of application is to be deprecated, and how much more dangerous, even disastrous, can be the idea of "Speech" as a lesson—something "taken" once a week on a certain day.

Ideally, every teacher should be equipped with the necessary training to correct bad speech habits as they occur in the classroom. Failing this there should be among the staff of every school one teacher who is also a specialist in Spoken English and is fully qualified to train children's speech and detect speech disorders. Even here, however, results are not wholly satisfactory without the co-operation of the other teachers, who are themselves "good" speakers and sufficiently alive to the importance of good speech to insist on it in their lessons and to report difficulties to the teacher responsible for speech.

The fact remains, however, that at present it is often a choice between a visiting specialist in speech or no speech training at all, and there is no doubt that much good work is being done by visiting teachers, in spite of the fact that they seldom have opportunities of meeting the children in any other capacity, and also lack the influence which a full-time teacher is able to wield in so many ways outside the classroom.

Schools vary, of course, in the extent to which they are able to make use of the services of the visiting specialist. Some of the most interesting pioneer work in speech training has been going on for some time in the Technical Schools, particularly in the Day Departments of Commerce. The realistic approach to the subject demanded here is undoubtedly best made by those specialists who can also bring business training and experience to bear on their teaching. In this type of school, more perhaps than in any other, co-operation between the visiting teacher and the full-time staff is absolutely essential, and without it the work is foredoomed to failure. In the first place, considerable resistance to the idea on the part of the children—particularly the boys—has to be broken down; and without the help of the full-time staff here the visiting teacher is lost indeed! Secondly, the course lasts only two years and in that short space of time many and varied bad habits of speech must be broken and new ones formed. Thirdly, exigencies of time demand the close relation of speech work to the other subjects being taught. The emphasis is on "Spoken English," rather than on "Speech Training," and the eradication of bad speech habits, although the principal object, is only one item in a syllabus which includes training in oral self-expression, sight reading, oral summarising of typed and printed matter, dictation of letters from notes, telephone technique and committee procedure. In teaching each of these the specialist relies to an enormous extent on the co-operation of the full-time staff. The teaching of shorthand signs for the sounds of language links up with the study of these from the phonetic aspect in the speech lesson, and the introduction of shorthand to these children demonstrates forcibly the difference between written and spoken language. The fallacy that "we have five vowels—A E I O U" is realised by these children within the first week of combined shorthand and speech lessons. It often takes many weeks to eradicate the idea from children of the same age in other schools where the teacher of speech is fighting a lone battle!

Text-books in general subjects, e.g., geography and history readers, are brought into use in the sight-reading lesson. Speakers for the out-of-school debates are trained in oral expression lessons. Both shorthand and typing may be used in connection with oral summarising, dictation of letters and committee procedure; while the possibilities of linking-up written and spoken English are endless, given mutual confidence between the English staff and the visiting specialist. Nor are the æsthetic and social aspects of spoken English forgotten. In many of these schools, speech festivals are held regularly, with classes in dramatic recitation, verse speaking and original speeches, frequently with the entire staff acting as a board of judges. Productions of the plays of Shakespeare and Shaw, directed by the visiting teacher with the help of the other members of staff, reach a commendable standard. The detection of speech disorders and the discovery of special talent are two tasks for which the specialist is peculiarly fitted. On one occasion two children found their way to a speech clinic and another to Royal Academy of Dramatic Art in one term! In such conditions as these, the visiting specialist can do invaluable work of the widest scope.

Little mention need be made in this article of the work undertaken by the specialist in such ideal conditions as are to be found in most Public Boarding Schools. Here the specialist is often resident; speech habits are good to start with by reason of the cultured background of these privileged pupils; and the verse speaking and play production set a beautiful standard of voice and speech which it is well to have, even though circumstances at present make it extremely difficult for less fortunate schools to reach it.

There remain the private preparatory and private secondary schools, and here the difficulties are shattering. For the preparatory schools cram for entrance to the secondary schools, and the secondary schools cram for entrance to the University. Qualification for graduation at our Universities demands no standard of proficiency in oral expression and neither the School Leaving Certificate nor Matriculation requires any facility in the use of spoken English. So long as this anomaly continues, so long will the work of the visiting specialist in private schools be strictly limited.

In the majority of these schools, speech, still unhappily known as "Elocution," is an "extra," and the services of the teacher are confined to private teaching of those children who are talented in this direction or of those whose speech habits urgently need correction. Valuable as this work is, it must always be unsatisfactory as it is totally unrelated to the rest of the school work, and in the task of raising the standard of speech as a whole the visiting teacher can take no part. Nor is she in a position to watch for speech disorders throughout the school and arrange for their treatment. Co-operation between the visiting teacher and the full-time staff is impossible because they seldom meet. "Elocution classes" are usually held after school hours, on Saturdays, and during school time specially set apart for this and other "extras."

There are, however, a number of progressive private schools where speech training is a part of the curriculum and is even continued without interruption right through to the "Scholarship Sixth," in spite of the Universities! This article would not be complete without mention of the work they are doing in the cause of spoken English. Given as much co-operation as is possible from the rest of the staff, the visiting teacher here has more promising conditions. The very fact that she *is* a specialist can sometimes be turned to advantage and the children impressed by the knowledge that, so important does the school consider good speech to be that it sets aside a special period for it and engages the services of a specialist to teach it. Other factors, too, help the visiting teacher to take a fuller part in the school life. The full-time staff, for example, is generally only too ready for the visiting teacher to take her share of school duties, and such tasks as lunch-supervision and house-meetings afford the specialist many opportunities of meeting the children outside the classroom. And although the visiting teacher is forever waging war against the use of good speech only in the speech lesson, she has weapons to her hand which are denied her in the Technical School. The standard of speech is usually better here and the schools themselves often have a tradition of good speech to which their pupils quickly conform. Greater attention can be given to raising the speech standard through voice and speech work over a period of upwards of five years, as against two in the Technical Schools. The work of the visiting teacher in these enlightened private schools, where speech training is a curriculum subject, has, also, a cultural aspect which is not affected so much by its being a form-room "subject." The arts of verse and prose speaking and dramatic performance, for example, which are unhappily crowded out of the technical school time-table, can be raised to a very high standard; and training in oral self-expression and reading aloud can develop along more advanced lines than is possible with the material available in the Technical School.

It is not the fault of our schools that spoken English is ignored in the training of Britain's professional classes, and tribute must be paid to the great efforts they are making, in face of official apathy, to restore the spoken word to its proper place among the necessary accomplishments of a cultured democracy.

The Speech of Deaf Children

By IRENE EWING

In the Report of the Committee of Inquiry into problems relating to Children with Defective Hearing, deaf children are classified under three heads :—

Grade 1. Children with defective hearing who can, nevertheless, without special arrangements of any kind, obtain proper benefit from the education provided in an ordinary school—elementary, secondary or technical.

Grade II. Children whose hearing is defective to such a degree that they require for their education special arrangements or facilities, but not he educaional methods used for deaf children without naturally acquired speech or language. These facilities range from a favourable position in the ordinary school classroom to attendance at a special class or school.

Grade III. Children whose hearing is so defective, and whose speech and language are so little developed, that they require education by methods used for deaf children without naturally acquired speech or language. This grade includes the totally deaf.

Speech of Children in Grade I

As a rule the speech of children in this grade does not suffer from abnormalities or defects which are due to an impairment of hearing. Their speech may be said to be normal to their environment.

Speech of Children in Grade II

Here the crucial factors are the cause and degree of deafness from which a child suffers. If it is caused by disease or obstruction in the middle ear, loss of hearing would probably be for sound throughout the whole range of pitch required for hearing speech (i.e., the speech range). This would reduce the loudness of ordinary speech to the deaf child and also probably prevent him hearing some of the quieter consonants such as *f, th, t, k,* or from distinguishing between them. For this reason a Grade II child who suffers from middle-ear deafness is apt to develop two tendencies in his own speech :—

(1) to speak too quietly, probably at much the same loudness as *he* hears other people speak;

(2) to slurr, mispronounce or omit some consonants.

On the other hand, if a child's deafness is due to disease or injury of the internal ear, his loss of hearing will be more severe for the upper than for the lower part of the speech range. Such a child's capacity to hear his own speech by bone conduction may also be impaired. This kind of deafness has been described as high-tone deafness. In this condition two common tendencies are often noticeable in a child's speech.

(1) He may use too loud a voice because he naturally wants to hear the sound of his own voice clearly;

(2) He may hear a somewhat distorted version of some words or vowels or consonants.

In fact he may hear the majority of words and yet be unable to hear clearly some others. As would be expected, therefore, he is likely to imitate in his own speech the imperfect versions he hears.

In these ways the speech of the Grade II deaf child is often characterised by defects that are directly attributable to deafness.

Appropriate remedial speech training should be based on accurate knowledge about the child's capacity or incapacity to hear and differentiate the consonants in speech. Those which he cannot hear or be enabled to hear with a suitable hearing-aid must be made known to him through his senses of vision and touch. Constant practice will be needed to perfect any consonants that are defective or omitted when he talks, but in the course of time by constantly associating the versions he can hear, feel and see, he should gradually acquire accurate habits of speech.

Speech of Children Classified as Grade III

Investigation has shown that approximately seventy per cent. of children in this grade are not totally deaf, but that they possess some capacity to hear loud sounds. This varies in degree and range. Some can catch the sound of a speaker's voice and odd words here and there in ordinary conversation, others can hear only very loud noises; some can hear loud sounds of low pitch but not of high pitch; others can hear high pitched better than low pitched sounds.

Amongst Grade III children in a special school for the deaf there are three main groups :—

(a) Those who can hear the sound of a speaker's voice and perhaps some of his words. These children fall into Grade III (a), approximately 35 per cent.

(b) Those who can only hear the mere sound of a speaker's voice when he talks in an ff voice or directly into their ears. These children are classified as Grade III (b), approximately 35 per cent.

(c) Those who are totally deaf, approximately 30 per cent.

The majority in each group have been born deaf or have become deaf before learning to talk.

The problem of the development of their speech therefore is bound up with and dependent upon their knowledge and use of words. This is nil except in relatively few cases in which a child has just enough hearing to pick up odd words. Apart from such exceptions it is true to say that children in Grade III, irrespective of their age, are dumb until they are taught to speak. But that it not to suggest that they are silent—far from it. Most of them use their voices in shouting and play, but until they are taught by special methods of education words play no part in their thinking, in their comprehension of the thoughts of other people or in the expression of their own thoughts.

Does the egg produce the hen or the hen produce the egg? A similar problem has to be faced in relation to the development of lip-reading and speech in a deaf child. The purpose of speech is made known to him in the first place through lip-reading. His acquisition of vocabulary to use in thinking and in the expression of thought is brought about by the interaction of his native urge to get something he wants and his aptitude for learning. His use of voice is instinctive, but the shaping of a word that he has seen on the lips of other people is evidence of capacity to imitate words, which of course involves learning words through the sense of sight instead of hearing. A deaf child's first attempts to speak follow his beginnings in lip-reading, but his ultimate success in lip-reading will depend mainly upon the extent to which he uses words in thinking and upon the range of his vocabulary and knowledge of English. These in turn depend upon his intelligence and all the opportunities he gets in his school and home environment of acquiring, using and comprehending speech.

It is now known that the majority of infants who are born deaf use their voices naturally in crying, laughing, gurgling, cooing, etc., during their first year. It is very important therefore that during the pre-school years (one to three years) a deaf child be encouraged to continue to make use of his voice to attract attention to his wants. If a child can hear at all, parents and other people should train him to listen to sounds they know he can hear and to learn to use his hearing by "singing" close to his ears. He should be encouraged also to "sing" to others. Both the pre-school child who can hear a little and the one who cannot hear at all should be encouraged to watch the faces and the facial expression of those who talk to them. This habit of watching faces is the first step towards lip-reading and speech.

All this fits the pre-school child for the special teaching he will get when he goes to a school for the deaf. There, speech will be developed through that form of training which is most suitable for the individual child, e.g., the speech of children in Grade IIIa will be developed through the combined means of hearing (with the help of special hearing-aid apparatus) lip-reading and sense of touch. In this case hearing is the dynamic which promotes and quickens the child's acquisition of speech. Lip-reading and perception of speech movements through touch supplement hearing and clarify word patterns which are only heard indistinctly.

Children in Grades IIIb and IIIc face a much harder task in learning to talk. In the one case only very loud sounds can be heard, and in the other case nothing at all. For both groups lip-reading is the dynamic which promotes the acquisition of speech. The actual articulation of words is aided by the tactile perception of speech movements. Nevertheless, the child who can be enabled to hear the mere sound of a speaker's voice has two advantages over the one who is totally deaf. The sound of voice stimulates the use of voice, and the use of voice is a natural and instinctive basis from which to develop speech. Human experience is enriched by capacity to hear even a few loud sounds. At least the Grade IIIb child will know the difference between sound and vibration, and between sounds of different loudness, and perhaps between some which differ in quality. This knowledge is important to the development of his speech and to the formation of habits which will enable him to control and modulate his voice when he talks.

Apart from ear and voice training such as can be given to the Grade IIIb child, the method of speech training is the same for him as for the totally deaf child. Both learn to articulate through their senses of sight and touch. Some speech movements are visible : others can be felt as they are made by lips or tongue, etc. Some, but not all, can be both seen and felt. In any case, it takes intelligence to perceive and recall, and to learn to make automatically all the quick delicate movements required for speech.

Learning to talk under the conditions which deafness imposes demands intelligence and good powers of concentration. It is not surprising, therefore, that all deaf children do not achieve intelligible speech. Neither do all children nor all adults who can hear. The wonder is that so many born deaf children do succeed in learning to talk intelligibly. Is the struggle towards this goal worth while? It must be confessed it is hard and long.

What is the alternative? To rely upon gesture and finger-spelling, ways of communication that few can use or understand.

Deafness inevitably limits social life, but dumbness adds a barriers that few can cross effectually enough to allow of free interchange of thought. To live like this is to be in a world of people who can hear but to have access only to a trickle from the vast stream of human companionship, accumulated knowledge and experience.

The value of the speech of deaf children should not be judged by its aesthetic qualities but by the part it plays in developing their minds.

BIBLIOGRAPHY

The Backward Child. C. Burt (Univ. of London Press, 7s. 6d.)

Speech in Childhood. Seth & Guthrie (Oxford, 10s. 6d.)

Survey of American Schools for the Deaf. Day, Fusfield & Pinter (Washington)

Report of the Committee of Inquiry into Problems Relating to Children with Defective Hearing. (H.M. Stationery Office, 1938)

Aphasia in Children. A. W. G. Ewing (Oxford Medical Publications)

The Handicap of Deafness. I. R. & A. W. G. Ewing (Longmans, out of print)

"Deafness in Infancy and Early Childhood" (*Journal of Laryngology and Otology.* 58/4, 1943)

The Teaching of Speech. Sibley Haycock (Hill & Ainsworth, Stoke-on-Trent)

Hearing and Speech in Deaf Children. P. M. T. Kerridge (Medical Research Council, Report 221, 1937)

Opportunity and the Deaf Child. I. R. and A. W. G. Ewing (University of London Press).

For addresses see page 212.

School Broadcasting

By DOUGLAS ALLAN

A STORY is told about the early days of School Broadcasting of a class of Scottish children listening on a closed circuit in a studio to a recording of a talk previously broadcast in England.

To the surprise of the B.B.C. officials present, the children went into uncontrollable fits of laughter (the speaker had not intended anything she said to be amusing). When the children at the end of the talk were asked why they had laughed, they said it was because "the lady's accent was that funny"! There is no evidence that the lady's voice was in any other way amusing—it was just that her accent, to children brought up in a Scottish environment and with few opportunities at that time to hear Southern English, seemed odd and unusual, and, therefore, something to laugh at.

It is inconceivable, I imagine, that that could happen now. Broadcasting may not have brought us an inch nearer that uniformity of speech which the dialect lover feared it might, but it has made most of us much more aurally aware than we were in pre-broadcasting days. It has brought about a familiarity which has not bred contempt. No regional speaker is likely nowadays to find anything amusing in the speech of, say, the news readers, and no speaker of southern English accustomed to listening to first-hand war "actualities" or features from the regions, is likely to regard the tongue of Yorkshire or Lancashire or Scotland as fitted only for the music-hall stage.

That effect of broadcasting has never been part of the B.B.C.'s deliberate intention. It has been an accidental by-product of the B.B.C.'s policy in other directions—its policy in choosing as news readers and announcers those who are likely to be understood by the greatest numbers; its policy of reflecting the life and, inevitably therefore, the language of the regions. It has resulted from an objective display of the linguistic goods of the British Isles without other intention.

AN EXPERIMENT IN SPEECH TRAINING

But two deliberate attempts have been made, one in England, the other in Scotland, to make listeners in schools aware of the differences in these linguistic goods, and, by implication at least, of certain values that go with these differences.

The English experiment began in 1927. Eight years before, in 1919, the Board of Education report, *The Teaching of English in England,* had recommended that standard English should be taught in the elementary schools.

Many thought that broadcasting might have something to contribute in this direction. Mr. A. Lloyd James, then Lecturer in Phonetics at the London School of Oriental Studies, was invited to give a series of weekly talks for schools on speech and language.

In his experimental lessons Mr. Lloyd James "felt obliged to refrain from any attempt to impose the received standard on the schools or to discourage the use of local pronunciations." His aim was limited to that of "interesting children in the problems of speech and language, awakening in them the desire to understand how they themselves pronounce the sounds in English speech, and imparting some elementary instruction in the general principles of spoken English."

Courses on these lines were broadcast from 1927-1930. In that year there was a change of intention. The Central Council for School Broadcasting decided to experiment with broadcasting as a medium for more precise instruction in spoken English. While no-one wished to discourage the use of dialect as spoken in the playground and the home, it was, however, felt that in view of the conditions of the modern world the children had a definite right to instruction in the form of English that is most widely understood. The main aim of the new series was, therefore, to give children regular practice in making accepted vowel and consonant sounds, and its main emphasis was on the pronunciation of individual sounds.

Then a number of questions naturally arose in the minds of those responsible for the course. Were pupils sufficiently trained by a twenty-minute broadcast for any difference to be noticeable in their speech at all? Was there any evidence that the work was continued in the schools? Was there any evidence that the broadcasts did in fact have any effect in changing children's speech? Some of these questions could be answered easily by enquiries on the spot, or by correspondence from teachers, but no method had yet been tried by which the result of the broadcast lessons could be measured on reliable scientific lines. In 1931 a scheme was considered for testing the results in this way. Without going into the detail of the experiment, it was, in short, this: that the speech of eighty-four pupils from two classes in a London County Council school should be recorded at the beginning and the end of one broadcasting year; one of the classes (the wireless class) having listened to Mr. Lloyd James's talks and carried out the suggested drill after the broadcasts; the other (the control class) having followed only its ordinary time-table of English work and having had no systematic instruction in speech.

The recordings were made in September, 1931 and in June, 1932, and the records were then submitted to an outside expert in phonetics, precautions being taken, of course, against his being able to identify the class or pupils to whose recordings he was listening. Having devised a system of marking, he then prepared tables showing the improvement in the making of speech sounds in the members of the wireless class and the control class. His tables were then submitted, for analysis to four statisticians. After testing the reliability of the figures, Professor Burt was able to conclude that "the main result of the experiment—a superior improvement in the class trained by wireless—is statistically reliable. This conclusion is confirmed by studying the progress of the individual boys in detail."

But the results of this enquiry were not regarded as sufficient in themselves to justify the continuance of the experimental course in speech training. The Central Council for School Broadcasting in 1933 came to the decision to abandon the attempt to give broadcast speech training in the National Programme. The difficulties and dangers were many. There was the difficulty of bad reception, with consequent distortion of the sounds made by the broadcasters. There was still a lack of an exact set of rules which would help teachers to take practical work after the broadcasts. There was still a strong body of people who resented the formulation of any such rules, fearing it might result in a dull uniformity.

The investigation itself had sampled only one school, and the evidence collected from it could not be regarded as nearly wide enough to prove anything. Besides, it had confined itself to the examination of a few sounds only, and had not covered, for example, matters of rhythm and intonation. At the school end, too, there was the time difficulty. Unless the teacher could find time (and had also the necessary training himself) to continue the speech exercises recommended by the broadcaster, little of value could be looked for from the twenty minutes devoted to the actual lesson.

In 1937 Miss Mary Somerville, Director of School Broadcasts, reported in a lecture to the Speech Fellowship conference, "I do not think they (the difficulties inherent in the broadcasting of lessons in speech) can ever be solved save with the co-operation of everyone interested in speech—in which case the decisions (i.e., as to a set of rules) on which the solution of the problem depends must be public decisions. They cannot properly be made either by the B.B.C. or by the Central Council."

THE SCOTTISH EXPERIMENT

In Scotland, on the other hand, it was found possible to get agreement as to what sounds should be taught. A small National Committee agreed to give guidance on the problem of vowel sounds, and after a considerable amount of experiment had been carried out at Jordanhill Training College, Glasgow, in the summer and autumn of 1934, a series of Speech Training broadcasts for children began in the spring of 1935.

The Special Committee's view was that the primary function of the broadcasts was to help teachers to train the children to speak clearly and precisely. And, while the Committee did not want uniformity or to impose a rigid "standard" Scots, it did agree that no attempt should be made to teach the accepted sounds of "standard" English—that for example, nothing should be done to interfere with the Scottish *"r"*, and that Dr. McAllister should not attempt to replace Scottish "pure" vowels by southern English diphthongs.

A second course for pupils from seven to nine was started in 1938. The broadcasts in both series (as in the English series too) were meant to be used in conjunction with the illustrated pamphlets issued by the B.B.C.

The Scottish experiment had one advantage and one promise of success that the English experiment had not. The Scottish educational system being what it was, it was certain that the great majority of teachers taking the broadcasts had been trained at one of the colleges administered by the National Committee for the Training of Teachers, and had themselves a certain amount of speech training from Dr. McAllister herself or one of her colleagues.

With the outbreak of war, and the discontinuance of regional broadcasting in its pre-war form, when only one programme (later two) was provided for the whole country, the two Scottish series were suspended.

So much for the attempts made in this country to give direct instruction in speech by wireless.

PROBLEMS OF SPEECH IN THE STUDIO

It is probably easier to say what kind of voice one would not use in a broadcast for schools than to say which would be acceptable. It would be obviously impossible to admit a slip-shod voice which slurred its consonants, and, on the other side, equally impossible to admit one that was over-careful and spat out all its "*d*s" and "*t*s". We would certainly shun the voice that appeared to be affected in any way or "genteel." Certain voices are pleasanter to listen to than others, and these are usually to be found within a limited range of frequencies—a range which would include the Radio Doctor, Mr. Churchill and Mr. Middleton at one end, and the voice of H.M. The Queen at the other. Voices that are too deep tend to sound pompous. Voices that are too high in pitch are a permanent irritation to the ear—that is why it is, generally speaking, much more difficult to find acceptable women broadcasters than acceptable men. But the one thing those of us who are responsible for broadcasting to schools would avoid like the plague is the voice that in any way "comes down" to the children. That effect may be merely vocal or it may be, and frequently is, the result of the speaker's attitude to children. The good speaker to schools will address his audience in terms that they can understand and on their own level, but without whimsy or condescension.

And again the question of accents arises. There are teachers whose contention is that we should never allow any but "standard" English speakers to broadcast, and would say that the authority given by the B.B.C. to a broadcaster whose own English was off standard might be likely to weaken the influence of the school in its attempt to lead the children on to a "higher" and "better" plane of speech. Now it is obvious that when one is broadcasting *A Midsummer Night's Dream* or a poem by Tennyson, one does want actors or readers whose speech is free from personal peculiarities or dialect characteristics. But, on the other hand, I can see no good reason for depriving children in schools of the first-hand experience of a man who can give them a vivid picture of Nigeria, or of the mental stimulus that can be imparted by a scientist, or of the knowledge of the best methods of pruning an apple tree, just because the speakers have the accents of Gloucestershire or the East End of London, or the Scottish borders. Provided always, of course, that they are intelligible—and intelligible all over the country. But within that field of intelligibility a great number of voices using Professor Wyld's "modified standard," or a trace of actual dialect, do prove acceptable to the great majority of listeners. Dr. Ida Ward, in a broadcast in the "To Start You Talking" series, used the phrase 'utility English' to describe the form of English used by such speakers.

All these considerations are, of course, those that would be held in mind by B.B.C. officials choosing speakers for any purpose; but they must be held in mind more particularly when one is choosing a broadcaster for young children. An adult (unless he is a tap listener) switches on his radio for a special purpose, because this is something he wants to listen to. He begins, that is, with something himself to contribute to the talk or feature to which he is listening, and a willingness to accept certain difficulties within reason. In the schools, however, unless interest and excitement are present because of the re-appearance of a personality whom the children have come to love, or unless an expectation has been aroused by the teacher in his preparatory work before the loud-speaker is switched on, the children may begin to listen in a state of apathy—we hope never antipathy. Interest, therefore, must be captured at the beginning and held throughout the twenty or twenty-five minutes of the programme. A dull voice will lose it; a voice too difficult to understand will lose it; a voice which sounds snobbish will lose it; a voice without variation of speed and volume will lose it; a voice that gabbles at too great a speed will lose it; a voice that sounds interested neither in the subject nor in the children themselves will lose it.

DRAMATIC WORK FOR SCHOOLS

In dramatic work again the fundamental issues are those affecting all broadcasting of plays and feature programmes. Acting that is suitable for the stage, dramatic reading that is suitable for the concert platform, just will not do for the microphone. Fortunately the B.B.C. can call on actors who have made it their business to learn the technique of the microphone; who have learnt to scale down their vocal range to reach an audience only, in effect, a few feet away from them; who know that in radio acting much can be achieved by a tiny inflection which would be lost between the stage and the back rows of the stalls, and that the essential characteristic of broadcasting is its intimacy.

Apart from that, our experience of the reactions to the broadcasting of plays and feature programmes for schools has led us to impose on ourselves certain restrictions which might not be so commonly imposed by the producers of a programme for evening consumption. Sound effects and music are never allowed to interfere with clarity of speech. Dialect, when used, must be toned down to a mere suggestion. The over-all speed should be slightly slower. And in a dramatic interlude, where the significance of certain points is intended to be grasped by the children, these points must be made by the use of some device in the writing or speaking of the script, or both, which will plant them firmly in the children's minds.

THE READING OF POETRY

The choice of poems to be broadcast, and of readers to broadcast them, is one of the biggest headaches that any B.B.C. official can have. In nothing is there so much difference of opinion. Comments from schools are never so contradictory as when directed at poetry broadcasts.

Without going into greater detail than the length of this article will allow, it is impossible to say what should guide one in one's choice of poems to be broadcast. There are certainly some which no one should try to speak over the microphone, since that was never the poet's intention. Of the readers of poetry I would personally avoid those who adopt a parsonic voice, and those who adopt a wailing voice—both, unfortunately, common. Many readers approach their job with an attitude of false reverence. One should never be aware, when listening to poetry on the air, of the intrusion of a personality with all its tricks and personal peculiarities—the poetry should seem to flow through the voice delivering it. But that is not to say that the poetry reader is merely an instrument; he is the instrument plus the player. And, for myself, I can count on the fingers of both hands those who have so trained their instrument and have such technical facility that they can read verse at the microphone to my satisfaction.

Among others, Mary O'Farrell and Carleton Hobbs have given children many memorable experiences in their reading of poetry for schools programmes.

BIBLIOGRAPHY

"School Broadcasting: Some Problems of Speech." Mary Somerville. *Good Speech,* Jan. 1938

"The Influence of Radio on Speech." C. S. March. *Educational Broadcasting* (University of Chicago Press)

"The King's English." Broadcast Talks to Schools by A. Lloyd James, later printed as *Our Spoken Language* (Nelson, 3s.) and *Exercises to Our Spoken Language* (Nelson, 1s. 6d.)

"Speech Training." Broadcast Talks and Lessons to Scottish Schools. Pamphlets edited by Anne MacAllister, later incorporated in *Steps in Speech Training* (University of London Press)

Children and Radio Programmes. A. L. Eisenberg (Milford, 15s.)
School Broadcasting. International Institute of Intellectual Co-operation (Allen & Unwin, 7s. 6d.)
Broadcasting and Education. Howard Whitehouse (Oxford, 3s.)
Evidence Regarding Broadcast Speech Training. (B.B.C., 6s.) (out of print)

Youth Organisations

By DIANA CARROLL

If one were to ask a number of club leaders at random whether they include speech education in their programmes, the reactions of many would probably be, "Oh, no, our members aren't interested in elocution"; but further cosideration would reveal many activities in which speech plays a vital part. Drama, Youth Parliaments and Councils, Discussion groups, Brains Trusts, Committees, Services—through all these speech education is being given indirectly, developing confidence and opening wider interests.

This informal approach is a distinctive mark of educational work in youth organisations. It recognises the needs of the girls and boys who, in their clubs, look for something different from classroom methods. The pendulum has swung over from childhood to assumed sophistication, and anything that smacks of school will be rejected as "kiddish." Approach is all-important, for the whole basis of a club is voluntary, and if subjects are presented dryly, no matter how great the qualifications of the teacher, the group will dwindle. A valid *reason* for anything is a valuable factor. Girls and boys who would never take speech training as an isolated interest, look upon it very differently if introduced in a dramatic setting, or when the excitement of debate calls for clear thinking and expression. Often after the first attempts comes a sense of limitations, and then the demand for help, opening the doors to direct teaching.

The following instances are chosen from many that are being tried among youth. The emphasis may vary according to the part of the country, whether the club is rural or urban, and above all according to the gifts of each leader, but a great similarity of pattern is to be found throughout.

DRAMA

This has many aspects and standards. It ranges from informal acting to finished festival productions. Action generally precedes speech, in the form of charades and mimed improvisations on characters or situations. Impromptu dialogue can be added, and tongue-twister competitions, sentences spoken in the manner of a given adverb, and "I want to be an Actor" sketches are light-hearted introductions to articulation and inflection.

Play-reading tends to be a preliminary to production rather than a separate activity in many groups, who find it too sedentary, and too revealing of their limitations. But there are numerous exceptions to this general trend. Some clubs have Sunday night readings, or read plays from other countries for international programmes. A club with microphone and amplifier broadcasts plays from one room to another. A group at Sheffield under the Religious Drama Adviser has given moving readings of *The King of Sorrows* by Dorothy Sayers. These relied entirely on the voices of speakers and crowd, and a few sound effects, the readers being unseen behind the audience. Some music groups have read L. du Garde Peach's plays, *Music Makers,* illustrated by records or songs.

Considerable help over speech can be given in the normal course of play rehearsals. The Drama Adviser of the National Association of Boys' Clubs sounds a warning against too conscious elocution, stressing that the first necessity is that the young actors should make themselves heard and understood by the audience. Better an imaginative performance in dialect than devitalised refinement. Even so, much can be done to correct sloppy, slurred speech, and to show the value of varied inflections, pace, and power, especially where the ear is quick to detect differences. When certain characters have gripped the imagination of the players they will be the keener to make their speech consistent. A mixed Y.W.C.A. group at Wolverhampton became interested in the Brontës after seeing and discussing the film *Wuthering Heights.* With their leader they borrowed books from the library, and collected pictures showing the costume and manners of the time. Finally they decided to produce the play *The Brontës.* Contemporary furniture was lent by a local shop, and a hairdresser copied pictures of the sisters for the correct styles. At rehearsals the players came to realise the influence that dress, deportment and speech have on one another, and how they vary with different periods.

Changing manners in speech were brought out in a Festival of English Comedy held between clubs in the London Division of Y.W.C.A. when scenes from Shakespeare, Sheridan, Shaw and Priestley were linked together by contemporary music. One actress was heard to say, "The old plays take ten words to say what could be said in one," thereby betraying our modern utilitarian attitude to speech. Others enjoyed the play of words, though sometimes lacking the technique to point a phrase.

Most club members have to rehearse their plays in a small room, only reaching the hall for one or two last rehearsals, where it takes all the producer's exhortations to prevent them sounding like conversational mice.

Diffidence is sometimes overcome by group-speaking, for which a dramatic setting is valuable. A feature programme *I*

*Hear America** included dialogue, songs, dances and mime, showing the contribution of many nationalities to America's population. It ended with "America has taught us the language of liberty, and we speak it with one voice!" Then followed part of the Declaration of Independence and speeches by Lincoln and Roosevelt, chorally spoken. Mixed casts with no previous experience in choral speaking have given this and similar theme-programmes without any self-consciousness.

Verse-speaking for its own sake appears to be more popular with girls than boys, in England at least. Festivals of spoken poetry give an incentive and a standard. A Nottingham club's speech choir combined with singers to give a World News-Reel of poems, songs, and news flashes from many countries. At Christmas they provided the narration for a mime of the Christmas story. The same leader, moving to Cheshire, introduced verse-speaking to girls of elementary education, and found them keen after the first giggles had worn off. She adds, "I tried to start a boys' choir, but failed completely."

In Wales, with its eisteddfod tradition, there is less sense of unfamiliarity. The Welsh League of Youth finds that recitation competitions are enjoyed by performers and audiences, the most popular being those in which eight or twelve young people recite together a poem or passage of prose or Scripture. One of their choirs has reached the highest place in the National Eisteddfod. Less formal is the Noson Lawen (Happy Night) held at a farm or hall, where everyone has to contribute by song, recitation, or telling a story.

An impressive contribution to choral work has been made by The Grail, the youth movement of the Roman Catholic Church, in its large-scale productions in London and elsewhere. In these, which have included *Everyman, The Hound of Heaven,* pageants, and nativity plays, groups of performers numbering several hundreds, using choral speech and symbolic movement, have replaced individual actors. "They do not present things which, though beautiful in themselves, have no bearing on their ideals . . . . They believe that they have a message to get over to those who listen, and while a single voice may make some impression on a large audience, yet the effect of the combined voices of 100, 200, or 500 is immeasurably greater." Music, dancing, movement, and lighting are used in combination with the groups of voices to build up the full effect.

Through religious services in the club, members can contribute much, in arranging the order and taking part. The final service at a school of voluntary youth organisations in Somerset is only one instance of many. The lesson was read by one boy, and a modern poem, "I have lain in the sun" by another; a girl led the responses after intercessions. Choral speaking of psalms, the introduction of modern prose or verse, and readings from

*In *To Meet the Occasion.* (Samuel French, 3s. 6d.).

modern translations of the Bible as commentaries or alternatives to the original, can bring new meaning to these services.

Youth Parliaments and Councils help their members to sort and express their views, and make them alive to the activities of their own club, as well as to a larger sphere of interests. A mixed club at Smethwick reports: "When we first started our Parliament the girls said nothing, but as they got used to procedure they found their voices, and now make a useful contribution. . . . The Speaker, who was a very reserved boy, has lost all trace of shyness and conducts the Parliament ably." Exeter has a town Youth Parliament, its House of Commons having representatives from local youth organisations, the House of Lords consisting of leaders and clergy. East Sussex youth held a Council to summarise their daily discussion groups at a week's conference. A boy was chairman, a girl secretary, and each of the four proposals had two speakers before being thrown open to general discussion.

"Hat Nights," Mock Trials, and the giving of Introductions and Votes of thanks to speakers, all encourage confidence. These last two particularly have a significance out of all proportion to their length. Through them, however halting, girls and boys express their responsibility as hosts in their own club, and the value of words in showing courtesy from one person to another.

See bibliographies to "Discussion Groups" (page 109), "Choral Speaking" (page 146), and "Amateur and Experimental Drama" (page 158). A list of youth organisations will be found on page 215.

Adult Education

By KATHLEEN STONE

IDEALLY, speech education is a continuous process. It begins in the Infant and Junior school, where helping the child to express himself should be the teacher's main concern; it continues through the Senior, Secondary or Technical school, where there should be regular opportunities for using this acquired skill; and confirmed in Youth Clubs and other organisations for the adolescent. So that, ideally again, the expression and communication of ideas through the voice should be the natural accomplishment of every adult.

In actual practice unfortunately, as organisers of W.E.A., Women's Institutes and Adult School classes know only too well, this is very seldom the case. Speech has been neglected for writing before the child is halfway through his education, and the average boy or girl, young man or woman, is unable to speak effectively. Even among students at Teachers' Training Colleges and Universities the standard is often deplorably low. In a recent article in the *Times Educational Supplement,* Mr. Roy Pascall described an oral test for students taking the course on Modern Germany at Birmingham University. They were given fifteen minutes in which to prepare a ten-minute talk *in English.* "Of the twenty students (almost all of whom are candidates for an Honours Degree) only one spoke with any fluency and sequence. The great majority found it difficult to utter more than two or three consecutive sentences. The examiners had continually to prompt, to ask leading questions, to help clear up confusions and contradictions in the candidates' sentences. The candidates who talked most easily used slipshod, colloquial and slang expressions to a large extent." It is hardly surprising if many of the men and women coming to an Adult School or Evening Institute (who may be employed in mechanical or routine jobs) are even less articulate.

Speech is therefore one of the great problems of the adult class. Most educationists are aware of this, and know that the nation cannot afford to leave its people with their ideas only half-formed and half-expressed. There can be no democracy of the inarticulate. But we shall not get far towards a solution of the problem unless we ask ourselves what we mean by "Speech," and come to some agreement about the answer. If we consider it merely as a synonym of "pronunciation" we shall fail, and fail hopelessly. Speech is a far bigger thing than that. It is part of our personality, and part of our thinking. It is the means by which we communicate our ideas and emotions to other people. Through it, a large part of our life is lived. So that speech education is not a matter of changing "accents"; it means enabling us to relate thought to language, and feeling to language, and to convey these thoughts and feelings simply, clearly and easily.

It follows, then, that speech education cannot be limited to a single class labelled "speech training" or "elocution" or "verse speaking." It should be one of the first considerations of any teacher or lecturer, whatever his subject, and it cannot safely be ignored in any section of adult education. We are slowly realising the value of the spoken word, and beginning to place less reliance on the written. We are encouraging adult groups to think for themselves and to talk for themselves, and not to sit back with a notebook and pencil taking occasional notes—which is a temptation after a hard day's work. There needs to be an alternating flow between the lecturer and the members of his class; the current should not be all one way.

But it is one thing to get the lecturer to realise this; another to persuade the student. We get accustomed to our own speech, and as it is efficient enough to obtain for us the necessities of life—beans-on-toast or a seat at the pictures—we seldom realise its deficiencies, and resent these deficiencies being pointed out to us. So before much can be accomplished for speech in adult education, the student must be helped to realise these deficiencies for himself. Perhaps the most effective means of doing this, and at the same time providing opportunities for improvement, is the Discussion Group, with which Mr. A. J. J. Ratcliff deals at length in another article. This is a very valuable feature of adult education, and one growing in popularity since the war. It is receiving the serious attention of the Bureau of Current Affairs, the Industrial Discussion Groups Experiment, the Association for Education in Citizenship, and similar organisations. They find it teaches coherence, self-expression, self-control and tolerance. It broadens the mind, by bringing it into contact with other minds, with new information, and with new ways of looking at old facts. It is both an aid to speech and an aid to personal knowledge and development. But discussion is not confined to the Discussion Group. There is also the discussion- or question-period at the end of every adult class. Rightly used, this can be the most profitable part of the lesson—the ten minutes or so in which the lecturer discovers how much of his talk has been really assimilated. Some lecturers prefer the whole period to be alternate lecture and discussion, so that the group never feels that he is merely giving out information while they are merely absorbing it. This is an excellent plan, though it requires considerable tact and leadership if the thread of the subject is not to be lost. It is interesting to note that both our Army and that of the United States consider the discussion group so important that it has been made a "function of command," and stress the point that it is more valuable for the men to talk than for the leader to address them.

BRAINS TRUST

The Brains Trust is a variation on the discussion theme. It has "caught on" extraordinarily since it was first introduced into broadcasting in the United States and later in England. The element of spontaneity has created its popularity. Listeners, or those present in the room, feel that there is always a chance that even Dr. Joad may be "floored"! But more important still is the freshness and life which is given to the voices of Brains Trusters compared with many ordinary speakers. Where a prepared lecture may be delivered in a dull fashion, with an even *tempo,* a regular intonation-pattern, and a general sense that the lecturer knows only too well what is coming next, an impromptu answer is varied in pace, in the length of pauses, and in range of intonation, so that the speaker is often in a more direct and intimate touch with his audience. There is also a more immediate connection between what he thinks and what he says.

The chief disadvantage of a Brains Trust is that it turns one group of people into the know-alls, and the listeners into the know-nothings. This segregation is not good, and, though it cannot be avoided in broadcasting, in adult education it can be mitigated by changing the constitution of the Trust regularly and bringing in the audience, one by one, as answerers; or else by having an answering-back period at the end of each session.

With a little experience of discussion, members of the group should become aware of speech as a vehicle for ideas. They should have realised the difficulties of communication and how much they depend on speech not only for expressing thought but even for thinking. To increase this interest, "Speech" might be chosen as one of the subjects for discussion, keeping the definition as broad as possible; that is, speech in the world of to-day, the recent return to the spoken word in preference to the written—radio, gramophone, telephone, cinema—and their effect on the world. (A useful book is *Our Spoken Language,* by A. Lloyd James.) Then from the effect on the million to the effect on the individual and his relationships with other people: speech in the shop, factory, office or at home, the values and the dangers of the spoken word. Some of the members may begin to realise the deficiencies in their own speech and start looking for some means of remedying them. This cannot be done in the discussion group itself because the emphasis there must always be on ideas, not on the delivery of ideas; any consideration of speech, as such, is bound to interrupt the flow of talk.

SPEECH CLASS

Now that the need has been created and understood, there should be some period set aside for speech. In the larger type of Institute there may already be a speech class to which those interested can be referred, but whether the class is newly formed or well-established, it calls for a teacher with many varied qualifications:—

(1) Tact and understanding, for an individual's speech is as personal as his table-manners.

(2) An outlook that is wide enough to view speech as part of daily life, and able to relate it to the problems and pleasures of to-day.

(3) An up-to-date knowledge of the subject, with sufficient understanding of phonetics to be able to analyse, *accurately,* the speech of the members.

(4) The ability to translate technical knowledge into terms understandable and interesting to the class.

(5) Enough artistic ability to appreciate the use of words in English poetry, drama and prose literature, and to be able to speak it beautifully yet simply; and yet broad-minded enough to recognise the value of rough simplicity.

(6) Sufficient humility to realise that his own speech is not perfect, and to regard it not as a pattern on which the

members should model their speech, but simply as one example of good speaking.

At the first lesson the question might be discussed: "What do we want to achieve? Where shall we aim?" In my opinion, it should be clearly stated that one does not intend to teach "better class" speech. The question of pronunciation will have to be dealt with here, but it should be constantly stressed that pronunciation is only one part of speech. It could be explained that there is a particular type of pronunciation which is readily understood all over the country, and gives no indication of the speaker's district or education; and it could be suggested that this type of pronunciation might be useful and worth acquiring for certain purposes. But every endeavour must be made to encourage the class in pride and appreciation of any type of good speech, and not merely "standard English"; and the teacher, as well as the class, needs to remember that the first purpose of speech is communication. They need to be shown how much more they can achieve even with the type of speech already at their disposal—by good, unstrained voice production; clear, vigorous articulation; the right use of emphasis; livelier and more varied tone and inflection; and greater fluency in delivery.

There will thus be a continual give-and-take between this class and the Discussion Group. The former will help them to express themselves more accurately and more interestingly. The Discussion Group will give a purpose to the speech class. For that has to be borne in mind continually—speech must never be allowed to become an end in itself, and the more opportunities that can be found for *using* speech, the better. The London Co-operative Society, for instance, arranges Public Speaking contests. If the judge is wise, this will show those taking part how good ideas and well-constructed speeches can be wasted because the speaker has not learnt how to use them effectively. Adult groups, such as political organisations, who are anxious to further their cause, will quickly see the value of putting their case to the best advantage. On the other hand, we need to be sufficiently educated in *listening* to assess how much of a public speaker's effect comes through good ideas, and how much through good presentation, and to be able to separate true reasoning from emotional appeal. (Thouless's *Straight and Crooked Thinking,* and J. W. Marriott's *Q.E.D.* would be helpful here, and contain the bases of several interesting discussions.) We need to impress upon the class that good presentation alone is not enough; a speech must be built upon truth and sincerity.

Drama, Play-Reading and Choral Speaking are other activities which provide opportunities for using speech—all of which art discussed in other sections of this book (pages 151 and 141). Principals of evening Schools and Technical Institutes might do more to encourage their students to join one of these groups, even if their normal studies run on scientific lines—perhaps even more so then, because there is a great danger of technology becoming divorced from art and ethics. Drama and Choral Speaking are great "humanisers," and they can also help the individual to develop his character and personality to a surprising extent. Anyone who has taught adults knows the way in which even the most unpromising student may suddenly find his feet as a result of a dramatic group, speech choir, or discussion group; and how his entire life may take on a new direction and purpose. The satisfaction felt by the lecturer, teacher or leader when this happens will amply repay him for the time and patience needed to achieve it.

Discussion Groups

By A. J. J. RATCLIFF

Discussion groups of sorts have existed since man could talk, and more definitely since neighbours could get together across the back fence. All great ages of talk and thought—the Age of Louis XIV and the Hôtel de Rambouillet, for instance—have been ages of discussion groups unaware of themselves. Formal debating too was discussion work, but discussion groups in stiff corsets. The Discussion Group proper, fully conscious of itself, is a modern stripling fathered by adult education and in this country mothered (and carefully nursed) by the B.B.C. The story of the prodigy is indeed worth a moment's attention.

It begins in 1924. The B.B.C., feeling it had a duty to discharge towards adult education, approached the appropriate bodies as to what first steps it should take, and as a result of the consultations decided on arranging a syllabus and organising a series of talks in connection with it, suitable for discussion by voluntary groups of listeners. The talks, given in the autumn of the year, were sufficiently successful to warrant the undertaking of a number of further series, and to prompt the setting up of a special Adult Education Section of the B.B.C. Later, a Committee of Inquiry under the chairmanship of Sir Henry Hadow issued a report on the contribution that broadcasting might make, through the discussion technique, to the general sum of adult education, and on the administrative machinery that would be necessary to bring the B.B.C. and the listening groups constructively together. Accordingly a Central Council was set up, supported by Area Councils each served by a paid Education Officer. The Area Councils were (and are) directly concerned with the organisation of discussion groups, the selection of leaders, and the arrangements for holding local conferences to stimulate interest. The Education Officers were to seek out leaders, help them to form groups, pass on to headquarters the leaders' constructive criticisms of the talks, serve as connecting links between groups and the Area and Central Councils, and promote the new educational development generally.

Soon it became apparent that leaders and prospective leaders would need some form of guidance and training. For discussion groups proved themselves to be not a vague and temporary *pis aller* for a study class but a new teaching mode with a definite function of its own. Group leading was not a casual or instinctive process but had its own rationale and technique, which needed to be explored, defined and taught.

So came into existence a succession of training courses: the first week-end school in April, 1929, at Thwait Hall, Cottingham, under the auspices of University College, Hull, and the first full-length school in August, 1930, at the North Yorkshire District W.E.A. Summer School at Saltburn-by-the-Sea, when two weekly courses were held, each for nearly a score of leaders, under the joint direction of Professor T. H. Searls and the present writer. Others followed, and the first National Summer School (50 leaders), held at New College, Oxford, from June 27th to July 4th, 1931, set the pattern for a regular institution.

In 1932 the Board of Education recognised the importance of this new medium of adult education by publishing pamphlet 92: *Adult Education Wireless Listening Groups* based on Inspectors' reports. The number of groups, the pamphlet declared, was rapidly increasing; thus from September-March, 1930-31, 261 groups had been reported, and for the same period, 1931-32, the number was 369. "A movement, which has already enrolled some 4,000 members in the parts of the country dealt with in this report, and which has enlisted the voluntary services of some hundreds of leaders, must be satisfying a real need; and no one can visit these groups without being impressed by the fact that [they] are playing a very important part in the lives of their members."

This is no overstatement. Nor was the success surprising. Universal elementary education preparing the ground, after slow beginnings adult education began to make headway—particularly as organised by such bodies as the W.E.A. Then, in the ferment after the first World War, when large numbers of people were beginning to read and think about national and international affairs, the need was disclosed for *social* and *sociable* thinking: the fortunate answer to which, as suggested above, was the discussion group—at that time the broadcast discussion group.

Up to 1939 the B.B.C. Discussion Group movement continued to spread and flourish. The support of a large organisation was decisive in lending persistence to it. Study pamphlets of first-class quality were devised and distributed. The future looked bright. Then in 1939 came the war, and with the dislocation of all normal arrangements the wireless discussion group abruptly lost much of the ground it had gained, and indeed every form of organised adult education suffered. But only for a time. The need was genuine, and the later phases of the war saw the sudden and amazing development of groups, whether in the Army, Navy, Air Force, Civil Defence and National Fire Service, or in civilian life (for example, the Co-operative Groups, Y.M.C.A. Groups, and the Industrial Discussion Clubs Experiment). A great tide of group-work and discussion swept everything before it, aided by the theatrical success of an allied educational technique, the Brains Trust. As for the B.B.C. groups, in October, 1944, for three series of talks only—Getting Things Done, To Start You Talking, and Friday Discussions—the number of groups functioning was well over 1,500.

The future promises well, especially if more is done to show group members how to make their thinking and their decisions affect actual practice in the several spheres of work, leisure, local and central government, and international relations.

PURPOSE AND TECHNIQUE

The purpose of the members of a discussion group is not to acquire a given body of information or to have their interest awakened in a set subject, as with students attending lectures; nor is it to practise the opposing of two parties in debate so as to get a majority decision on an issue; nor again is it to be encouraged in mere talk. The immediate purpose is to consider, as partners in a social group, some particular matter in a way that will stimulate the individual members' ideas on the issue concerned, and make explicit the group's total considered reaction to it. The long-term purpose is to promote a habit of approaching all questions actively, keeping an open yet curious mind, and striving to see every aspect of the problems involved and not merely a single, personal aspect; in short, it is to promote practical judgment and *wisdom*.

The technique varies under the influence of subject, group, leader and other factors, but in the main a meeting comprises three parts: listening to a short talk (15-20 minutes) by an informed speaker (lecturer, broadcaster or the leader himself), subsequent formulation by leader or group of three or more questions for discussion, and then the discussion proper, when the questions are taken up in turn and tossed about from member to member as the spirit moves or as the leader skilfully directs. This discussion, which may last anything from half an hour to an hour and a half, is closed by the leader, who sums up and expresses the sense of the meeting as manifested in the course of argument, counter-argument, and statement of opinion. The leader, who is rather a host and chairman than a teacher, and prefers his group to sit in a circle and not as a compact audience before a rostrum, has to keep things going, maintain what relevance he can in the argument, make plain how contributions relate to the issue and advance or retard the process of orderly thinking, and generally keep the discussion unified and organic.

In practice, discussion groups work amazingly well; and any normal group under a satisfactory leader can be counted on to function actively and usefully on any reasonable issue. Individual performance and group competence increase surprisingly with regular group meetings, which in the long run tend to affect the thought and outlook of the members in the direction of stability and breadth. Power to speak increases, and capacity to think, to co-operate, to be adaptable and yet to take a stand, to understand oneself and others, and to exercise judgment; moreover, new interests are aroused. Discussion has a wider purpose than study and absorption of principles: a discussion group is a school for active citizenship.

EFFECT ON SPEECH FORMS AND HABITS

Discussion group speech lies somewhere between public-house argument and table talk. In the quality of order, it is above chit-chat, which is unpooled and unchairmanned; in formality, below the lecture and the debate; in compellingness, below good story-telling. It is simple and natural but urgent. It should be clear, direct, short, and live; not rhetorical or passionate, rather factual and normal with a pipe-smoking ease. Discussion is a thinking aloud in company; not imperative or formally consecutive. It is a softener of prejudices, a schooling in adaptability and social collaboration. Discussion group work can thus play a crucial part in the process of readjustment required in our time of startling transitions and reversals of customary practice and precept.

Discussion speech should be quietly expressive and not narrational or descriptive or atmosphered or hortatory, but a mixture of exposition and interpretation, suited to express facts, opinions and incidental personal experiences in relation to the techniques and pressures of modern society. The discussion group offers an appropriate democratic speech pattern, though limited to the persuasive and consultative aspects of speech. A near historical parallel is that of the speech in the coffee-houses of Queen Anne's reign, with the exchange of modern scientific and sociological subjects for manners and the arts; and it is noticeable that coffee-house talk formed a prelude to the good sense and plain speech characteristic of the Eighteenth Century, the Age of Reason.

SOME BOOKS ON DISCUSSION GROUPS

How to Lead Discussion Groups. E. M. Hubback. (English Universities Press, 4d.)

The Discussion Group Leader. Kenneth Spreadbury. (Harrap, 2s.)
Discussion Groups for Citizenship. E. M. Hubback. (Association for Education in Citizenship, 9d.)
Discussion Groups and Their Leadership. W. E. Lloyd. (Workers' Educational Association, 3d.)
Arguments and Discussions. J. W. Marriott. (Harrap, 2s. 6d.)
Something to Argue About. W. M. Ballantine. (Craig & Wilson, 1s.)
Q.E.D.—Some Hints on Arguing. J. W. Marriott. (Harrap, 1s. 6d.)
Talk it Out. H. Newman. (Alliance Press, 1s. 6d.)
The Adult Class. A. J. J. Ratcliff. (Nelson, 3s. 6d.)
"Industrial Discussion Clubs." *Times Educational Supplement,* July 1st, 1944.
Discussion Clubs in Factories. Folder issued by the Industrial Discussion Clubs Experiment.
To Start You Talking. (Pilot Press, 6s.)
Organised Discussion. J. Windsor Musson. (John Crowther, 5s.)
Talking Things Over. R. G. Martin. (Religious Education Press, 3s. 6d.)
Discussion Method. (Bureau of Current Affairs, 1s.)

B.B.C. Pamphlets

Adult Education Wireless Listening Groups. (Board of Education Pamphlet, No. 92.)
Argue it Out: Hints on running group discussion on broadcasts. Patrick Thornhill. (British Broadcasting Corporation, gratis.)
Listening Groups. Folder issued by the B.B.C.
Wireless Discussion Groups: What they are and how to run them. (British Broadcasting Corporation.)

Discussion Series

"Charter for Youth." (Nelson, 5s. each.)
"Democratic Order." (Kegan Paul, 1s. each.)
"Digests on Current Affairs." (Staples & Staples, 2s. each.)
"Discussion Books." (Nelson, 3s. each.)
"Home University Library." (Oxford, 4s. 6d. each.)
"Pamphlets on World Affairs." (Oxford, 6d. each.)
"The Thinker's Library." (Watts, 2s. each.)
Annual Discussions Handbook. (National Adult School Union, 1s. 6d.)
"Booklets for Discussion Groups." (Harrap, 1s. 6d. and 2s. each.)
"Discussion Circle." (Craig & Wilson, Glasgow, 1s. 6d. each.)

"Handbooks for Discussion Groups." (English Universities Press, 3d. each.)

"Pelican Books" and "Penguin Specials." (Penguin Books, 1s. each.)

"Topics for Discussion." (Workers' Educational Association, 3d. each.)

List of Discussion Group Organisations, page 210.

TRAINING

FOREWORD

Most of the following organisations offer training courses for the prospective specialist in speech training. More detailed information and advice on this matter will be found in *Speech Training as a Career* (Vawser & Wiles, 5s.)

General teachers who are working in Primary and Secondary schools and wish to receive instruction in speech training for classroom use are referred in particular to the Speech Fellowship, 9 Fitzroy Square, W.1., and the Incorporated Association of Teachers of Speech and Drama, 'Oakhurst,' Steep, Petersfield, Hants.

Members of the public wishing to improve their own speech will be interested in the spare-time classes arranged in the evening institutes of most large towns, particulars of which may be had from the County Education Office. Addresses of private teachers will be found in the lists issued by the Incorporated Association of Teachers of Speech and Drama (address above), and the Lamda Teachers' Association, Tower House, Cromwell Road, S.W.5.

Vacation Schools are listed on page 209.

Central School of Speech Training and Dramatic Art

By GWYNNETH THURBURN (*Principal*)

The Central School of Speech Training and Dramatic Art was founded in 1906 by Elsie Fogerty, C.B.E., to promote the knowledge, study and practice of speech and dramatic art in England, and became incorporated in 1925.

The first Patron of the school was H.R.H. Princess Louise, Duchess of Argyll; and the first President, Sir Frank Benson. The School is at present under the patronage of H.R.H. the Duchess of Kent, and the Right Hon. the Earl of Lytton, K.G., G.C.S.I., G.C.I.E., is President of the Council.

In the early years of the school much of its work was devoted to the study of fundamental principles underlying movement and speech, and in this connection Dr. Hulbert contributed valuable assistance. The work of Dr. Aikin, in later years, established the principle of a scientific approach to the human voice in speech and song.

Conferences on Speech and Speech Training were organised by the Central School in 1912 and 1927.

In 1923 the University of London, in response to a petition, instituted the Diploma in Dramatic Art. This was followed in 1928 by the institution of a Certificate of Proficiency in Diction and Drama, which is intended for teachers who do not aim at being specialists in the subjects of the certificates, but require a working knowledge of items such as would be of special value to them in educational work. The Diploma in Dramatic Art, with the endorsement of the supplementary course for Teachers, is recognised by the Royal Society of Teachers. Particulars of both these examinations may be had from the University Extension Registrar, University of London, Imperial Institute Road, S.W.7.

POETIC DRAMA AND BROADCASTING

The Central School has played an important part in the production of plays in verse. It has produced or been associated with, among many others, productions of : *Atalanta in Calydon,* by Swinburne, *Boadicea,* by Laurence Binyon; and *The Rock* and *Murder in the Cathedral,* by T. S. Eliot.

In 1912 the Central School invited a group of poets to test the verse-speaking of the students, and since that time it has had the advantage of close association with many poets, including John Masefield, Laurence Binyon, Gordon Bottomley, Richard Church and L. A. G. Strong.

The School's connection with the B.B.C. has developed to a remarkable extent during the last few years and many calls have been made upon its students past and present. Students have taken part in almost every type of broadcasting from choric-speaking and announcing to play-production.

TEACHERS' COURSE

Opportunities are given to students to develop their own artistic work—a high standard of performance being required—and at the same time training is given in the teaching of all subjects related to spoken English. It seems probable that the demand for specialist teachers will increase, particularly if the recommendations on speech in the Report of the McNair Committee are fully implemented. Hitherto the work of specialists has been largely confined to public, private and secondary schools, whereas it is in the elementary schools that they are so badly needed. It is to be hoped that the new orientation of school work which will result from the Education Act will allow for the specialist teacher of speech and drama as well as providing facilities for the equipment and knowledge of all teachers in matters relating to speech.

Qualified teachers are in demand for work in the following categories :—

(1) Full-time resident posts in schools to take charge of speech and dramatic work and possibly spoken English.
(2) Visiting posts as teachers of speech and drama in schools and training colleges.
(3) Evening Institute work.

(4) Posts as Lecturers, Drama Tutors and Organisers in Clubs and Institutes.

The course, which lasts three years, includes: Theory and Practice of Voice Training, Elementary Anatomy and Physiology, Elementary Psychology, Phonetics, History of Drama, History of Theatrical Art, English Poetics, French, Verse-speaking, Acting and Rehearsal classes, Dancing and Mime: and in the third year teaching under supervision in elementary and secondary schools and play production in Clubs.

Students sit for the Diploma in Dramatic Art of London University at the end of their second year and the Supplementary Subjects at the end of their third year.

The Diploma of the Central School is taken in the third year and students are not allowed to proceed from one year to the next unless their work, both theoretical and practical, has reached the required standard. Students holding this Diploma qualify for admission to the Incorporated Association of Teachers of Speech and Drama and the course is recognised by the Royal Society of Teachers.

Flexibility is ensured by the fact that members of the staff are in constant touch with practical and experimental work outside as well as inside the school.

STAGE COURSE

Training for the stage includes both practical and theoretical training in acting and the arts of the theatre. It has always been the policy of the school that teachers of acting should have active connections with the theatre and have had experience in acting and producing on the professional stage.

Students who hold the requisite educational qualifications may enter for the Diploma in Dramatic Art of London University.

The stage course lasts for two or three years and includes: Acting and Rehearsal classes, Production and Stage Management, History of the Drama, History of Theatrical Art, English Poetics, Voice Production, Diction, Dancing, Mime, Phonetics, Fencing, Make-up, Stage Lighting.

SPEECH THERAPY COURSE

Many changes have taken place since the first clinic for the treatment of defects of speech was opened at St. Thomas's Hospital under the direction of Elsie Fogerty in 1913, and Speech Therapy is now recognised as a separate profession, auxiliary to medicine.

The School's training is in accordance with the requirements of the College of Speech Therapists, full particulars of which are given on page 200.

Enquiries should be addressed to the Secretary, Central School of Speech Training and Dramatic Art, Royal Albert Hall, London, S.W.7.

Royal Academy of Music

By L. GURNEY PARROTT (*Secretary*)

THE study of speech and drama has spread astonishingly in the past twenty years. Speech training (or Elocution) is becoming increasingly important in the schools as it is realised how much the life and character of the individual may be affected by good or bad habits of speech. The proper use of the voice is not only of importance to those whose profession largely depends upon it, such as actors and actresses and public speakers of all kinds; it is of value in every walk of life.

The study and development of the speaking voice means not only correct enunciation and the removal of speech defects; it includes the study of volume, quality, pitch, rhythm and inflection; the understanding of and artistic response to the subtleties of poetry and prose, with the broadening and deepening of the mind which the love of great literature can engender.

Associated with speech training is the study of the drama. In schools this has not for its primary object the performance of plays. In learning to act the student learns to control mind and body; to develop poise and sensitivity. The study of great plays, involving as it does characterisation, interpretation, and team-work, develops the student's own personality.

In the Royal Academy of Music the value of speech and drama has long been recognised. The original Regulations of 1822 state that :—

> "The first object in the education of the Students is a strict attention to their religious and moral instruction. *Next,* the study of their own and the Italian language . . "

English, in fact, appears as the first lesson on the first day of the first Students' Time-Table of those distant days. The curriculum was designed to cover the whole education of the students, who were also boarded in the Academy. Later on, boarding was discontinued, and the three R's, religious training and other subjects were dropped, it being found that a complete musical education fully absorbed the teaching facilities of the Institution.

In 1828 an Opera Class was begun, and it was probably due to this that by the middle of the century Elocution had become a part of the curriculum. The first dramatic performance was given in St. James's Theatre in 1853, and from this date the study and performance of plays became increasingly important in the Academy. The earliest course of training in Elocution and Dramatic Art of which any record remains is detailed in the prospectus for 1880. This included private lessons in Elocution, Drama Class, a musical subject, Deportment and Dancing, and a language.

Since those early days there have been many changes to meet changing needs and conditions. The following three-years course, specially designed to bring the study of speech and drama into line with modern developments has been instituted at the Academy :—

SPEECH TRAINING AND DRAMATIC ART

1. *Speech Training.*
   Two private lessons weekly of 30 minutes each.
2. *Weekly Classes.*
   Choral Speech; Verse Speaking; Voice Production; Dancing (Classical); Dramatic Rehearsal; Fencing; Mime; Phonetics; Public Speaking; Stage Lighting and Make-up.
3. *Lecture Classes.*
   Drama; Theatre; Costume; Poetry, Principles of Teaching; Psychology; Remedial Speech; Broadcasting Technique.
4. *Teaching* (under supervision).
5. *Recitals.*
   Informal Recitals of Lyrical and Dramatic Speech in the Theatre, in addition to the terminal performances of plays.

The inclusive fee is twenty guineas per term (plus an Entrance Fee of two guineas).

For internal students who take the complete three-years course, there are the grades described as Divisions 2, 3 and 4 (Certificate of Merit, with or without distinction) being respectively 1st, 2nd and 3rd year awards at the annual examinations.

L.R.A.M. IN SPEECH AND DRAMA

This Diploma for Teachers and Performers (originally the L.R.A.M. in Elocution, instituted in 1916) is open to any person wherever trained. The examination fee is five guineas.

These examinations may be briefly described as follows :—

Teachers' Examination

A. *Paperwork* : Two papers of three hours each. One deals with the use of the Voice, methods of training and interpretation, etc.; the other with the literary side of the subject, such as the History of the Drama, Theatre, Costume and Poetry.

B. *Practical* : This is divided into three sections : (a) Performance of *three* pieces and a sight reading test; (b) Teaching of a class; (c) Viva-voce.

Performers' Examination

A. *Paperwork* : One paper of three hours, dealing with the use of the voice, interpretation, repertoire, etc.

B. *Practical*: This is divided into four sections: (a) performance of *four* pieces; (b) a prepared Mime scene; (c) Reading at sight; (d) Extempore speaking.

Further information is obtainable from the Royal Academy of Music, Marylebone Road, London, N.W.1.

London Academy of Music and Dramatic Art

By WILFRID FOULIS (*Governing Director*)

L.A.M.D.A.—The London Academy of Music and Dramatic Art—is an amalgamation of four schools of music, the oldest of which, bearing a similar name, was founded in 1861. I believe that the Royal Academy of Music is the only institution of this nature which can claim an earlier inception. Its Patrons are the Rt. Hon. Lord Brabazon of Tara, M.C., P.C., who led the joint deputation of L.A.M.D.A. and the L.A.M.D.A. Teachers' Association to the Board of Education in 1943, the Rt. Hon. The Viscountess Buckmaster, Mrs. Theodore Cory, Arundell Esdaile, Esq., Litt.D., Miss Beatrice Forbes-Robertson, Robert Perkins, Esq., M.P. and Ronald Simpson, Esq.

More than fifty-five years ago the London Academy of Music inaugurated the first public examinations in Speech, and their popularity is proved by the ever-increasing flow of candidates. The examinations are held three times a year throughout the country, and even war-time conditions did not interfere materially with them. The Academy has its accredited local secretaries in most important provincial centres, and is always pleased to send examiners to schools and colleges where numbers justify special adjudications.

The Elocution Examinations consist of six Grades, the Bronze, Silver, and Gold Medals, and also a Teacher's and Performer's Diploma—"A.L.A.M. (Eloc.)"—which satisfies the conditions of the Royal Society of Teachers' in respect of attainments. The newly-constituted *Teacher's Certificate in Speech and Drama* represents the highest possible attainment in this branch of the teaching profession.

In addition there are three Grades in Reading, four in Choral Speaking, and in Public Speaking an Introductory Grade, Silver and Gold Medal examinations. By means of a thorough examination in prepared and extempore speaking the Academy's Diploma of Associate "A.L.A.M. (Public Speaking)" may be obtained.

The examining staff of the Academy for these branches of Elocution consists of: Rodney Bennett, Miss Esmé Beringer, Mrs. Eve Acton-Bond, Frank Cellier, Miss Kathleen Cunningham, Arthur Fayne, Frank Freeman, Miss Stella Hackman,

Mrs. Frieda Hodgson, Musgrave Horner, Henry Oscar, Miss Beatrice Rose, Miss Beatrice Forbes-Robertson, Clive Sansom, James Stephens, Miss Kathleen Stone, Ben Webster, and Ernest Wellbeloved.

DRAMA

Some years before the war the Academy inaugurated public examinations in Acting, and these have become a very considerable and popular part of its activities. In the Junior Examinations, for boys and girls under sixteen years of age, certificates are offered in five Grades. The selections are chosen from representative modern plays suitable for children, mostly in prose. Simple make-up is expected, no costumes, and but few properties. The Senior Acting Examinations comprise three Grades, Bronze, Silver and Gold Medals, and a Teacher's or Performer's Diploma—"A.L.A.M. (Acting.)" This examination is of thirty-five minutes' duration, and the following great artists form the panel of examiners: Frank Allenby, Miss Peggy Ashcroft, Miss Joyce Barbour, Frank Cellier, Miss Viola Compton, Miss Beatrice Forbes-Robertson, Leslie French, Nicholas Hannen, Walter Hudd, Miss Ursula Jeans, Miss Agnes Lauchlan, Miss Beatrix Lehmann, Miss Curigwen Lewis, Miss Olga Lindo, Miss Marie Lohr, Miss Eva Moore, Miss Cathleen Nesbitt, Miss Marie Ney, Henry Oscar, Miss Winifred Oughton, H. Kynaston Reeves, Milton Rosmer, Ivan Samson, Miss Margaret Scudamore, Miss Athene Seyler, Ronald Simpson, Reginald Tate, Miss Mabel Terry-Lewis, Ernest Thesiger, Austin Trevor, Dame May Whitty, Harry Hanson, J. Baxter Somerville, etc.

The certificate "A.L.A.M. (Acting)" states that in the opinion of two of the above artists the candidate is capable of appearing in a West End (London) theatre with a professional cast. Obviously a very high standard is necessary for this Diploma. The Teacher's section of this Diploma requires the working of a 3½-hour theory paper in addition.

During their visits to examination centres in all parts of the country, examiners keep a keen eye open and report to headquarters in London all cases of exceptional talent, and in many cases special auditions have been granted in London, often resulting in the award of Dramatic Scholarships at the Academy's acting school.

The Academy's headquarters are in Kensington, where a comprehensive curriculum is in force, providing complete training for stage and screen, with parallel courses for teachers of speech and dramatic art.

Particulars of these activities may be had on application to the Secretary of L.A.M.D.A., at Tower House, Cromwell Road, London, S.W.5.

The Guildhall School of Music and Drama

By E. GUY PERTWEE

THE School was founded in 1880 by the Corporation of the City of London, with Mr. H. Weist Hill as Principal. The original premises were in Aldermanbury, but it soon became clear that they were inadequate for the continually growing number of students, and that more spacious accommodation would have to be secured. As early as in 1884 the Corporation decided, in order to provide what was demanded by the evident prospects of the new School, to adopt the plans prepared by the City Architect, Sir Horace Jones, for the erection of a completely new building at a cost of £26,000. Three years were occupied by the necessary work, and the School was able to remove to its present site in John Carpenter Street in 1887.

Speech from the utilitarian and the artistic points of view plays a very important part in the work of the Guildhall School of Music and Drama. Students entering the School can study Verse Speaking, Drama or Public Speaking. Verse-speakers can undertake their studies as students of single subjects under specialised teachers, or they can take a comprehensive course designed for teachers or performers, comprising Voice production, Speech, Appreciation, Interpretation of Verse, Prosody, Outline of the History of Poetry and Drama, and the characteristics of poetry throughout its progress. Those students who have in view a teaching career can, after they have attained a certain standard, become members of the Teachers' Training Course, which comprises three terms' lectures, recognised by the Royal Society of Teachers. They can also belong to Rehearsal Classes which include Mime and production, both subjects taking an important part in the equipment of a teacher. Dramatic students, in addition to individual lessons in Voice Production, Interpretation and Verse Speaking, can become members of the classes which include Deportment, Make-up, Shakespearian production, modern Play Production, Play Reading, Stage design and décor. These classes in the main are conducted in the School's Theatre, so that those taking part can accustom themselves to working on an actual stage. The School is fortunate in possessing an excellent theatre with modern lighting equipment. Public performances are given each term.

The present Principal, Mr. Edric Cundell, was appointed in 1938. He was preparing still further to widen the scope of study by the introduction of special training for the films and television, for which purpose work had already been begun on a model film studio, when the outbreak of war caused the postponement of all such plans. They are, however, awaiting resumption until conditions are more stabilised.

Students can take advantage of the widely known series of Grade examination in Verse Speaking and Drama, leading up to the Diplomas, Teacher or Performer. The L.G.S.M. is open to the general public, but the A.G.S.M. only to those students of the school who complete three years' professional course. Both Diplomas are recognized by the Royal Society of Teachers (Teachers' Registration Council), and they are also recognized by the Scottish Education Department. There are additional examinations for Public Speaking and Choral Speech. All examinations are conducted by specialists in the subject. The Examiners include: Mr. Reginald Besant, O.B.E.; Miss Dorothy Dayus, L.R.A.M., F.G.S.M.; Mr. E. Guy Pertwee, A.R.A.M., F.G.S.M.; Mr. John Holgate; Mr. Daniel Roberts, F.G.S.M.; Mr. Nicholas Robson; Mr. Clifford Turner.

Enquiries should be addressed to the Secretary, Guildhall School of Music and Drama, John Carpenter Street, Victoria Embankment, London, E.C.4.

Royal Academy of Dramatic Art

By Sir KENNETH BARNES (*Principal*)

Of all professional careers for which a good standard of speech is required, the Theatre is the most exacting. The actor, whose words fail to be heard by every attentive member of the audience in all parts of the Theatre, is a positive nuisance unworthy of his or her salary. The exacting circumstances consist in the dual responsibility demanded of the actor, whose first aim must be to convey the motive and emotional state prompting the character to say just what it does at that particular moment of its existence in the play. To accomplish this, exceptional proficiency in voice control and clarity of ennunciation is needed. The attention of the audience has to be held; and the talented actor realises his business is not merely to be heard, but to interest the audience in the feelings of the acted character. Not only vocal tone, flexibility and articulation have to be studied, but timing, and a sense of rhythm and beauty in speech. It is obvious that any reputable school for the Theatre must regard speech training as a matter of the first importance.

At the R.A.D.A. a distinction is made between voice production and what is termed, for lack of a better word, Diction. The teacher of voice production concentrates on breathing, placing, vowels, ear-training, modulation, tone, pronunciation, and precisely those elements in the process of speaking that can be assisted by means of exercises, and which do not include expression, but only the making of sounds and the forming of words as Nature intended. The Diction Teacher's sphere is expression and correct interpretation of memorised passages, but there must be mutual understanding between these teachers in the treatment of each individual student. Some students need special remedial treatment—for "accents," squeakiness, soft "s" sounds, nasalities and other habitual defects, which have to be removed before the "patient" can qualify to take a part in a public theatre. Extra time has to be devoted to these faults; and here the study of Phonetics is valuable.

Further, just as the baby feels before it squawls, so must the actor assimilate the imagined mood before he speaks the words which express that mood in the character; so mime will always occupy an elemental place in the training of an actor. As expression through mime is not voice but gesture, control of the outward physical form of the personality must be mastered; and a sense of rhythm, significance and grace of movement be acquired. A knowledge of the manners and gesture habitual to each historical period in necessary; and closely connected with them are the ever-changing fashions in dress. The R.A.D.A. possesses a very good wardrobe, fortunately not destroyed with our Malet Street Theatre by enemy action in 1941. The cultural background of the Drama is studied through lectures on its history, from the points of view of literature and theatrical representation. The study of Shakespeare occupies a central place in the curriculum—special tests are arranged to provide opportunities for leading members of the Old Vic Company to select promising recruits. The Academy is a National Institution, granted a Royal Charter (1920), and later the patronage of their Majesties the King and Queen. An annual subsidy is voted by the Treasury. Instruction in Broadcasting is given under the direct supervision of the B.B.C.; and opportunities provided for training in Youth Leadership. Scholarships, with maintenance grants from the L.C.C., the Leverhulme Trustees, Sir Alexandra Korda and the Halford Trustees, are open to competition, as well as many other scholarships and prizes. The R.A.D.A. has been the means of training a great number of successful actors, actresses, producers and dramatists.

Enquiries should be sent to the Secretary, Royal Academy of Dramatic Art, 62 Gower Street, London, W.C.1.

Trinity College of Music, London

By ALEXANDER T. REES (*Hon. F.T.C.L. Secretary*)

THE skilful use of the speaking voice as a solo instrument requires training and practice. The importance of early training in this subject cannot be over-stressed, neither can the advantage which attaches to such a sound foundation be over emphasized in relation to subsequent study.

As far back as 1879 the College instituted a course of study in English Literature. From that time there has been a progressive development in speech training in its fullest interpretation, leading in later years to preparation for public-speaking—the effective use of the voice towards a command and resourse of language that will give fluency of expression. The foremost aims of the Teaching Department are:

To develop the speaking voice to the best advantage in daily life;

To cultivate a love and appreciation of the English language; of all that is best in English literature, poetry, drama and prose;

To study the art of self-expression through the medium of public speaking, and to acquire self-confidence.

In the year 1918 the College instituted a series of local examinations, and within two years the syllabus was extended to provide for Teachers' diplomas of Associate and Licentiate. Over the period of the past 27 years the graded examinations, Practical and Theoretical, have been further expanded, and now cover all stages in a student's career to the Diploma of Fellowship, including examination for Teacher and Performer. An interesting and unique alternative syllabus of examinations in Spoken English was instituted in 1935. For some years prior to that time examiners (from overseas) reported that increasing numbers of foreign students presented themselves for examination on the basis of the original syllabus. In adopting that syllabus such candidates laboured under a disadvantage, since, however excellent their achievements, they suffered by comparison with British candidates of English speech taking the same Examination. In order to provide for the needs of such foreign students, the syllabus of Examinations in Spoken English was designed to include tests appropriate to the peculiar difficulties of those whose mothe tongue is not English. As a counterpart to these Examinations there is also a series of written Examinations embracing tests in grammar, composition and style.

The Elocution syllabus, necessarily a work of compilation and selection, is designed to encourage progressive study of the art of speech. The matter of grading is one which calls for special comment. Of the wide field of the subject-matter from which Examination material has been collected, the difficult task of fitting selected works, appropriate to each successive division, has not been achieved without considerable thought and research. The College has consistently observed the policy of entrusting such important work to persons of acknowledged educational status and experience, possessing specialized knowledge of the subject for which their services have been enlisted.

To those about to embark on a teaching career this syllabus is an invaluable guide to an appropriate and wide choice of material for students of every degree of ability and learning; and the opportunities which the College provides for the furtherance of the study of the subject are extended to teachers and students alike, in the sincere belief that their work will thereby be assisted and encouraged.

As a post-script to the foregoing it may be said that, to those who value the companionship of books, the College syllabus may well be regarded as the nucleus of a good collection.

Address for enquiries: Trinity College of Music, Mandeville Place, London, W.1.

New Era Academy of Drama and Music

THE New Era Academy of Drama and Music (London) Ltd., of 17 Cavendish Square, W.1, pays special attention to Voice and Speech Training for the platform, stage, pulpit, broadcasting and film work and are peculiarly fortunate in having on their staff teachers who specialise in Tone Production and Speech, and an authorised teacher of Sinus Tone Production (speech), the revolutionary method now being applied with ever-increasing success in voice culture and remedial work.

Both individual and class tuition in Elocution and Stage Technique, and public examinations in Elocution, Stage Technique, Public Speaking, Choral Speaking and Examinations for Foreigners held at regular intervals in London and other parts of the country, and so making a solid contribution towards voice and speech training development by setting a high standard both for examinees and pupils.

The Academy is run for the sake of art and not profit, and it is hoped in time to offer scholarships. The Elocution and Stage examinations comprise standardised Grades from 1 to 6, Bronze, Silver and Gold Medals and Diploma, the latter, in the Elocution and Drama sections, covering separate examinations for Teacher and Performer.

The Directors of the Academy are Doris Buckley, Douglas Stevens and G. Gordon Harvey. Its Patrons are Maurice Codner, R.P.S., C. E. M. Joad, D.Litt., Augustus John, O.M., Claire Luce, Flora Robson, Frank O. Salisbury, Maude Salisbury, and Dame Sybil Thorndike.

The teaching staff are Grace Beale, Doris Buckley, Ann Clark, Eileen Elsworth, Margaret Halstan, Horace Sequeia, Elsie Starkey and Douglas Stevens. Examiners include Mary Clare, Nigel Clarke, Madge Compton, Edith Evans, and Baliol Holloway.

A twelve-week course of stage training, taken by professional artistes, takes place each term. Full particulars may be had from the Secretary.

The Speech Fellowship

THE Speech Fellowship is a society working for the general improvement of speech education; it is not primarily a teaching body. In response to requests, however, it organises classes and lectures whenever a particular need is felt. The most frequent of these have been its London courses for Primary and Secondary school teachers who wish to learn the fundamentals of speech training, verse speaking and choral speaking for the classroom. These are held in the evenings, or during school vacations. There are also occasional week-end courses in the Provinces.

Other classes are arranged, from time to time, in public speaking, verse drama, and movement and speech. Lecturers at recent courses have included Miss Hilda Adams, Mr. Rodney Bennett, Miss Isabel Chisman, Miss Marjorie Gullan, Miss Elizabeth Loe, Mrs. Rachel Marshall, Miss Constance Rennie, Mr. Clive Sansom, Mrs. Ruth Sansom, Miss Kathleen Stone, Miss Barbara Storey, Miss Mona Swann and Mr. Norman Wright. Enquiries should be addressed to the Secretary, Speech Fellowship, 9 Fitzroy Square, London, W.1. (See also page 52).

Incorporated Association of Teachers of Speech and Drama

Courses are arranged for Primary and Secondary school teachers on evenings during the school term, and there are short vacation courses for members of the Association as well as non-members. (See page 54).

Further information is obtainable from the Secretary, I.A.T.S.D., 'Oakhurst', Steep, Petersfield, Hants.

School of Oriental and African Studies

(UNIVERSITY OF LONDON)

THE School of Oriental and African Studies was founded in 1911. Its lectures and classes are open not only to University students, but also to those who have not matriculated and do not wish to follow a full University course—especially to those who are going to the East or to Africa in any capacity, whether in the service of Government, or as missionaries, or to engage in a profession or in commerce; and to those who have temporarily returned from the East and wish to continue their studies while in England.

Instruction is given in the following languages and dialects:

SEMITIC

Arabic: Classical, *Aden dialect, Egyptian, *Iraqi, *Moroccan, *Sudanese, Syrian.

**Amharic, Aramaic, Ethiopic, Modern Hebrew.*

AFRICAN

Bantu : Bemba, Kikongo, Kikuyu, Kingwana, Ganda, Lamba, Lingala, Nyanja, Shona, Sotho-Chwana, Swahili, Zulu-Xhosa.
Sudanic : Efik, *Ewe, Fante, *Ga, Ibo. *Mende, Moru, Twi, Yoruba, Zande.

*Instruction arranged when required.

Nilotic : Acholi, Bari, Dinka, Nuer, Shilluk.
Unclassified : Hausa.

TURCO-TARTAR

Western Turkish (Anatolian branch).
Eastern Turkish (Turki-Chaghatai-Tartar branch).
Early forms of both branches (Kök Turkish-Uighur).

*GEORGIAN

INDO-EUROPEAN

Armenian
Iranian : Avestan, Old Persian, Persian, *Pashto, Saka, Sogdian, Parthian, Middle Persian, Pahlavi.
Indo-Aryan : Sanskrit, Pali, Prakrit, *Assamese, Bengali, *Gujarati, Hindi, Hindustani, *Kashmiri, Marathi, *Nepali, *Oriya, Punjabi, *Shina, *Sindhi, Sinhalese, Urdu.

DRAVIDIAN

**Kanarese.*
**Malayalam.*
Tamil.
**Telugu.*

SINO-TIBETAN

Tibeto-Burman : Tibetan, Burmese, *Old Burmese, *Chin, *Kachin.
Tai : *Shan, Siamese.
Chinese : Classical, Kuo Yü (Pekingese), *Cantonese, *Amoy, *Swatow, *Foochow.

MON-KHMER

*Môn, *Old Môn.*

FAR EASTERN

Japanese.
**Korean.*
Manchu.
Mongolian.

AUSTRONESIAN

Indonesian : Malay.
**Micronesian Languages.*
**Melanesian Languages.*
**Polynesian Languages.*

* Instruction arranged when required

The work of the School covers practical and theoretical phonetics; the culture and history of Oriental and African countries; comparative grammar; and general linguistics, including phonology. Intensive courses, vacation courses, and private lessons may be arranged for students who require them. In addition, there are special Commercial Courses, which enable students to acquire a knowledge not only of the everyday language of the people, but also of the particular phraseology and idioms of commercial life.

There is a Library, temporarily at Clarence House, 4 Central Buildings, Matthew Parker Street, S.W.1, and a Gramophone Record Library in the Department of Phonetics and Linguistics. Recordings may be made in connection with intensive language courses in Japanese, Turkish, Hindustani, Persian, and certain East European and Balkan languages.

The School issues an occasional *Bulletin,* price 15s. a part, containing contributions to the knowledge of Oriental and African languages, book reviews, etc.

Enquiries should be addressed to the Registrar, School of Oriental and African Studies, University of London, W.C.1.

School of Slavonic and East European Studies

(UNIVERSITY OF LONDON)

This School was founded in 1915 for the study of the history, culture and languages of Slavonic and East European countries. There are day and evening courses, and the subjects taken include:

Comparative Slavonic Philology.

Russian. Special courses in translation, the training of personnel for foreign trade, language study for scientific purposes, and Russian phonetics.

Polish.

Czechoslovak.

Serbo-Croat.

Bulgarian.

Hungarian.

Roumanian.

Private lessons and courses may be taken by arrangement. All enquiries should be addressed to the Secretary, School of Slavonic and East European Studies, London, W.C.1.

Department of Phonetics

UNIVERSITY COLLEGE, LONDON

It is thirty-nine years ago that Mr. Daniel Jones was appointed as Lecturer in Phonetics at University College. The full Professorship was inaugurated in 1921, and from then until now there has been a staff of ten full-time lecturers, in addition to the Professor. The work of the Department consists largely in the scientific analysis of spoken languages, with three main objects: (1) to enable English people to speak foreign languages accurately, (2) to enable people of other nations to speak English accurately, and (3) to invent or improve the orthography of various languages. Much work has also been done on the languages and dialects of Africa and the Orient; carried on, by phoneticians who trained under Professor Jones, at the London School of Oriental and African Studies. (See page 126).

The Department was closed on the outbreak of war, but it returned to its original home in Gower Street in the autumn of 1943, and has already resumed its former activities. Courses are given in the phonetics of French and German, and others in English Phonetics and Spoken English for foreigners, Certificates of proficiency being offered in all these subjects. Courses are also given in the phonetics of Spanish, Russian, Italian and Greek.

In addition, there are special classes in the phonetics of English for English students — one for undergraduates taking Phonetics as their special subject in the B.A. Honours Degree in English; another for Speech Therapists; and an evening course which is intended for teachers of English. This last course is particularly useful as a preliminary to speech training in schools. An examination for the certificate of proficiency in English Phonetics is conducted at the end of each session. It consists of a written test, with phonetic dictation, phonetic transcription, a paper on phonetic theory, and an oral test which includes reading aloud from prepared and unseen texts, and questions on phonetic theory and its practical applications. Candidates are also expected to answer questions on the best methods of teaching an acceptable pronunciation to those who have notably dialectal or defective speech.

Further information may be had from the Secretary, Department of Phonetics, University College, Gower Street, London, W.C.1.

Department of Spoken Language
(UNIVERSITY COLLEGE, NOTTINGHAM)

THE Department provides courses in the theory and practice of spoken language, and attention is given to defective speech. A student in any department of the College whose speech is likely to prove a hindrance in his subsequent career may have an individual course of treatment from a qualified speech therapist.

There is a course in general phonetics for students preparing for degrees in English, Modern Languages, or Classics. Those in the Department of Education, who are preparing for the

Teachers' Certificate and whose own speech is of a good standard, may prepare for a Certificate in Methods of Speech Training in Schools. This course consists of the physiology of language and the principles of speech; English phonetics; the physiology of speech; and methods of speech training in schools. Actual practice is given in the teaching of spoken English in schools.

In addition, all those who take the special English Courses for Overseas Students at the College attend lectures on English speech and phonetics in this Department, and also receive individual attention according to their needs.

Enquiries should be addressed to the Registrar, University College, University Park, Nottingham.

Certificates and Diplomas in Speech and Drama

**A.G.S.M.* Associate of the Guildhall School of Music (page 121).

**A.L.A.M.* (*Eloc.*). Associate of the London Academy of Music. Performer's and Teacher's Diploma (page 119).

A.L.A.M. (*Acting*) London Academy of Music and Dramatic Art (page 120).

**A.L.A.M.* (*Public Speaking*). London Academy of Music and Dramatic Art (page 119).

A.R.C.M. Associate of the Royal College of Music.

A.S.S.T. Associate of the Society of Speech Therapists. Superceded by *F.C.S.T.* and *L.C.S.T.*

**A.T.C.L.* Associate of Trinity College, London (page 123).

**Central School Diploma.* Central School of Speech Training and Drama (page 116)

Certificate in Methods of Speech Training in Schools. Department of Spoken English, Nottingham University (page 129).

Certificate of Merit. Royal Academy of Music (page 118)

Certificate of Proficiency. Incorporated Association of Teachers of Speech and Drama (page 56).

Certificate of Proficiency in Diction and Drama. University of London (page 116)

Certificate of Proficiency in English Phonetics. (English Students), University College, London (page 129).

Certificate of Proficiency in English Phonetics. (Foreign Students), University College, London (page 129).

Certificate of Proficiency in Spoken English. (Foreign students). University College, London (page 129).

**Diploma in Dramatic Art.* University of London (page 116).

Diploma in Elocution. New Era Academy (page 125).

F.C.S.T. Fellow of the College of Speech Therapists, page 200).

F.G.S.M. Fellow of the Guildhall School of Music (page 121).
F.T.C.L. Fellow of the Trinity College of Music (page 124).
F.R.A.M. Fellow of the Royal Academy of Music (page 117).
Marjorie Gullan Certificate. See Speech Fellowship
International Phonetics Diploma. International Phonetic Association (page 64).
L.C.S.T. Licentiate of the College of Speech Therapists (page 200).
**L.G.S.M.* Licentiate of the Guildhall School of Music (page 121).
**L.R.A.M.* (*Eloc.*). Licentiate of the Royal Academy of Music. Superseded by the *L.R.A.M. Speech and Drama.*
**L.R.A.M.* (*Speech and Drama*). Royal Academy of Music (page 118).
**L.T.C.L.* Licentiate of Trinity College, London (page 124).
Speech Fellowship Certificate for Teachers (pages 52 and 125).
Speech Institute Diploma. Discontinued
Teachers' Certificate in Speech and Drama. London Academy of Music and Dramatic Art (page 117).
Teachers' Diploma in English Phonetics. University College, London. (See *Certificate of Proficiency in English Phonetics*).

*Accepted for registration purposes by the Royal Society of Teachers.

THE ART OF SPEECH

Spoken Poetry

By RICHARD CHURCH

It is really a most extraordinary, a most abnormal state of affairs, that the matter which I am discussing in this article should need to be discussed at all. To me, it is just as trite as if I were to go to a body of orchestral players to point out to them the necessity of music being performed rather than merely read in silence from the printed score. In no country in the world other than our own would my obvious bit of pleading be tolerated. In France, for instance, I should be referred to Molière's character, M. Jourdain, who discovered that he had been speaking in prose rhythms all his life.

And what is the matter of my article? It is the suggestion that our English words, the myriad billows, waves, lappings and scuts of foam which make up the ocean of our superb language, should be spoken by us. And when I say spoken I mean spoken with deliberate and proud consciousness, as Pavlova danced, and as Melba sang. "How dreadful!", some may say; "How artificial!" Yes, but we English have allowed ourselves, or probably driven ourselves, to take for granted a sub-normal attitude toward our speaking of our native language, and we need, for a time at least, some sort of remedial process before we can make the most of our English word-music in a free unconscious way, as the blackbird sings, or as the Frenchman orders his luncheon.

We have inherited a language as beautiful in tone even as French, as subtle and full of aural innuendo as Gaelic, as emotionally naive as the Teutonic tongues, while it transcends them all in range and adaptability. But all these other peoples, when speaking their languages, do so with a sense of artistry, a tacit acknowledgement that they are taking part in the ritual display of a unique mystery—human speech, the fulcrum on which man heaves himself out of darkness into light, out of the animal stage into the divine.

With us it is no such thing. For some reason or other we have degenerated, during the past century, into inarticulateness. We have even made an art of it, developing a trick of litotes, of flat understatement and diminished symbols, that has found an almost comically appropriate vehicle in a form of speech clipped off by closed teeth and a sort of semi-paralytic convulsion of the mouth and larynx. It has a negative charm, perhaps; but we have overdone it. The device has affected our state of mind, and the time has come in which we have had to set up, by Governmental action, political machinery known as the British Council and the Ministry of Information, intended to counteract the mischief done abroad by our laryngeal modesty.

That is the general state of our speech. What concerns us here is the effect of that state upon our attitude to English verse, and our way of speaking it. The usual effect it has is to deter us from speaking English verse at all. The majority of English people still, in spite of the brave efforts of the B.B.C. and other bodies, prefer to read verse with the eye, rather than to hear it with the ear. In self-defence, they quote Keats, "Heard melodies are sweet, but those unheard are sweeter," but they know that this is a bit of special-pleading, to cover up a slight sense of shame, and the awareness that something is wrong.

And most emphatically it is wrong. What does the poet work for, if not to make a music of consonant and vowel, a pattern of verbal shapes with length, depth and thickness; using the arts of the composer and the painter in order to fill abstract ideas with sensation, and morals with passion? Shelley rightly claimed that the function of the poet was more exalted than that of the practitioners of the other arts. I believe that exaltation is due to the fact that his medium of words is the latest and most detached of any available in nature. Paint and stone are inert; the notes of the musician's scale are fluid; but words have both these attributes and more besides; so much more that a whole science has still to be created in order to explain the difference; a science embracing philology, psychology, anthropology, and other of our clumsy tools for analysing the special nature of man.

One of the greatest of all mystics said that "the Word was in the beginning" and we have still to explore the full significance of this saying. It should remain the first axiom in the poet's horn-book, urging him always to absorb into himself the whole universe so far as he can experience it upon his nerves, senses and intelligence, converting all into a verbal form so that nothing of himself, and nothing of the multitudinous life around him, remains inarticulate, without a word-shape that can be projected from the tongue in the superb mystery of speech. It seems that we have lost our awareness of this mystery; that as civilisation comes over us with too much custom, too much safety and social habit, we take for granted a function that in the early days of human intercourse was recognised as a powerful weapon towards the making and breaking of human destiny, and the control of nature. Merlin, and the more historically authentic utterers of incantation, the prophets and the priests, are not wholly archaic and discredited. Indeed, we have learned to our cost just lately how much the uttered phrase can work upon a people's will and turn it to deeds, tearing up history by the roots, and treading through the quiet garden where thought and love have worked together to control the wilderness.

But all this is so obvious, so trite. Again and again men rise up to warn us not only of the efficacy but also of the dangerous power of Words. Remember what Milton said about books "But books are the flat score of the spoken word, a mere latter-day convenience for preserving their fiery magic from generation to generation." Publishers and booksellers are a kind of coal-merchant, purveying for the soul a fuel in which the sun, the life-force, is latent too, but now the Sun of Suns, that archetype faintly glimpsed by Plato. Words are God, are Life made mineral, docile and latent to the hand of man. But speak them, burn them, and what coals of fire they become, warming us into divinity; and if we are not skilful, consuming us as they have nearly consumed Europe today.

I have touched on this aspect merely as a reminder of what lies behind this subject of speech-craft. I want to point out again what dangers and miserable deprivations lie in our national habit of denying ourselves the full gesture of speech. When we mince out our teeth-clenched understatements, with vowels emasculated and consonants elided, we are guilty of more than a mere social self-consciousness. We are breaking the biological unity of body and mind. *Reading* poetry! Does a man love a woman and beget children by post?

Now all this is more teleological than practical. I expect that readers of this book know all about the practical aspect of the problem. But from time to time we all need a reminder of the source from which our energies, our principles, are forever springing. As for the art of speaking verse, I have neither cause or opportunity to discuss it here. We have textbooks which are useful to us, and they are constantly being mentioned in Speech Fellowship circles. We know too what was being done before the war to offer opportunities for the practice in public of verse-speaking. John Masefield started the annual Festival of Spoken Poetry at Oxford, and other poets took on the direction of it from him. This has now been revived in London, and we hope to enlarge its scope to meet the needs of a people so much more experienced and aware of the spoken word than were pre-war peoples. The British have woken up indeed and amongst their great achievements in the agony of war was the discovery that they carry magic in the mouth, the great and special magic of English, an inheritance of poetry that craves to be performed.

POETS READING

W. H. Auden. Poems from "Journey to a War," "Another Time," etc. 1 record (Harvard Film Service, U.S.A.).

Laurence Binyon. "For the Fallen." (H.M.V. Not yet released).

Walter de la Mare. "Music," "Farewell," and other lyrics. Two records. (H.M.V.).

John Drinkwater. "Mrs. Willow," "Anthony Crundle," and other poems. Two records. (Columbia).

T. S. Eliot. "Gerontion" and "The Hollow Men." (Harvard Film Service, U.S.A.).

Paul Engle. Poems from "West of Midnight." 1 record. (Harvard Film Service, U.S.A.)
Robert Frost. "Death of the Hired Man," "Mending Wall," etc. Four records. (Erpi Picture Corporation, U.S.A.).
Christopher Hassall. Poems from *Crisis, Penthesperon,* etc. Two records. (Columbia).
Vachel Lindsay. "Congo." (National Council of Teachers of English, U.S.A.).
Henry Newbolt. "Drake's Drum," "He Fell Among Thieves," etc. Two records. (Columbia).
V. Sackville West. Passages from *The Land.* Two records. (Columbia).
Edith Sitwell. Poems from *Façade,* with accompaniment of William Walton's music. (Decca).

OTHER VERSE RECORDS

Edith Evans. An Anthology of Recorded Verse. Six records. (Columbia).
John Gielgud. Poems ranging from Elizabethan lyrics to Eliot's "Journey of the Magi." Six records. (Columbia).
Margaret Gowings. Five lyrics. One record. (H.M.V.).
Marjorie Gullan. Readings from Keats, Blake, Wordsworth and the Scottish Balladists. Four records. (Halligan Studios, Madison, New Jersey, U.S.A.).
Ion Swinley. Grey's "Elegy in a Country Churchyard." (Columbia).
Clifford Turner. Poems of Milton, Keats, Shelley, and Tennyson. Two records. (H.M.V.).
See also under "Choral Speaking," page 147, and "Speech in Our Theatre," page 154.

Verse Speaking To-day

Mr. T. S. Eliot, discussing the poetry of the last twenty years, has described it as "belonging to a period of search for a proper modern colloquial idiom."[1] These years might also be considered as a period of search for a proper method of speaking poetry. There have been a variety of techniques, from gushing vowel-consciousness to a matter-of-factness more suited to business conversations than to the expression of any deep emotion. Somewhere between these two extremes, one feels, is the true style—one that rises spontaneously from the poet's mood having been caught and imaginatively re-created by the interpreter.

Discovering this style has been a matter of trial and error. There is—perhaps luckily—no Royal Academy of Poetry. There are no sets of rules, not even an accepted tradition such as has

1. *The Music of Poetry.* Jackson, Glasgow

existed in music. And although the English genius is a poetic rather than a musical one, as a nation we are, as Mr. Church has suggested, suspicious or even contemptuous of verse. "Poetry's unnatural," Mr. Weller told his son. "No man every talked poetry, 'cept a beedle on Boxin' Day. . . . Never let yourself down to talk poetry, my boy." And the average Englishman has taken his advice.

Even poets have been affected by this suspicion. Some have composed in print; their poems have meaning to the eye, but little to the ear. Others, like the earlier Auden, have written for a private circle of friends, and so widened still further the gulf between the poet and his audience. The verse-speaking movement owes a great deal to poets like John Masefield, Gordon Bottomley and the late Laurence Binyon, who co-operated with some of the leading teachers of speech to found the English Verse-Speaking Association in 1929. This organisation, which later carried on and extended the poetry festivals established in Oxford by Dr. Masefield, summarised its views as follows :—

"Disheartening things had been done in the name of elocution in the nineteenth century; and the practice of recitation had—for two reasons—lost sight of its justification : its practitioners had concentrated on acquiring an equipment of tricks and recipes for delivery that should fulfil their every requirement; and, in choosing material on which to exercise that technique, they looked for pieces that lent themselves to sensation and effect, and neglected the cultivation of that fine taste and exacting judgment which alone could have justified them.

"The Association's first principles are two : fine verse speaking can only come from those who have acquired a habit of fine speaking and utterance; and only fine verse is worth fine speaking. The finer the verse, the more compelling it is to the perfecting of speech for its sake.

"The judges hope to hear speakers whose earnest aim is to display the poem and not themselves : who have sought to discover what the poet has put into the poem as a guidance to what they should get out of it : who realise that metre and rhythm and rhyme are so many guides to the poet's intention, and that to disguise or neglect or improve them is to falsify or injure the meaning : and who, as the very foundation of their work, understand that the sound of a poem is part of its meaning, and needs a vocal cultivation for its revealing that shall be as exacting as a great singer's, and as undemonstrative as the singer's often is demonstrative."

Unfortunately, owing to internal difficulties, the Association was dissolved in 1936. There is still the need for an independent organisation that can provide a meeting-ground for poets, speakers and listeners, arrange experiments in the speaking of different types of poems, or the same types under different conditions—concert hall, open air, radio, etc.—and act as a general clearing-house for ideas on the subject.

There are, however, several societies interested in the speaking of poetry. Among them is the Speech Fellowship—its original title was "The Verse Speaking Fellowship"—which has put the encouragement of verse speaking among its major aims. It performed a healthy task in its early days by linking verse speaking to phonetics, to ensure that the speech employed in the interpretation of poetry obeyed the natural laws of speech and did not indulge in artificial pronunciations and intonations. Many of the Fellowship's monthly meetings have been devoted to recitals of verse, chorally and individually spoken, and to lectures on the subject.

The Association of Teachers of Speech and Drama, and the directors of the English Festival of Spoken Poetry, have also played a prominent part in the verse speaking movement; and the Poetry Society has done a useful service with its Friday afternoon readings, and monthly recitals at the Comedy Theatre, London. Further particulars of these societies will be found elsewhere in this book, and a list of other organisations interested in verse speaking is given on page 210.

The Arts Council of Great Britain (formerly the Council for the Encouragement of Music and the Arts) has done very little for poetry. Either poetry is not regarded as an art, or it is not considered worthy of encouragement. Scattered poetry readings have been arranged at the Lyric Theatre, Hammersmith, and at one or two provincial theatres, but, compared to its magnificent work in the field of music, the Council's contributions to verse-speaking have been negligible. It is curious that an organisation which was established to serve all the arts, should possess a Music Panel, an Art Panel, and a Drama Panel, but has not a single council member to represent poetry.

BROADCASTING POETRY

The strongest potential agent in verse-speaking to-day, and another which has not yet realised its responsibility towards the greatest of the English arts, is the British Broadcasting Corporation. One remembers gratefully some programmes arranged by such sensitive producers as Stephen Potter, Patric Dickinson and Edward Sackville-West, and readings by Robert Harris, Jill Balcon, Cecil Day Lewis, and others. But these are small things compared with the possibilities of broadcasting. For it might be the means of bridging the enormous gap that exists between the poet and the public. In fact, under present conditions, it appears to be the only one. It could take into the people's private rooms poems which are unsuitable for the concert hall, speaking the words as if it were the poet himself thinking aloud. It could bring to the microphone the finest speakers and the finest poets—they do not always inhabit the same body! It could make ordinary men and women realise the beauty and the value of poetry, as it has convinced a large minority in this country of the importance of good music. And it could persuade, indeed compel, poets to write for the ear again; and to write plays, as Shakespeare wrote, for the gay and the bawdy as well as for the literary. Instead, the B.B.C. has given a few cramped minutes to poetry, usually at the end of the day's programme, reminding one of the familiar phrase: "Too little and too late."[1]

There was a discussion in the *Listener* some time ago, in which poets put forward some interesting suggestions for verse broadcasts. The late Robert Nichols advised, "Begin with narrative poetry, and don't play down—that is, don't substitute amusing tosh such as "Frankie and Johnnie" for "Clerk Saunders" or "Kirkonnell," however "proletarian and all that" such stuff may be. . . . Attempt to destroy in the public mind the notion that poetry and "uplift" are Siamese twins, and poetry a low-down dodge for getting folk to feel what isn't natural to them. . . Give humorous poetry—not facetious verse—a chance." Geoffrey Grigson complained about background music for poetry—what would the music-lover say if some announcer softly recited Gray's "Elegy" while one of Beethoven's symphonies was in progress?—and he thought that there was a lack of adequate and systematic rehearsal. Herbert Read's view was that the actual voices were not chosen with sufficient care. "We have fruity voices," he said, "and commanding voices, manly voices and coaxing voices, but rarely the poetic voice. . . . The ideal to aim at is a voice that is almost disembodied, the very opposite of the assertive and all-too-solid voices that seem to put us in physical contact with the personality of the popular broadcaster." He advocated the formation of poetry groups, like the discussion groups already organised by the B.B.C., and continual experiment.

Without the help of the B.B.C. the verse-speaking movement will remain useful but remote, and not socially significant. But if the B.B.C. gave to poetry a fraction of the time, thought and hard work which it has given in the past to serious music, poetry would again have meaning in the common life of the people.

C. S.

SOME BOOKS ON VERSE SPEAKING

The Speaking of Poetry. W. B. Nichols. (Methuen, 4s. 6d.)
The Speaking of English Verse. (Elsie Fogerty. (Dent, 6s.)
The Speaking of Verse. John Drinkwater. Two records by John Drinkwater. (Columbia).
With the Living Voice. A Lecture by John Masefield. (Heinemann, 1s. 6d.)
Spoken Poetry in the School. Marjorie Gullan. (Methuen, 4s. 6d.)
A Commentary on Prose and Verse Speaking. Drew & Robinson. (Harrap, 5s.)
The Speaking of the Ode. Elsie Fogerty.
The Speaking of the Sonnet. W. B. Nichols.

[1] Written before the dawn of the Third Programme

The Speaking of the Ballad. Dulcie Bowie.
English Verse Speaking Association pamphlets (out of print).
Poetry and Contemporary Speech. Lascelles Abercrombie (English Association.)
Speaking Lyric Verse. Clive Sansom. (Lamda Pamphlets, 6d.)
On the Speaking of Shakespeare. Clive Sansom. (Lamda Pamphlets, 6d.)
Elocution Examinations: Examiners' Criticisms. (Lamda Pamphlets, out of print.)
Chapter X in *Poetry for You.* C. Day Lewis. (Basil Blackwell, 4s. 6d.)
See also Bibloography to "Choral Speaking," page 146.

Choral Speaking

By MARJORIE GULLAN

THE case for choric speech was well put by Elizabeth Adams who, at a meeting at Lincoln School, Rhode Island, in 1939, said: "Choral speaking is providing a form of artistic expression for hundreds of boys and girls, men and women, who, though they are deeply sensitive to the appeal of poetry, are too reserved or too self-conscious to speak it alone." This new form of art has taken root among us because it fulfils real needs in the life of the community—cultural, psychological and social.

In its social capacity it has already done much to develop in the ordinary man and woman, boy and girl, a vital interest in speech, and a realisation that speech is the chief medium in human intercourse. Members of a group will practise exercises for articulation, pronunciation and tone—which will help them to master this medium—with real enjoyment, when, left to themselves, nothing would have induced them to do so.

Psychologically, the value of group work can hardly be overestimated. Speakers, unlike musicians, have never, up till now, known the stimulus and the artistic discipline which comes from working in and for a team. Through this new experience, the egotist learns to curb his desire to "star," and the shy and nervous find possibilities within themselves of which they had not dreamed; and the powers of every member are increased.

But none of these things could happen if it were not for the fact that each one in the group is enjoying that deep satisfaction which comes from sharing an artistic experience. There is no better way of getting into touch with literature (and by literature we mean anything that *is* literature, from a "Mother Goose" rhyme to an epic poem) than by speaking it. But the speaking of it must be an art. We must not mistake cheerful shouting, or musical moaning, or mechanical repetition for choral speech.

This is the conductor's responsibility. He must know how infinitely flexible and varied and sensitive speech and voice should be if they are to convey the language of imagination. He must know not only the technique, but the artistry of speech, and be able to share it with his choir. He should help them to achieve, as another writer has expressed it, "strength without loudness, agility without blurring, and precision without regimentation."

The choice and arrangement of material will have much to do with the development of free and varied speech and tone. Ballads, lyrics, narrative verse and prose, nonsense verse and choric drama should all find their place at different times in the choir's programme. The speaking notes to *The Poet Speaks,* and any reliable textbook on the subject, will suggest many varieties in the arrangement of material, from solo speaking with refrains, through dialogue, sequence, accumulative and group work. But, above all, the speech choir must be democratic in outlook. If the speaking is to have spontaneity and conviction, it must be the result of argument and of free discussion between conductor and members. An imposed interpretation on the part of the conductor means nothing but slavish imitation from the group, and the loss to each member of what he should be getting from choral speech —a liberal education in spoken English.

HISTORY OF THE MOVEMENT

Choral speaking in this country had its beginnings in Scotland in 1922, when a group of young Scotswomen, at Dr. John Masefield's suggestion, spoke some choruses from *The Trojan Women,* in the verse-speaking section of the Glasgow Musical Festival. This group, known afterwards as the Glasgow Verse Speaking Choir, gave many demonstrations in Scotland, England and Northern Ireland.

In 1924 a series of lectures were given in London at the request of the New Education Fellowship. School teachers were quick to realise the value of choral speaking in encouraging a love of poetry among large groups of children, and very soon scores of schools in the Home Counties and elsewhere were developing these ideas, searching for new material of a suitable kind, and making their own experiments. It is no exaggeration to say that choral speaking has revolutionised the teaching of English poetry in the average elementary school, where it had formerly been too often a task and a burden.

But side by side with its appeal to children went the interest in choral speaking shown by the adult speaker. In 1926 was founded the London Verse Speaking Choir, which has carried on the work of the Glasgow choir, giving numerous recitals in London, Bristol, Oxford, and elsewhere. Other choirs were started in Scotland and Ireland—outstanding among them the Falkirk High School Choir under Duncan Clarke, and the Stranmillis Training College Choir, Belfast, under Evelyn Abraham.

Mona Swann, of Moira House School, Eastbourne, had begun as early as 1917 to experiment in what she then called Language

Eurhythmics, but which later developed into full choral work throughout the school. It was due to her teaching and influence that Eric Laming, headmaster of Neville House School, Eastbourne founded his boys' choir.

Soon, too, musical festivals began to include choral speaking in their programmes. Enfield Musical Festival, Middlesex, organised by Ethel Woods and Margaret Bidwell, was one of the first. It did a great service to the movement by the high standard of work it maintained and by the wide range of ages and types of schools and associations it included. The London Speech Festival—promoted by the Department of Speech at the Regent Street Polytechnic in 1928, and later continued by the Speech Fellowship—was essentially a choral speaking festival, and it gave special encouragement to the work of London elementary schools. To this festival, Barry Training College, Glamorganshire, sent several choirs which delighted the audience with their interpretation of Welsh poetry. At Bingley Training College, Miss Brooke Gwynne (afterwards to be associated with the Institute of Education) started a choral speaking festival in which all the elementary schools of the area were invited to take part. And later, the Oxford Festival of Spoken Poetry included choral speaking, and we heard the work of Headley Goodall's boys from Bristol, Phyllis Turner's boys from Ryde School, Isle of Wight, and other excellent groups, drawn mostly from private schools, from all parts of the country.

Some schools hold their yearly festivals. Perhaps the most interesting of these, and one which has had a profound effect on the speech of the pupils, was that first promoted by Elizabeth Loe at St. Albans Grammar School for Girls in 1939, after four years experimenting with choral speech. In this festival the work is chosen, planned and conducted by the pupils themselves. Every girl in the school takes part, and the choral work includes verse and prose in French, German, Greek and Latin, as well as in English.

So to-day, little more than twenty years after its modest beginnings, choral speaking is included in the syllabuses of schools, colleges, academies and evening institutes—an indispensible part of speech education.

CHORIC DRAMA

The rise of the speaking choir in Britain coincided with an impulse towards the revival of the chorus in drama. As Mr. Ashley Dukes expressed it in 1938, in his article "Re-enter the Chorus": "Twenty years ago or thereabouts the idea of choric speech or the language of exaltation, of dramatic poetry finding impersonal utterance, was beginning to be formed afresh."[1]

The first modern poet to be struck by the possibilities of the chorus in drama was Dr. Gordon Bottomley, whose *Scenes and*

---

[1] Theatre Arts Monthly.

Plays, Lyric Plays and *Choric Plays,* based upon old Scottish legends and written between 1929 and 1939, were actually inspired by the speaking choirs he had heard. Many of his choruses were unusual. They represented, not persons, but elemental forces, and called for a free imaginative movement quite unlike that of classic drama and more akin to the continental Dance Drama. Two of these plays, acted by the Falkirk High School Choir, scored a great trumph for choric drama by winning first place two years in succession at the British Drama League contest over 500 competing teams. The same author's *Acts of St. Peter,* sponsored by the Religious Drama Society, was first played in Exeter Cathedral in 1933, and then repeated at St. Margaret's, Westminster, in the following year, when the choruses were taken by the London Verse Speaking Choir. The reception given to it showed how great was the interest already aroused by this form of art.

Two years later came another play which was to become one of the outstanding successes of the English theatre during this period, and one which did more than anything else to excite interest in chorus work—T. S. Eliot's *Murder in the Cathedral.* First produced, under Martin Browne's direction, in the Chapter House of Canterbury Cathedral in 1935, with a chorus from the Central School of Speech Training, it was later performed at the Mercury Theatre, London, and all over England and overseas. Mr. Eliot has written several other poetic dramas in which the chorus has been used with varied intentions—*The Rock,* where the choruses far outweighed the play itself; and *The Family Reunion,* an experiment in poetical-colloquial speech which has never received the attention it deserves.

In her choric plays adapted from the Bible, Mona Swann has offered great opportunities to speaking choirs. These plays, the best known of which is *At the Well of Bethlehem,* were first originally written for performance by her own choir at Moira House, Eastbourne. One also remembers her work in choral speaking at the London Theatre Studio before the war, including the beautiful production of Carl Wildman's *Judith.* On a smaller scale, there are Clarissa Graves' one-act dramas, *Three Biblical Plays,* written for and acted by the London Verse Speaking Choir. Other choric plays on religious themes are *The Rite of the Passion* by Charles Williams (adapted for choral speaking when produced by Lorna Davis at St. Anne's, Soho); *The Boy with a Cart* by Christopher Fry, which was performed at Steyning in Sussex; and R. H. Ward's *The Holy Family,* written for the Adelphi Players.

But the chorus has also been used very effectively on political themes. W. H. Auden has made most striking use of it in *The Dog Beneath the Skin* and *The Ascent of F.6,* and the same medium has been explored by Stephen Spender in *Trial of a Judge,* by Cecil Day Lewis in *Noah and the Waters,* by Sean O'Casey in *Within the Gates,* and (in the United States) by

Archibald MacLeish in *Panic*. All these plays, it is interesting to note, have a social purpose, and choric drama in these authors' hands has been given a political twist. Akin to this type of drama is the "Mass Recitation" of the Young Workers' Group of Unity Theatre, London, directed mainly by Margaret Leona. This is a form of chorus work, begun in 1937 with group-arrangements of a very vivid dramatic nature, using propaganda material most effectively. The outstanding examples were *Salute to Spain, Salute to the Soviet Union* and (most remarkable of all) *The Agony of China,* which was performed entirely by Chinese students speaking in English.

A similar experiment was part of the workers' movement which grew up in the United States as a result of the economic crisis of 1929. Here "Mass Recitation" was carried out under the Works' Project Administration, and used the themes of unemployment, land-hunger, and housing needs. One of the most memorable of these was the crowd-drama *A Third of a Nation,* which has since been staged in London by Suria Magito and Margaret Leona.

EUROPE AND OVERSEAS

To the United States choral speaking made an instant appeal. In 1931 the first choirs appeared at North Western University, Cleveland, Ohio, under Dean Dennis, and at Pasadena Junior College, California, under Elizabeth Keppie. Now, some fifteen years later, Primary and High Schools, Colleges and Universities all have their speech choirs, and the subject is regarded as an essential part of a teacher's training.

Among those who have developed this form of art in the United States, Miriam Gow of Chestnut Hill College, Philadelphia; Agnes Curren Hamm of Mount Mary College, Milwaukee; and Cécile de Banke of Wellesley College come immediately to mind as three conductors who, by books, lectures, demonstrations, festivals and broadcasts, have made choral speaking known far beyond their own states.

Melbourne and Sydney, both started speaking choirs as early as 1929, with Eileen O'Keefe and Grace Stafford as conductors. The work appears to be progressing steadily in Australia, though without the speed of the movement in the United States.

Canada had its first choral speaking festival in Winnipeg, Manitoba, in 1934. Since then, Windsor, Ontario; Calgary, Alberta; and Vancouver, British Columbia, have introduced it into schools and training colleges. Calgary had its first radio broadcast of choral speech in 1938, the choir being introduced by Olive Fisher of the Normal Training School, and conducted by Mr. Miller, principal of the Normal Practice School.

In Europe the movement took place simultaneously with that in Britain, though it was not until some years later that either knew of the other's activities. It played a great part in the

Germany of the Weimar Republic. Regular lecture-courses were given in 1929 by Herr Wittsack in Halle University; and the speech choir of Professor Leyhausen at Berlin University was producing many of the Greek plays, parts of Goethe's *Faust*, and passages from Hölderlin. It also travelled to Greece to give exchange performances with a Greek choir of *The Persians* by Aeschylus.

At the Munich Exhibition of 1930 appeared *The Totenmal*, described as "a choric vision for speech, drama, light and music," written, composed and conducted by the Swiss poet, Albert Talhof. This made use of mimers and speakers with accompanying orchestral effects, and employed some two hundred players. It was a daring and original venture in the new medium, and had been ten years in preparation.

Besides these purely artistic types of choirs, there were in Europe at this time two other kinds. One was devoted to religious or ethical purposes, such as the Goetheanum Choir from Dornach, Switzerland, and the Youth Movement Choir in Holland, which developed the Dutch Community Drama. The other belonged to the Proletarians of Germany. These young workers began to train themselves in 1924 in combined speech and movement—the movement being based on the famous Laban "dance drama"—in order to present such plays as Ernst Toller's *Requiem* and his *Masses and Men*. These choirs were to be found at the time of the Weimar Republic in all the Workers' Institutes, and the beauty and strength of some of their work was very striking.

The last news received of choral speaking in Europe before the war was in the summer of 1938 when Josef Boon's religious play, *Sanguis Christi* was performed (in Flemish) by more than two thousand speakers, singers and musicians in the main square of Bruges, with the famous belfry as its background. A friend who saw this performance expressed the hope that it would became a traditional part of the life of Bruges, just as the Passion Play is a part of Oberammergau or Tiersee. The war interrupted that, but one hopes it will not be long before choral speaking takes its place again in the cultural life of all these countries.

BOOK LIST

GENERAL

Choral Speaking. Marjorie Gullan. (Methuen, 4s. 6d.).

An Approach to Choral Speech. Mona Swann. (Macmillan, 4s. 6d.).

Poetry Speaking for Children. Marjorie Gullan and P. Gurrey. (Methuen), Part I, Infant, 2s. 6d.; Part II, Junior, 3s.; Part III, Senior, 4s.

The Art of Choral Speech. Cécile de Banke. (Baker Plays, Boston, U.S.A., $1.75, A. & C. Black, London).

Choral Speaking Technique. Agnes Curren Hamm. (Tower Press, Milwaukee, U.S.A.).
Choral Speaking: Suggestions for Its Practice and Study. Clive Sansom. (London Academy of Music pamphlet, 6d.).
The Teaching of Choric Speech. Elizabeth Keppie. (Expression Co., Boston, U.S.A., $2.25).
Choral Speaking: *Study Aid.* Edited, Georgia Corp. (University of Winconsin, 40c.).
"Mass Recitation by Workers in U.S.A." Susan Shepherd. *Good Speech,* July 1935.
"Mass Recitation." Margaret Leona. *Good Speech,* April 1939.
"A Letter against 'Harmonising' in Speech Choirs." "Vox." *Good Speech,* October 1936.
"Choral Speech." Mona Swann. (*Spoken English,* Methuen).

ANTHOLOGIES

Poetry Speaking Anthology. Hilda Adams and Anne Croasdell. (Methuen, Book I, Infant, 1s. 6d.; Book II, Junor, 1s. 6d.; Book III, Senior, 2s. 6d.).
Many Voices. Mona Swann. (Macmillan). Part 1, Part 2.
The Poet Speaks. Marjorie Gullan and Clive Sansom. (Methuen, 5s. 6d.).
The Speech Choir. Marjorie Gullan. (Harper & Bros., New York, $1.75).

CHORIC DRAMA

"Re-Enter the Chorus." Ashley Dukes. *Theatre Arts Monthly,* May 1938.
"The Place of the Speech Chorus in Modern Drama." John Garrett. *Good Speech,* January 1937.
"Choric Speech and the Stage." Gordon Bottomley. *Theatre Arts Monthly,* July 1935.
List of plays-with-choruses suitable for Junior and Senior Schools. *Good Speech,* April and October 1936.
List of plays-with-choruses, suitable for Adults in *The Poet Speaks.* (Methuen).

GRAMOPHONE RECORDS

Choral speaking is a new art, and neither speakers nor technicians have so far mastered the difficulties of recording it. The following records are by no means perfect examples, but they must suffice until gramophone companies and speaking choirs are prepared to give the subject more consideration:

London Elementary Schools. A set of 3 records, supervised by Marjorie Gullan. Classroom recordings in Infant, Junior and Senior Schools. (H.M.V., B.8268-70).
Channing School, Highgate. Conductor: Hilda Brettell. Junior and Senior Choirs. (H.M.V., B.8962).

Moira House School, Eastbourne. Conductor: Mona Swann. Choral Speaking by Girls. (H.M.V., B.8671-2).
Neville House School, Eastbourne. Conductor: Eric Laming. Choral Speaking by Boys. (H.M.V., B.8857-8).
The Individualists. Conductor: John Laurie. A group of adult speakers from the Oxford Festival of Spoken Poetry. (H.M.V., B.8870).
The London Verse Speaking Choir. Conductor: Marjorie Gullan. Adult Choir. (H.M.V., B.8271).

Speech Festivals

By DULCIE BOWIE

In 1919, Miss Marjorie Gullan induced the organisers of the Glasgow Music Festival to include a section for the speaking of verse, and this lead was soon followed by other Music Festivals all over the British Isles. The new section was called the "elocution section." The word "elocution" is now outmoded and scorned, because it has unfortunate associations for many people; but it has a clear and precise meaning—"the art of oral delivery"—and it was, and is, in fact, this art, in its many aspects, which the Festivals aimed to develop. In some districts, and in some years, elocution was the Cinderella of the festival; the entries were small, or the speakers were ill-equipped, or the contests poorly attended; the audience was more accustomed to listening to music or to drama than to poetry or prose. But in other centres, especially in the North, where literature is a living tradition and there are people passionately concerned for fine speech, the elocution section was as large and as popular as the music classes.

In any case, without the enterprise and devotion of the organisers of the Musical Festivals, I doubt whether the later Speech Festival—the Festival devoted entirely to speech—could have come into being. Dr. John Masefield, the Poet Laureate, organised the first of these at the Examination Schools, Oxford, on the 24th and 25th of July 1923. He called it "The Oxford Recitations, a Verse Speaking Contest." Dr. and Mrs. Masefield, with Professors George Gordon and Gilbert Murray, formed the executive; the adjudicators were Laurence Binyon, Professor George Gordon, John Masefield, Professor Gilbert Murray and Sir Herbert Warren. Later, other poets and scholars took part—Gordon Bottomley, Lascelles Abercrombie, Walter de la Mare, Harold Monro, Robert Trevelyan, John Buchan. Finally, the contests were abandoned and the Festival moved to Dr. Masefield's own little theatre on Boar's Hill, where speakers who had become known at the contest were allotted poems to speak and parts to play in programmes devised and rehearsed by the poets. To many of us, these Festivals brought our first experience of people who considered that the speaking of poetry was neither daft nor strange, but as natural an impulse, almost, as the need of food and sleep. This was the peak of the year, a period of excitement, of fulfilment, of stimulation and inspiration, not found elsewhere. These meetings were held simply for the delight of poetry; and this aim seems to have been somewhat obscured since the Recitations ended in 1931. We have not known the same singleness of purpose and achievement since that source was closed to us.

In 1922, the Scottish Association for the Speaking of Verse was founded, with Dr. Masefield as its first President, and by 1924 there were branches in Edinburgh, Glasgow, Firth and Aberdeen, which organised their own Festivals, adjudicated by visitors from England as well as from Scotland, and visited by pupils and students from many types of schools and many sections of the community. In 1927 the first London Speech Festival was organised by the Speech Fellowship, under the direction of Miss Marjorie Gullan. Choral Speaking was the main feature of this Festival from the first year, and attained an increasingly high standard. Children from state schools, and adults from Training Colleges and Evening Institutes, came to take part.

In 1932 the young English Verse Speaking Association held its first Festival of Verse Speaking at Rhodes House, Oxford, with Laurence Binyon, Gordon Bottomley, John Drinkwater, Alida Monro, Professor Oliver Elton and Professor Ernest de Sélincourt as judges. The contests were based on the lines of the Oxford Recitations and had the blessing of the Poet Laureate. Four years later, Laurence Binyon and Gordon Bottomley, with Richard Church and Wallace Nichols, took over the Festivals, and carried them on when the E.V.S.A. was dissolved, with the help of an executive, and a panel of judges on which served for the first time Clifford Bax, Austin Clarke from Ireland, and L. A. G. Strong. The principle of having poets to adjudicate remained, and in 1937 W. H. Auden, Wilfred Gibson and Victoria Sackville-West, and in 1939 Cecil Day Lewis and Sylvia Townsend Warner, joined the galaxy. In 1946, the Festival was held in London, re-named the English Festival of Spoken Poetry. The death of Laurence Binyon during the war, and the ill-health of Dr. Gordon Bottomley, deprived the directorate of two experienced and valued leaders and friends. The resumption of the Festival was devised as a "devout tribute" to the work done by these two poets. The building, the competitors and many of the judges were new, but the old enthusiasm and friendliness remained.

SCHOOL FESTIVALS

Meantime, the schools had not been idle. The Association of Teachers of Speech and Drama, founded by Miss Elsie Fogerty, had for a long time held annual Festivals in London and in

Northern England, for the pupils of members. Miss Mabel Gulick, at Roedean; Miss Mona Swann, at Moira House School; Miss Nancie Smith, at Highbury Hill High School; and the St. Albans Grammar School, invited poets, scholars and speakers to judge the work of the year within the school. Miss Woods and Miss Bidwell organised Speech Festivals at Enfield, which included classes for the speaking of foreign, as well as English, poetry. This Festival, and the Stewart Headlam Foundation Festivals under the auspices of the L.C.C. Education authorities, have survived the vicissitudes of the war years.

SPEECH FESTIVALS OVERSEAS

In Sydney, Australia, a "A Good Speech Festival" was first held in 1930. In 1936, the city of Winnipeg, Manitoba, held the first Canadian Speech Festival; it was non-competitive, and for choral speech only. The following year, Marjorie Gullan was in Canada on a lecture tour, and spoke of the "very great interest in speech education" throughout the country. In Wellesley College, Massachusetts (Alma mater of Madame Chiang Kai Chek and her sisters) Cécile de Banke, Head of the Speech Department, crowned her work with a festival programme of American poetry, choral and solo, spoken partly by her students and partly by the poets concerned. This was in 1942, and again in 1943. Her speech choir is well known in America and has done several world broadcasts over the American radio. Miss de Banke uses choral speech extensively in training her students.

FUTURE FESTIVALS

The speech festival, however, is still in its infancy. Now that the war is over, we must have more and better Festivals. I would like to make some suggestions for these:

The aim of every festival should be the enjoyment of fine speech and language.

Unity of performance is probably best achieved under the leadership of one person, whether man or woman, though the executive work, which is heavy, must be done by a committee or some group of helpers.

The festivals should be non-competitive. Competition endangers unity, and is a severe handicap for many performers. People should come together to exercise themselves in the "art of oral delivery," to receive advice and guidance, and to see and hear what others are doing.

Set pieces should be chosen from the poetry which makes universal appeal, especially poetry which makes its effect largely through sound; the more eclectic and intellectual poetry should be avoided, or used only for a special reason. Those who come to listen should be drawn in and made to feel that they have a definite part in the occasion—as indeed they have.

The poets should be brought in more and more, as directors and as critics.

The issue between dialect speech and what is loosely (and rather offensively) called "Standard English," should be clearly stated everywhere. In centres where the common speech is dialect, the speaker should be given a chance of handling both forms to the best of his ability.

There should be some method of exchange—of ideas, of adjudicators and of performers—from time to time, between the speech festivals of the United Kingdom and, as soon as possible, the United States of America, the Dominions, and the Colonies.

I am sorry that restrictions of time and space prevent me from naming and paying tribute to many other fine people—poets, teachers, speakers and actors, education authorities and private individuals—who have devoted their time and talents and energy to speech and Speech Festivals for the past 25 years, and have shown us how lovely and how inspiring speech can be. The way has been hard at times, and their labours have not met always with the appreciation they deserved. In particular, perhaps, is this true of the poets. A section of the community inside and outside the festivals, seemed unable and unwilling to accept guidance and criticism from the poet; yet he is the creator, in his own medium, as the musician in his, and the policy of inviting musicians to judge music-making seems to create little or no antagonism by comparison. I am quite sure we should see to it that the poet is more, not less, concerned in the Festivals of the future, leading, hearing, questioning and learning with the rest of us.

BIBLIOGRAPHY

Yearbook of the British Federation of Music Festivals, 106 Gloucester Place, London, W.1.

Syllabi of the London Speech Festival, 1927-1939. Out of print.

Syllabi of the Oxford Festival of Spoken Poetry. Out of print.

"The Ideal Festival." Marjorie Gullan. *Good Speech,* Oct. 1935.

"The Bingley Speech Festival." M. Brooke Gwynne. *Good Speech,* Oct., 1933.

"Speech Festivals." Lucy Story. Speech Fellowship *News Letter,* July, 1944.

"Leigh and St. Albans Speech Festivals." Marjorie Gullan. Speech Fellowship *News Letter,* July, 1944.

Speech in Our Theatre

By E. MARTIN BROWNE

CHOOSE any year in the period between wars: look through the files of any leading newspaper for its dramatic critic's views on speech: more than half his references will be to inaudability. This complaint has never been heard in the theatre before. It means that the actor is trying to do with his voice something never before attempted in the theatre—and that, for the most part, he is not yet sure of the means to do it. We should enquire what this something is: whether the attempt is a right one and likely to continue: and if so, what the actor needs for success in it.

During most of the century our drama has become increasingly naturalistic. That is, it has sought to establish conventions, not of a ritualistic kind (as in Greece) nor an heroic kind (as in Shakespeare's theatre), nor of an elegant kind (as in Congreve's or Sheridan's), but of an approximation to ordinary life. Its speech, therefore, has not been song or verse or rhythmic prose, but a selected and concentrated version of conversational talk. Someone wickedly said of the most naturalistic of all our dramatists that his dialogue consisted of "Oh, I'm sorry"—and this considerable exaggeration does suggest the clipped and inexpressive medium which our writers, however high their skill, have set themselves to use. They have required the actor to express himself as if he were not in a theatre, but in a room. This sets him a difficult problem, for he is in fact speaking for hundreds, or even thousands of people to hear. He must find means of enlarging the sounds comprising his author's version of natural speech so that they can be heard throughout the theatre, without losing the effect of natural behaviour or contradicting the feelings from which that behaviour springs.

This problem has not yet been successfully solved. The tradition of the theatre is all against its solution—for thousands of years the actor used a declamatory form of speech, suited to the carefully patterned and highly rhythmic diction of his author's writing. He took it for granted that the speech of the theatre was completely different from that of real life, and regarded his script just as the singer regards his music. At times, however, his delivery would become divorced from the thought and feeling it was to express. (Such a divorce afflicts all the expressive arts by reason of the repetition they demand). Then the test of "reality" would be applied as a corrective, to bring his speech back into relation with the life of his character: but no one ever supposed that this "reality" was that of ordinary daily behaviour, nor denied to the theatre a speech of its own. So the actor's instinct, founded on long tradition, taught him a speech belonging to his art. And in facing the demand of the naturalistic play for an approximation to the speech of ordinary life, he was further handicapped by having to go on playing older plays written in palpably artificial speech. Shakespeare still held the stage that made room for Mr. Lonsdale and Mr. Coward.

So great became the difference in the requirements of the poet and the "drawing room dramatist," that Shakespearean actors were considered old-fashioned, and few of them could get work on the modern stage. Conversely, when the modern actor stepped from his drawing-room to the battlements of Elsinore, he was apt to pale into insignificance. To make the poetry "real" to himself, he would deliberately clip phrases and destroy the structure of the verse: so that I have been assured by a pillar of the pre-war Old Vic that the right way was to disregard the line-endings and "speak it as if it were prose." The modern actor fits his emotional make-up to the range of Shakespeare's passion by reducing that range to the compass of his own "childish treble." He achieves a truth of feeling within that small compass : but at what a cost! It is true that often he would wish, if he knew the way, to increase the compass to something like its original vastness : but he does not know the way : and after all he spends most of his acting-time in the parlour with Mr. Coward's Queen instead of on the throne with Shakespeare's.

Of late years a reaction has been setting in. Great events have cast their shadows on the theatre, and people have discovered that they need great drama. Mr. Gielgud has found a huge public for the classical play : and it is noteworthy that his own delivery of the classics has become more and more oratorical. His recent Macbeth had the grandeur and sweep of which one hears in the giants of the past : and at the same time it was so packed with concentrated thought as to compete with any subtlety of the naturalistic stage. Who that saw and heard it will ever forget the speech that ended with that gigantic pause in which the word of finality was sought for and found :

Signifying . . . . nothing.

The two London Repertory Companies, Mr. Gielgud's and the Old Vic, have led the way to a theatre in which the plays are chosen from the best of every age : and that, as we have seen, is going to demand a speech which can rise to the heights of poetry or descend to the intimacies of naturalism : which can be audible in both and be the vehicle of real feeling in things of ephemeral as of immortal significance.

How is the actor of the future to equip himself for this task? It is a bigger one than actors have ever had before. First, he can no longer rely on his natural gifts alone. The day is gone when a handsome youth could walk straight on to the stage and make a career by "just being himself," or a pretty girl succeed on a pleasant voice. Training is essential—the laborious process of becoming conscious of one's own equipment in order to master it, of taking it to pieces, so as to speak, in order to re-fashion it as the instrument of one's art. That process will go on all through the actor's life : in speech, as in movement, the good actor will be constantly increasing his mastery. But the basis of mastery must be established before he first treads the boards.

To find the right way to mastery over the varied kinds of speech needed on our stage, we may well go to our greatest living dramatist, Bernard Shaw. Throughout the period of extreme naturalism, Mr. Shaw has always written in an oratorical style. He has always demanded of the actor agility of mouth as well as of mind. He has truly said that while he never asks an actor to do the impossible, he does demand that the actor should know his job and exert his powers to the full. The actor must, in short, be a trained orator before he is an actor.

This is sound doctrine, for the drawing-room as for the throne-room play. Every play worth playing is a microcosm of human life : nothing in it is without significance : and to throw anything in it away is to cheat an audience which still comes to the theatre trusting it to reveal the meaning while it unfolds the tale. So every sound set down for the actor must be heard. His first requirement is sufficient muscular power and control to make every word fully audible and telling. Physical training, then, comes first.

But when articulation is mastered, there follow rhythm and inflection. Here we have made a mistake in our training. It is wrong to let the student use speech in acting before he has mastered speech as such. No man is in full command of speech until he can express a full range of thought and feeling in speech alone : and that command will never be attained unless its foundations are laid before speech is applied to characterisation. The student should be able to deliver fully expressive speech before he is allowed to act.

This is a hard doctrine : but a necessary one. It is doubly important because to-day speech is the distinctive province of the stage. The film can do the visual part better : it has a wider range and a greater technical power : but in the film hearing is always subordinate to seeing. It is only on the stage that the riches of speech are completely revealed. So to the actor of the future speech will be all-important.

The naturalistic dramatists tended to make the actor distrustful of speech. In portraying the ordinary man, they inevitably cast oratory into disrepute : and only the most sensitive of them managed to preserve any rhythm in their writing of prose dialogue. The poets too were affected : the iambic had become foreign to ordinary speech rhythm and hence was unsuitable as a dramatic medium, but the attempt to find another verse-form was pursued through many uncertainties. Only now do we begin to see what that new-old medium is. Dr. Gordon Bottomley has done thirty years of pioneering in discovering it. Mr. T. S. Eliot has defined it in *The Family Reunion.* Even during the war, a small but steady stream of plays in this "new" verse emerged, and it is evident that more are to come. So the actor will have once more the poetry of his own day in his mouth. This is essential to good speech in the theatre. The poet is the arbiter of speech standards : and only the actor who speaks a living poetry can speak also a prose worthy of the stage. If the too-long gap between poet and dramatist is securely bridged, we shall have again a fully expressive speech in our theatre.

SOME ACTORS' VOICES

Henry Ainley. Excerpts from *Hamlet.* Two records. (H.M.V.).
Edith Evans and John Gielgud. Scene from *The Importance of being Earnest.* (H.M.V.)

Maurice Evans. Scenes from *Richard II.* Five records. (Columbia.)
Johnston Forbes-Robertson. From *Richard II, Macbeth* and *Hamlet.* Two records. (Columbia.)
John Gielgud. Lines from *Richard II* and *King John.* One record. (H.M.V.)
A set of 5 records from *Merchant of Venice, Hamlet, Othello, Richard II,* etc. (Linguaphone.)
Sybil Thorndike. Scenes from *Macbeth.* (H.M.V.).
Flora Robson. Three Scenes from *Macbeth.* 2 records. (Harvard Film Service, U.S.A.).

For addresses of Drama Societies (see page 212).

Amateur and Experimental Drama

By MARGARET LEONA

THERE is scarcely a small town or village without its own company of players. It is true that many of these do not aspire beyond *Rookery Nook* or *The Ghost Train*; and the standards of producing, acting and speaking are often such as could only be endured by an audience of relations and friends. But there are others attempting plays of Shaw, Galsworthy, Bridie and Priestley of our own time, and some of Shakespeare's, Goldsmith's, Sheridan's and Wilde's; and frequently they give pleasure to those listening as well as to those taking part. There are also a small minority of amateur groups who present plays of an experimental type which the commercial theatre would never consider—verse drama; "psychological" drama; plays with a strong political or social bias; dialect plays; religious drama, the revival of nativity plays and new work by Gordon Bottomley or Laurence Housman, as well as translations from the Greek, French and German.

In all these groups, speech varies as much as the choice of play. But it is a mistake to expect perfect speech from the start, and disastrous to expect it in a newly-formed society. The amateurs' enthusiasm is important in the adventure on the stage. They will be discouraged if excessive attention is paid to the delivery of the words. The feeling of the part, the moves, and the bearing are no less important in a world of bewildering new values. The amateur "comes to" slowly, and time is needed before he is free to realise that it is not enough for the lines to be spoken; they must also be heard, and heard in a particular way, and that this is sustained throughout by the mood. The speed, intensity, phrasing and rhythm given to a line are an indispensible part of its meaning. In plays where the words themselves have great significance—whether it is *Twelfth Night, St. Joan* or *The Importance of Being Earnest*—even more depends on the style in which we interpret these to the audience. Teachers like Marjorie Gullan, Herbert Scott, and the late Elsie Fogerty, have all done much to improve the quality of speech in professional drama, and their influence has extended to the amateur theatre. We are coming to realise the value of effective speech, not for its own sake, but in order to convey more powerfully or sensitively the intention of the poet or playwright.

Before the war, drama in London received impetus from the formation of several experimental theatre companies—first the Group Theatre, and then London Theatre Studio and Unity Theatre. The earliest, the Group, under Rupert Doone's direction, produced several verse dramas, including Eliot's *Sweeney Agonistes,* Auden's *Dance of Death* and *Dog Beneath the Skin,* and Louis MacNeice's translation of the *Agamemnon.* The London Theatre Studio, which was a training school for the professional stage, experimented widely in acting and production. One remembers particularly their dramatised version of *Judith* by Carl Wildman, produced by Michael St. Denis with the students, the words of the Bible making the script—words beautifully spoken by a chorus under the direction of Mona Swann.

Unity Theatre was a working-class theatre addressed to a working-class audience. The little band of enthusiasts were keen lovers of the theatre—a few were keener lovers of politics, and got rather mixed in their issues! But all were united in needing material that reflected current political trends. Training and development as artists could come later; they had something to say and believed in the urgency of their outlook. They had no writers, actors or premises, until they found their own. They were fortunate in their dramatic leadership—John Allen. He set Unity on its feet, and by the quality of his productions made this theatre unique. He had a genius for bold presentation, and demanded that all theatre material should be given in the most imaginative and direct theatre idiom. He inspired Herbert Hodge and his friend, both taxi drivers, to write *Where's That Bomb?* which caught the imagination of the audience from the first night. It was a political cartoon, with racy speech, and given with great vitality.

There was no money at Unity and no stage—just a raised platform, improvised lighting, a few sacks, and wildly keen untrained actors—hairdressers, typists, factory-workers, shop hands by trade—all politically alive. In time they built their own theatre in Goldington Street, near St. Pancras Station. By then the actors were used to playing together and had developed more than one acting group. They felt the need for maintaining direct contact with the audience to help onlookers realise that they shared responsibility for events occuring in the world to-day. So Unity produced *Waiting for Lefty,* by Clifford Odets, followed later by *The Busman's Living Newspaper,* largely written and wholly directed by John Allen (a documentary concerning the busmen's strike at the time of the Coronation). In all these plays the language of ordinary daily conversation was used, and used with a strength and purpose often lacking in the normal professional theatre.

MASS RECITATION

With this work came Mass Recitation, and I was asked to help in its production. Speaking choirs, with a background of movement caught the fancy of some of the actors and many open-air audiences. The voices in the group were, on the whole, freer than most dramatic students'. Fear of addressing an audience or of speaking with strong feeling never occurred to them; they were used to it. But when it came to sustaining a mood, or speaking while performing an action, or modulating a sequence, then much practice and much rehearsal was needed. So eager and keen were they that often shouting was mistaken for emphasis, and key-words were hammered instead of being properly phrased, and it took time for them to hear the relationship of phrase with phrase. When they did, their response was whole-hearted. The value of these Mass Recitations for the untrained actor lay in the limitation of the medium. This work demanded disciplined attention and disciplined speech. There were no stage curtains or "props"; only the words to depend on, very little action, rhythmic grouping, bright costume, and the flag of the nation for whom the actor was speaking as background. Mass Recitations, such as Jack Lindsay wrote for Unity, seem to me to have a possibility of tremendous dramatic development.

PLAY-READING

Play-reading is another activity which lends itself to experiment. Some groups study the work of a particular playwright, or become interested in scenes of contrasting times—dialect, modern or period plays.

The chief advantages of play-reading are (1) It brings in everyone; there need be no audience. (2) It does not have to be rehearsed often; it can be fitted into two hours or two-and-a-half in the evening without leaving one's own building. (3) It can create an interest in drama among people who would not otherwise be brought in contact with it. (4) Women can read men's parts. (5) It makes those taking part realise the importance of the voice as a medium for expressing emotions and ideas. But a warning is necessary. The play chosen should be suitable for reading; some cannot be appreciated without the appropriate action. It is also important that the words themselves have been valued by the playwright, whether his purpose has been serious or humorous. And the leader should encourage those taking part to develop all the oral qualities of the play, not only the mood and variation of pace in speech, but all significant sounds, such as a door-bang, footsteps, a bell, wind, rain, etc.; to pick up cues quickly, and not pause to breathe after the last person has spoken; to keep their heads out of their books; and to speak directly to the other character, so that the tone is always lively. The whole play gains full value in sound by this treatment.

Other groups have taken play-reading into the hospitals. Dr. Casson and Miss Macdonald of the School of Occupational Therapy, Bristol, have tried this and other speech activities with their patients. It is difficult, at present, to judge how far social rehabiliation can be aided through speech, song and drama; but I feel sure that it could have much to give to patients convalescing. There is also work to be done with the blind, whose voices are often infinitely more sensitive than ours own. Very little has yet been tried, but these are lines which need developing.

ABCA (now the Bureau of Current Affairs) made an interesting experiment in the forming of Living Newspapers, which originated in America. These are Documentaries, presented dramatically, on subjects relating to current events. Documentary programmes dealing with *Lend-Lease, Japan, Where do we go from here?* were performed before various army units, and proved a tremendous success. The pointer lies here: people daring to speak for themselves, about things that matter, and in a way that matters. In this way we might develop an informed people, a creative approach—a critical audience making fresh demands on the professional theatre, and a greater contribution to the art of living.

BIBLIOGRAPHY

The Amateur Actor. Frances Mackenzie (Nelson. 3s. 6d.)
The Amateur Stage. F. Brotherton and A. Hobbs (Oxford, 5s.)
Acting Improvised. Robert G. Newton (Nelson, 3s. 6d.)
Amateur Acting from A to Z. John Bourne.
The Play Produced. John Fernald (Deane 3s. 6d.)
To Meet the Occasion. Carroll & Greenwood (French, 3s. 6d.)
Drama and Youth. Carroll & Thomas (Arnold, 1s.)
A Textbook of Stage Craft. Susan Richmond (Deane, 3s. 6d.)
Further Steps in Stage Craft. Susan Richmond (Deane, 3s. 6d.)
The Craft of Comedy. Stephen Haggard & Athene Seyler (Moller, 5s.)
Entertain Yourselves. (National Council of Social Service, 2s. 6d.)
Play-Reading Course. Mark Perugini (National Union of Townswomen's Guilds, 1s. 6d.)
A Textbook for Playwrights. E. D. Lewis (Heinemann, 2s. 6d.)
Twenty-Five Years of the British Drama League. (B.D.L., 1944.)
Let's Do a Play! Rodney Bennett (Nelson, 4s. 6d.)
Let's Get up a Concert! Rodney Bennett & H. S. Gordon (Nelson, 4s. 6d.)
The Concert Book. Ed. Sydney Northcote (Nelson, 3s. 6d.)
How to Make a Pageant. Mary Kelly (Pitman, 5s.)

A List of Plays for Boys and Men *The Players' Library* *A List of Plays for Girls and Boys* *Plays for Village Players*	British Drama League

Speech and Song

By RODNEY BENNETT

It may be as well to admit at once that to pretend, at the present date and in a few pages, to deal with the subject of "Words and Music"—or should one say "Words v. Music"?—is a species of dishonesty. In spite of the publication of several interesting and one excellent book upon the subject, the situation remains, in the word favoured by news announcers, obscure. The obscurity might perhaps be to some extent cleared up if someone who is at once a musician, singer, poet (or at least versifier), phonetician, writer, and thinker, girded his loins to the large task of exploring the relevant country, much of which is still virgin. But that is by no means certain. The subject is surrounded by such a jungle of real difficulty, muddled thinking, misconception, preconception, prejudice, and what may be called the vested interests of teachers of singing, a jungle which has developed such pretty new tangles during the last twenty years, that not even the emergence of that all-round paragon could be guaranteed to clear it. The following paragraphs must therefore be regarded as no more than a brief statement of the nature of the problem, and a consideration of how it came into being, and why so little has been effectively done to resolve it.

With troubadours and minstrels, one imagines, the story was the thing. Given four strong accents to the line, or four and three, they filled in with such syllables as sense, speed and atmosphere demanded, fortifying the total rhythmic effect with chords on the harp. Among folk-singers the mental attitude was much the same. In narrative songs the words ruled, but where atmosphere or emotion was more important, they were liable to be subordinated even to the point of *eheu o loro* and *fol the doddle,* emotional sound-carriers freed from any burden of mere sense. This happy harmony of voice and verse persisted in Elizabethan times. Lutenists often wrote their own words, and self-respecting poets did not think it beneath them to write especially for music, nor composers to set the result with genuine regard for the poet's intention. Lastly, and, perhaps, most important of all, music, including singing, was still regarded as an essential part of a liberal education for gentlemen. Poetry and music, in short, were still congenial and equal partners. As late as 1690 Purcell could assert, apparently without irony or wishful thinking, that "Music and Poetry have ever been acknowledged Sisters, which walking hand in hand support each other."

But the seeds of discord were already planted. Ruthlessly maltreating words to suit their melodic and harmonic devices, madrigalists had started a musical fashion which has increasingly alienated poets ever since, an alienation which, as recently at 1937, caused W. B. Yeats to assert, in a Broadside, that "the poet, his ear attentive to his own art, hears with derision most settings of of his own work," and that "the concert platform has wronged poets by masticating their well-made words and turning them into spittle." The division of the ways may be put at 1728, when *The Beggar's Opera,* in which verse was still treated more or less in the folk-song manner, dealt the more formalised type of opera a blow from which, at least in the English-speaking world, it has never entirely recovered. The battle was joined between poet and composer, and later the struggle was embittered by the emergence of two other combatants, the singer and the general public. Handel, while using words with what it is polite to call latitude, treated singers and their throats with as much consideration as his temper and their vanity allowed; but with Beethoven, who seems to have regarded voices merely as instruments, that consideration began to lapse into a decline to which many composers have vigorously contributed, especially young ones of the "advanced" type, who apparently hold the same view of a voice as the Murdstones held towards the former Mrs. Copperfield: that you should be firm with it, even if the subject dies under the treatment. Not a few composers, who would be ashamed to write for clarinet or harp with no regard for its peculiar genius, and who would not think of asking a tympanist to operate with a hammer, seem to delight in writing for that perishable mechanism, the voice, with the perverted ingenuity of a ski instructor who should train his pupils largely by making them plod up exhausting slopes.

The root of the trouble, of course, is summed up in Yeats's phrase, "his ear attentive to his art": composers, poets, and singers alike are apt to regard the problem of combining words, music, and voice too exclusively from their own point of view, to their mutual detriment. Nor have schools of music made any notable attempt to bring the combatants to an armistice, let alone an understanding. There may be schools of singing where the study of speech and of poetry is an obligatory part of the student's training—as it obviously should be—but they are certainly rare. In the same way those schools of composition are rare, even if they exist, in which intending writers for the voice are normally expected to study that instrument; to learn its reaction to various vowels; to know what it can do with comfort and effect, and what, with the best will in the world, it cannot; to acquire the rudiments of singing themselves, and to sing in a choir at least enough to know that such terms as vocal movement and *tessitura* have real meaning.

Conversely, it is reasonably safe to say that there is no place in the world where composers can receive precise instruction in the art of writing words to fit tunes—a strict and revealing discipline—or words which will be acceptable at once to composer, singer, and listener; or where the poet can pick up ideas about writing for music. That being so, it is not surprising that such writing is hardly at all regarded for what it is: as a separate art, difficult, austere, yet fascinating, in which clear, immediate, and uncomplicated statement, atmospheric suggestion, and rhythm are of primary importance, rhyme of comparatively little importance, and scansion and subtleties of no importance whatever. The amateur who tries to learn the art for himself is harassed on the one hand by the purists who complain that his metre is defective and that his work does not stand on its own poetic feet (in both senses)—which is precisely what a good song should not do; and on the other by the popular statement that composers should set only the finest poems to music, an argument which overlooks the obvious fact that the best poetry, being self-sufficient, neither needs nor can comfortably tolerate the amplification of music. The problem is partly but not entirely solved by poets like Walter de la Mare, who have themselves been singers, or like Gilbert, who, though they have little technical knowledge of music, yet have a lively sense of musical rhythm and style. Such men are not numerous, and composers make up for the scarcity of words expressly fitted for music by using the other kind. They fall into two main classes: those who sacrifice the spirit to the word, and those, the object of Yeats's spleen, who reverse the process, concentrating upon some feature of subject or rhythm, and subordinating the poem as a unity to it. Both are apt to lament that poetry "has so many syllables."

The appearance of the singer and the listening public in the lists was one of the immediate results of radio. The public, after centuries of tolerance to singers' words, or their absence, suddenly decided that two things were intolerable: a wobble and word mastication and swallowing. They demanded with unkind insistence that words should be not merely audible and understandable, but also natural-sounding. With this demand singers were by no means all prepared to cope, especially the many who had been trained by foreign teachers who found it easier to stigmatise English as unvocal than to learn it. The general basis of their teaching was that vowels are superior to consonants, and that the rich profusion of English vowels should be pruned more or less to Italian proportions. Of the sliding diphthong, that rich and unique English characteristic, few had apparently even heard.

The argument that English is unvocal overlooks two facts: that a vocally contemptible tongue could hardly be expected to produce a splendid body of poetry, especially dramatic poetry; and that, especially if the difference between speech and song is of degree rather than kind, a language that was grand to speak could hardly be vile to sing. It is worth note in passing that this confusion of thought is perpetuated by many singers of the more erudite sort, who, while regretting the naughtiness of English, revel in singing German, in spite of the fact that, in addition to most of the same consonantal difficulties, that language sports a glottal stop (*coup de glotte*) which, however effective as an emotional device, is vocally destructive and emotionally wasteful as a routine usage.

It would be of course absurd to deny that some pre-wireless singers, as do some today, solved with apparent ease the problem of making words at home with notes, because they combined a good vocal method with a lively ear for speech. But they were in a minority. The others garbled words, played strange tricks with consonants, and simplified vowels and diphthongs to such an extent that not a few, especially contraltos, may be said to have gone through life on virtually one vowel, with minor modifications for the sake of variety in fruitiness. Few modern singers dare go so far as that, but many use strange expedients. Some, in a new enthusiasm for consonants, make finals as strong as initials, or even stronger; others, determined that nothing shall be missed, give as nearly as possible equal importance to all syllables—two devices which, however audible, are certainly not English. The emphatic school tend to glorify *r* in all positions, while others, at the other extreme, subscribe to the regrettable southern English usage of treating that virile consonant as if it were not quite respectable.

Whatever the language, the difficulty of the sung word, except in patter songs, lies in the slow-motion of singing as compared with speech, and the fact that slow motion, whether physical or verbal, induces what may be called introspection, that notorious mother of self-consciousness and enemy of the spontaneous and instinctive. English adds a number of curious problems by reason of its richness in consonants, its range of vowels which are modifiable in relation to stress, its diphthongs, its treatment of *r* and *er,* and the high and fluctuating incidence of the neutral sound. To take two familiar instances from Handel:

a

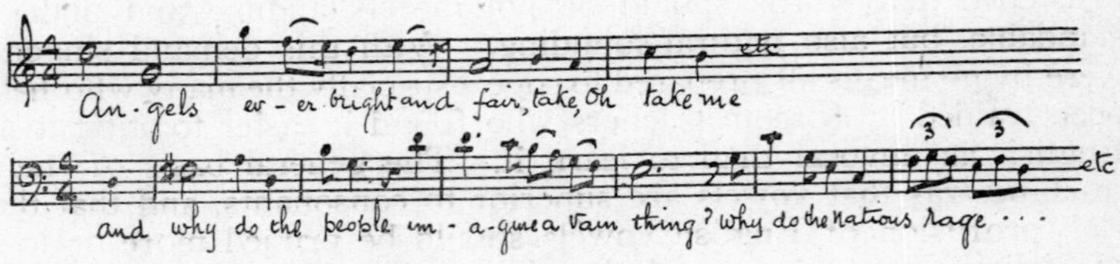

What compromise is to be made about the second syllable of "angels," since the normal speech neutral sound has a dull effect when thus unnaturally prolonged? What is the vowel value of the second syllable of "ever" and "people"? Is final "y" to be sung as short *i,* or is the *ee* so favoured by singers permissible? What is the value of the second element of the whole range of "air" diphthongs? What is the nature of the initial consonant, or consonants, of such words as "furiously," and of the first vowel of that and similar words? And exactly what is the first element of the *ay* in "rage," and, for that matter, of all diphthongs but *oy*, where it is unmistakable?

These problems are not incapable of solution. They are not even particularly difficult; but until they are solved, there is liability to distortion, which is probably uncomfortable for the slightly perplexed singer, and certainly for the listener. Much could be done by collaboration between a group of expert singers and some trained and sympathetic phoneticians. The former would certainly be roused, at least at first, to acrimonious comment and assertion, since it is notoriously difficult to distinguish between what one really does with words and what one imagines one does; but it should not be beyond wit and goodwill to work out a usage which would be acceptable to both throat and ear. Its general acceptance would be a comfort to perplexed singers, and even more to their hearers.

BIBLIOGRAPHY

A Key to Speech and Song. Barbara Storey and Elsie Barnard. (Blackie, 5s.).

Speech and Song. A. M. Henderson (Macmillan, 3s. 6d.).

Voice, Song and Speech. L. Browne & E. Behnke (Sampson Low.)

Pronunciation for Singers. A. J. Ellis (Curwen & Co.).

Singing Learned from Speech. Edward Bairstow & H. Plunket Greene. (Macmillan, 6s.).

Interpretation in Song. H. Plunket Green (Macmillan).

Voice Training in Speech and Song. H. H. Hulbert (Novello).

Words for Music. V. C. Clinton-Baddeley (Cambridge Univ. Press).

The Brain and Voice in Speech and Song. F. W. Mott (Harper & Bros., New York).

The Mechanism of Speech and Song. Douglas Guthrie (Royal Philosophical Society, Glasgow).

Public Speaking

By ARCHIBALD CRAWFORD

Our future as a free and democratic nation rests on an improvement in our public speaking. This has for long been at too low a level. This low level indicates slovenliness in thought and expression. A system of life—democracy—which depends on accuracy of thought and speech cannot long endure on a defective foundation.

The causes of deficiency are educational. We have not been taught to think before we speak, nor to seek how best to say what we do think. In talk we are as untidy as a bull in a china shop, and we carry our "crashings" on to the public platform so that our public controversies are conducted much as the said bull conducts his incursions. Until we are taught the once much-practised art of good conversation our platform attempts must of necessity by inferior. Conversation is the raw material of public speech and if it be an ill-conceived affair so will our speeches be much below what should be their normal quality datum line.

When I was in my youth audiences were still content with high-sounding phrases and rhetorical flows. Today they are more and more demanding clearness, precision and simplicity. Also their lives are so quick and so over-filled that they demand vivid word-pictures from their speakers. Which is one of the reasons why Winston Churchill has such a hold on his audiences. He is the master word-picture maker; the supreme user of metaphor. Consider this gem delivered on the 22nd October, 1940:—

> "Herr Hitler—has managed to subjugate for the time being most of the finest races in Europe, and his little Italian accomplice is trotting along hopefully and hungrily, but rather wearily and very timidly at his side. They both wish to carve up France and her Empire. Not only the French Empire will be devoured by those two ugly customers—Alsace-Lorraine will go once again under the German yoke, and Nice, Savoy, Corsica—Napoleonic Corsica—will be torn from the fair realm of France. But Herr Hitler is not thinking only of stealing other people's territories or flinging gobbets of them to his little dog—he is plotting and working to quench for ever the fountain of characteristic French culture and French inspiration to the world. It is not defeat that France will be made to suffer at German hands, but the doom of complete obliteration."

The House of Commons, restive at some seeming war failure in say Africa or Italy, demands the Premier's head on a charger. In five minutes the same House is listening meekly, acceptingly, to his explanation of seeming lapse which, seen in its true perspective, is made to seem no lapse at all but, on the contrary, the best of good conduct. Because he has created a picture!

Others who excelled in this picture or metaphor speaking were John Bright; listen to him now:—

> "The Angel of Death has been abroad throughout the land; you may almost hear the very beating of his wings. There is no one to sprinkle with blood the lintel and the side posts of our doors, that he may spare and pass on; but he calls at the castle of the noble, the mansion of the wealthy, equally as at the cottage of the humble and it is on behalf of all these classes that I make this solemn appeal." (On the Crimean War—House of Commons—23rd February, 1855).

And Abraham Lincoln; listen to him:—

> "Four-score and seven years ago our fathers brought forth on this continent a new nation, conceived in liberty and

dedicated to the proposition that all men are created equal. Now we are engaged in a great civil war, testing whether that nation, or any nation so conceived and so dedicated, can long endure. We are met on a great battle-field of that war. We have come to dedicate a portion of that field as a final resting place for those who gave their lives that that nation might live. It is altogether fitting and proper that we should do this. But in a larger sense we cannot dedicate, we cannot consecrate, we cannot hallow this ground. The brave men, living and dead, who struggled here have consecrated it far above our poor power to add or detract. The world will little note, nor long remember, what we say here, but it can never forget what they did here. It is for us, the living, rather, to be dedicated here to the unfinished work which they who fought here have thus far so nobly advanced. It is rather for us to be here dedicated to the great task remaining before us—that from these honoured dead we take increased devotion to that cause for which they gave the last full measure of devotion. That we here highly resolve that these dead shall not have died in vain—that this nation, under God, shall have a new birth of freedom—and that Government of the people, by the people, for the people, shall not perish from the earth." (The Gettysburg Oration).

In these speeches were that simplicity, neatness and pictorial clarity of outline that the man in the street can appreciate and, as he thinks back, recall. This brief and accurate clarity is one of the needs of democracy in this hurried machine age. All who run must be able to listen and "read."

Churchill is a model for all of our speakers, political religious, social and industrial. Above all, industrial. What a power for good and evil in industrial relations is the spoken word and how woefully the training in its technique has been neglected. There is a potential fortune in the right word rightly said and a potential crisis, human and economic, in the wrong word wrongly said.

We see all the main avenues of our living—political, religious, economic and social—dominated by thoughts expressed in words, and in hardly one of these do we find much time devoted to the training of the mind for speech or the training of the various aspects of the personality which go to the expressing of these thoughts.

What would we say to, e.g. Sir Cedric Hardwicke, if he lured us to the theatre and gave us a slovenly, amateurish rendering of the words of a great dramatist? We would hiss him from the stage. Why do we not hiss from the platform the many who shamefully let us down by their public utterances? Why? Because our own education in the matter has been so neglected that we are hardly aware that C3 goods are being delivered to us on an A1 occasion.

And this even in the sphere where expressed words are the

only coinage that passes for currency. I refer to the Bar, in which I and so many others pass their professional lives. The reader will find it hard to believe that the young advocate or barrister—*i.e.* the word—soldier—goes to his first case (like a lamb to the slaughter) without any compulsory training in the art and craft of the spoken word. Well I recall how I crashed in my early performances in Court. If this is so in the professional world of speech—as it is—what can we expect of the open forum!

Quite a lot can be done for young men and women and for those in later life by attendance at debating societies and so on, but the real cure lies in a new angle on the education of the youth of tomorrow. Training in Advocacy and Public Speaking should become one of the basic subjects for study, both at school and, better still, at the continuation vocational colleges which are being set up under the new Education Act.

Real mind training for speech making and discussion will be a service to our national life in all its aspects—political, religious, educational, economic and social. I do not mean loose and vague training. I mean training in precision of thought and expression, including word picture-making. Not only are the exercises involved fascinating and invaluable to the service of sound private and public expression but they are one of the best means of enlarging the outlook and giving a breadth and a depth to our thinking. I have lived an advocate's life. To have to attack, with a view to influencing the minds of experts or, indeed, of the now shrewd public, requires a concentration of knowledge and views and an organisation of thought such as cannot but be an educational exercise of the highest kind.

We may be slovenly in our private discussion and conversation and get away with it, but to be other than thoroughly prepared and skilful in our release of thought on public occasions is a public affront which will not for long be condoned. Good citizenship depends on sound speech training as much as on anything else.

For this reason I welcome the Discussion Groups so prevalent in these days, subject, however, always to this, that the group should have a trained leader and guidance. A group which lacks a trained leader is like a ship without a master and a helmsman. It will soon go on to the rocks. But subject to the presence and control of a leader who knows what is relevant and what is not, nothing is better for the build-up of a sound world of democratic expression than the Discussion Group method of approach. From it will come in the future many competent speakers. The more competent speakers we have the more surely will we retain our liberties and enrich our lives.

One aspect of speaking I keep to the end—speaking at dinners and other social occasions. Here again the level is deplorably low. How much real joy and pleasure is thus missed. A delightful after-dinner speech is a contribution to our social pleasure such as has few rivals. The art is not difficult to acquire. Some thought, some analysis of the occasion which draws us together, a little free run of humorous fancy, some mild chaffing of personalities and great delight and merriment will result. If only every speaker on every occasion would realise that he is more powerful than his audience, the devastating stage fright which does so much public harm would tone down to its right and proper size of a mild anxiety to do an important job well. Then confidence would come to speakers and so to audiences.

So, in conclusion, I exhort my readers to give to this matter of public speaking that serious and strict attention which it deserves. There is no activity more interesting or more stimulating and none of greater value to the body politic. A training in speaking does much to aid mind, body and morale, public and private.

BOOKS ON PUBLIC SPEAKING

History of Public Speaking. M. Platz (Noble & Noble, New York, $2.50).
Public Speaking. Archibald Crawford (Pitman, 6s.).
Speech Making. F. J. Griffiths (Oxford, 3s. 6d.).
Ladies and Gentlemen! Rosslyn Mitchell (Harrap, 2s. 6d.).
Hear! Hear! William Freeman (Dent, 5s.).
The Speaker and Debater. Gibson & Bennett (English Univ. Press, 3s.).
Hints for Platform and Parliamentary Speaking. Arthur Ponsonby (Allen & Unwin, 2s.).
Mind Training for Speech Making. Archibald Crawford (Pitman, 5s.).
The Psychology of Effective Speaking. T. H. Pear (Kegan Paul, 3s. 6d.).
Thinking to Some Purpose. Susan Stebbing (Pelican, 1s.)
Clear Thinking. R. W. Jepson (Longmans, 3s. 6d.).
Straight and Crooked Thinking. R. H. Thouless (English Univ. Press, 3s. 6d.).
Q.E.D.: Some Hints on Arguing. J. W. Marriott (Harrap, 1s. 6d.).
Pros and Cons. M. I. White (Routledge, 3s.).
The A.B.C. of Chairmanship. Walter Citrine (N.C.L.C. Publishing Society, 3s. 6d.).
The Chairman's Handbook. A. Palgrave (Dent, 3s. 6d.).
Conduct of Public Meetings. Cecil Newport (English Univ. Press, 3s. 6d.).
See also "Discussion Groups," page 106.

PUBLIC SPEAKING RECORDS

Winston Churchill. Nine albums of War Speeches. (H.M.V.)
Franklin D. Roosevelt. Address to Congress, Dec. 8th, 1941, two records (H.M.V.).

Field-Marshal Smuts. Address to both Houses of Parliament, Oct. 21st, 1942, two records (H.M.V.).
Neville Chamberlain. Broadcast from 10 Downing Street, Sept. 27th, 1938 (H.M.V.).
Frank Laskier. Broadcast of Oct. 5th, 1941, two records (H.M.V.).
Emlyn Williams. "Portrait of a Londoner," broadcast of Nov. 3rd, 1940 (H.M.V.).
Lincoln's Gettysburg Address. Spoken by Raymond Massey. (Linguaphone, U.S.A.).
Lecture Records. One hundred lectures, prepared for the International Educational Society, ranging from "Astronomy" to "Smells." A detailed list may be had from the Columbia Education Department.

The Use of the Voice in Church

By A. MAUDE ROYDEN

No use of the voice has been more criticised than church use. The criticism is often justified : but in looking for improvement one should try and realise the circumstances which gave rise to some at least of the faults which give most offence today. Otherwise we shall be very likely to fall into another and perhaps even more offensive error.

It must then be remembered that Christian churches of the Roman Catholic and Orthodox types were built for worship and not for teaching. The sermon, if sermon there were, was unimportant : the act was everything. There was therefore less need for the words to be distinctly heard in every part of the building and the building was not designed to make this easy. To overcome the acoustic difficulties which resulted from the fact that the church was built for worship the words were intoned. Intoning sounds to many people to-day "unnatural," but it was in fact perfectly "natural" for its purpose.

The Protestant or Evangelical church is built for the sermon. The pulpit occupies the central position at the end of the building and every line leads up to it. Anyone who has preached in Anglican and Free Church pulpits must have been conscious of this difference. In the typical Anglican church the pulpit is pushed to one side leaving the altar or East window or reredos to command the attention of the congregation. In the Free Church, the pulpit is so placed that not only the eye but the ear is satisfied. There is a marked absence of intervening pillars or piers and the acoustics are generally excellent. I have often reflected that if a preacher could not hold his audience from the City Temple pulpit, for example, he could not hold it anywhere.

Having grasped the nature of the difficulty and the reason for the "unnatural" intonation of many clergy trained in the old school, there still remains something to be learned of the actual use of the voice at the present day. Perhaps the matter which most interests the laity is the reading of the Bible, because this is a part of the service in which they have for a very long time been allowed to take some part.

I consider it exceedingly difficult to read the Bible rightly in church. Most of us fall between two stools. We read it either as though we had no idea that it contained any meaning at all, or we overburden the words with their meaning in such a way that we become theatrical. Which is the worse fault? I hardly know, but I am inclined to think that the theatrical manner is even more destructive of devotion than the one which is meaningless. I think it exasperates the congregation more.

It is of course due to the fact that unless one has some sense of drama one is likely to be a very dull reader (or preacher). Every speaker and every reader ought to have some dramatic sense and it is difficult to have this and not to overdo it. I am always conscious that my reading is apt to become too dramatic, and I exercise heroic restraint to prevent this from happening! Indeed, for most readers of the Bible in public, restraint should be the guiding thought.

Many years ago, when I was being guided into a better voice production by that master of voice production, Mr. Madoc Davies, I asked him to read to me the lessons that I was expecting to read on the following Sunday in the Guildhouse. His reading of the Bible was to my mind quite ideal. I have heard many beautiful readers, but never one who seemed to me to reach quite his pitch of excellence. I therefore, as I said, asked him to read the lessons for me. On one occasion the lesson I had chosen was the scene in the Garden of Gethsamene. He read it and then handed me the book and I began. The tragedy—the poignancy—of the scene overwhelmed me and as I read it my voice trembled. Mr. Davies immediately stopped me. "Don't be sentimental," he said, "this is something too great for you to be sentimental about."

This was a lesson I have never forgotten. I remember speaking to Sybil Thorndike about it and she entirely agreed with what Mr. Davies said. They both held that one should *have felt* all the emotion behind a tragic story, but when the time comes for reading it or speaking it to others one's emotions must be put aside and one must be content simply to be the speaker of the words. You are not reading for your own benefit but for those who hear you. The significance of this is, I think, best understood when one remembers that a speaker or reader who appears to be (and in fact is) on the point of breaking down creates intense embarrassment to those who listen. They cannot really listen to what is being said because they are in a state of nervous tension for fear the reader should break down altogether. This emphasises Mr. Davies's point that one must not allow his emotions to come between the hearer and the word.

My advice, therefore, to those who are to read the Bible in church is that they should read the passage over and over again; that they should study it with the help of different versions; that they should be quite sure that they have *realised* the meaning of what they are to read. They should further remember that their hearers are not nowadays all familiar with the Bible, and they should begin the reading in a way that makes it intelligible to those who are ignorant. For instance, we should not say "And he spoke to the multitude," even if that is in the Gospel. We should say "Jesus spoke to the multitude." We should stop at the right place, that is to say the place which carries the meaning that we want to convey. Instead of over-emphasis and theatrical delivery, these means should be used and will be found sufficient. For example, if you are to preach on "Hope" and you take as your lesson the passage beginning "Though I speak with the tongues of men and of angels and have not charity" the end of the lesson should be "And now abideth faith, hope and charity, these three." If you do what almost all readers do in these circumstances and continue the verse to the end—"but the greatest of these is charity"—it seems obvious to the hearer that it is charity you are to emphasise, and not hope. If you stop at the unusual place you concentrate the attention of the congregation on the fact that there are three theological virtues and that they are faith, *hope* and charity.

If one prepares for reading the Bible in church in this way, one has then really nothing to do but to let the words carry their own message. One should avoid, as in some passages of Bach's piano music I believe, wilful stresses and over-emphasis. Readers in English churches are blessed indeed in the beauty of the Authorised Version of the Bible. For my part, unless I am to read some of the more incomprehensible passages in the Epistles of St. Paul, I never allow myself to use the Revised Version though I always study it beforehand in order to get the full meaning of what I am going to read. No other version is so beautiful as the Authorised, and this is a sufficient reason for not using any other in public worship. If I am told, as I often am, that, for example, the Revised Version is more correct in certain passages I must of course admit it: but it is not so true. What is less beautiful cannot be more true. That would be a contradiction in terms.

I recognise the disadvantages of using a version of the Bible written in a language which is not that of the present day, but I believe they are not nearly so great as people suppose. Certainly we must admit alterations here and there, where the meaning of the text is not merely obscure but actually destroyed, as in the words "I know that my Redeemer liveth and that in my flesh I shall see God," which should read—"without my flesh I shall see God." *Job, XIX,* 25. But the alterations should be not only very sparingly made but should as far as possible be in accord with the cadence and rhythm of the old text.

To sum up. Let the reader be sure that he knows the meaning of what he reads, as far as careful study beforehand can reveal it: let him respect the beauty of the words too much to distort, them by over-emphasis or declamation: let him respect the intelligence of his hearers, but not take for granted their knowledge of the passage chosen or its context. He can then hardly go wrong.

The use of the voice in prayer is much more difficult, Liturgical prayers are the least difficult because, like the words of the Bible, they are generally beautiful. They are familiar also, and the one who speaks can be sure he is not praying *at* the congregation or giving the Almighty unnecessary information. He knows that, if they choose to do so, his fellow-worshippers can pray with him because they know the words. He knows that, whatever his own deficiencies in devotion and concentration he is bringing them to the throne of God by paths trodden by the feet of countless saints and worshippers before him, taking upon his lips the very phrases which were on their lips as they prayed. He should therefore be content, as when reading the Bible, with a quiet and reverent manner of speech.

This sounds very simple but in fact it is not quite so. The utterance of liturgical prayer easily falls into a most lamentable drone or even moan. Words of joyful adoration are pronounced as though they were a confession of sin or a cry for mercy, the Gloria in Excelsis as though it were a Penitential Psalm. Once more I can only urge that the one who prays in public worship should realise what he is saying and then say it. Drama, long pauses, heavily-emphasised words are unnecessary and distracting.

Far more difficult is the task of the *extempore* prayer. The speaker here has no beauty of phrase to help him but his own. Neither can he rely on the familiarity of his fellow-worshippers with what he is saying. He must not pray at them nor inform the Almighty. He must use words and thoughts so human as to fit the needs of all who wish to pray or praise, without the age-old and universal appeal of the great liturgies. He is to lift up to God the present and immediate needs of the congregation, their personal difficulties, their causes of thankfulness and joy. To do this without assuming either a sentimental or a jaunty tone is difficult. Both are odious.

I assume that the speaker of *extempore* prayer in public worship has considered deeply what he is to pray and give thanks about. I must therefore confine myself once more to the counsel to use the voice as simply as possible. I do not say "as naturally" because to many of us English people to pray aloud in public is not natural at all, and this is perhaps why it is generally done so badly. I say as *simply* as possible, for this is appropriate to the needs of the sincere and humble worshipper. Let the one who prays pause for a moment, consider Whom he is addressing—and speak.

It is perhaps otiose in an article on the use of the voice in church to speak of the use of silence! I cannot, however, refrain from remarking that words, however beautiful and ancient, or fresh and fitting, must always define and therefore in the nature of things divide. Silence unites. There should be periods of silence in every service of public worship.

Finally, there is the use of the voice in preaching. Here fashions change very much, and so do schools of thought. Congregations gravitate to the style they like best. It does not seem that many modern people like the oratorical style of a generation or two ago. The thunders of Joseph Parker, Spurgeon or General Booth strike coldly on our ears to-day when we try to recover their thrill through the medium of cold print or the recollection of one who actually heard them. Yet I incline to think they would still move us deeply if we could hear the living voice and experience the impact of the great personality. There are voices of such beauty as to cast a magic of their own, and there are personalities so powerful as to impose themselves and their message on their hearers of any generation. Listening recently to a broadcast on Anthony Trollope's method of writing novels, I realised how futile it is to object to a writer's methods so long as these are justified by their results. So it is with preaching. When I hear one who heard Joseph Parker in his prime rehearse at length one or other of his sermons forty or fifty years after hearing them, I marvel how anyone could sit through such harangues. To me their texts, headings, summings up and perorations seem more to resemble an acrostic than a sermon. Yet how can I criticise a method of preaching such that a hearer could repeat the sermon to me half a lifetime later? I well remember one man who had listened to Dr. Parker every Thursday—he lived out of London and could not attend the services on Sunday—and who described to me "the sense of desolation" which fell upon him when the end came and he knew it would be a whole week before he heard that voice again!

By way of contrast, R. J. Campbell crowded the same great building Sunday after Sunday and Thursday after Thursday for years, though his voice, silvery in quality, was never strong, and one listener told me that he rarely heard what was said. Asked why in that case, he went, he replied simply "I couldn't help it." I have not been fortunate enough to hear many great Free Church divines, but I heard Dr. Boyd Carpenter, the old Bishop of Ripon, whose preaching soared to great heights of eloquence and, when at Oxford, I used to go weekly to the Cowley Fathers' church where the preachers for the most part read their sermons from a manuscript without raising their eyes, in a voice almost entirely on one note. Yet such a man as Father Congreve, for example, made a profound impression on me by the very fact of this complete absence of dramatic appeal.

Certainly there can be no rule about the use of the voice by men of genius such as these. The shrill, almost strident voices of some, the glorious deep music of others—both are lost in the greatness of the speaker. I am, like many others, painfully sensitive to an unpleasing voice, bad accent or slovenly English, but let the speaker be great enough and I forget them all. For those, however, who are less than these, there is at least good counsel if no rules. It is always good counsel to make the best of such voice as one has, for who is the preacher to decide that it does not matter if he offends people's ears? And it is a fact that it almost always *is* possible both to improve a harsh or shrill voice and preserve and enhance a good one. To quote Mr. Madoc Davies again, he once told me that he could greatly help those whose voices were unpleasing; though, when asked whether he could give *anyone* a musical enunciation, he did ruefully admit that there were just a few—a *very* few—whose vocal chords seem to be made of old iron! Most people can, however, be helped to overcome such difficulties as are at least likely to create prejudice against them. And here—since women are likely in future to be more called upon to speak in churches than they have been in the past—I specially advise them to notice what note or notes they habitually speak on and if, as is often the case, it is unpleasingly high, train themselves to tune their voices down a tone or even more. It can be done and becomes second nature to the speaker. Men with rather high voices, verging on to a falsetto, should do the same. A shrill voice is hard to listen to. This is specially true in the case of a broadcast service.

People with naturally beautiful voices should be as careful to use them beautifully as singers are. They may think (probably mistakenly) that their voices can't be improved; but they can certainly be *preserved*, when they would otherwise suffer from fatigue or age.

Churches, as I have already pointed out, are often peculiarly awkward from the point of view of acoustics. Visiting preachers are therefore well-advised to enquire of its minister what the difficulties are. Some of us, endowed with good voices, are too conceited to do this. This is silly for it takes time to gauge all the possibilities and difficulties of a building not primarily designed to help the speaker, and the man who preaches in it habitually knows all its tricks. On the other hand, it is not invariably wise to take local advice as to how to get round them. I have often been entreated to shout because "the acoustics are bad," when shouting would really have been worse than useless. This is the case when a church is built with massive piers, as, for example, St. Giles' Cathedral in Edinburgh. The difficulty in such cases is not met by shouting, for this only creates an echo: it is necessary *not* to shout but to speak more slowly than in a clearer space, and enunciate even more carefully.

On the whole, and allowing for the wholly permissible eccentricities of genius, I hold that the speaker in churches should speak as is most natural to him but with greater restraint than he might on a secular platform. If he is naturally dramatic he should be more careful never to become melodramatic. If his voice has a great range he should nevertheless neither scream nor rumble. Let him remember that his congregation is not an audience; that its individual members are more reluctant than at a public meeting to show displeasure or to walk out. In short, let him be moderate in all things.

FOR FURTHER STUDY

Vital Preaching. Sidney Berry (Independent Press, 3s. 6d.).
Simple Addresses. Helen Cobbold (S.P.C.K., 2s.).
"Reading Aloud." Chapter in *Spoken English* (Methuen, 7s. 6d.).
Chapters on the Bible in *On the Art of Reading.* A. Quiller-Couch (Cambridge).
The Bible Designed to be Read as Literature (Heinemann, 12s. 6d.).
Bible Readings. A set of five records made for the B.B.C., with an introductory booklet on "pulpit English" by A. Lloyd James (Linguaphone).

First record	2 Samuel, I, 17-27
	Isaiah, XL, 1-11
	Isaiah, LV, 1-5
Second record	I Kings, XVIII, 22-39
	Ecclesiastes, XI; XII, 1-8
Third record	Job XXVIII
	Luke, XV, 11-32
Fourth record	Psalm 139
	I Corinthians, XII, 27-31; XIII
Fifth record	I Corinthians, XV, 38-58
	Hebrews, XI, 1-10, 32-40; XII, 1-2

Scripture Reading. Lewis Casson. Luke II, 1-20. Sermon on the Mount, Matthew, VI, 10-34 (H.M.V.).
London Verse Speaking Choir. Marjorie Gullan, solo speaker. David's lament for Jonathan. (H.M.V. B8271).
Christmas Morning Sermon from *Murder in the Cathedral.* Robert Speaight (H.M.V., 3s. 3d.)
The Preacher's Voice. W. C. Craig and R. Sokolowsky Wartburg Press, U.S.A., $2.00).

ENGLISH SPEECH ABROAD

English as a World Speech

By J. HUBERT JAGGER

"Universal English" is an expression that possesses two distinct meanings that are not always distinguished, and even by those who distinguish them the extent of the difference is not always appreciated. This difference is radical, and it is necessary to be quite clear about it.

A universal speech, in the first sense, would be a speech spoken by all mankind as their native tongue, all existing languages, or all but one, having been superseded. A universal speech, in the second sense, means a medium of intercommunication between nations. According to this idea, each nation would retain its traditional speech, but a second language would be universally known, or, if not universally known, would be available for those who needed or wished to write or speak to men of other nations.

When, therefore the enthusiast expatiates on the babel of today, and the disadvantages to commerce, to travel, and to the advancement of knowledge that arise from the difficulty men find in communicating with each other, and allows his imagination to play over a visionary world in which no such difficulty exists because all people speak the same tongue, he can be seen to be confusing the two meanings; for these disadvantages could be removed by the institution of a universal speech in the second sense, side by side with the 1,500 languages now spoken.

A subsidiary language for all men could be prescribed by a decree of governments. It could be an existing language like the living tongue French or the dead tongue Latin; or it could be a manufactured article like Esperanto. Except for those who happened to speak it as their native tongue, it would be of little or no literary use, but it would be of immense value for the purposes of communication. It would have little or no effect upon the personal character or ideals or modes of thought of those who adopted it as their auxiliary language. It would be a code of symbols; it would not be the breath of the spirit.

There have been in the past many international media of this kind, operating over limited areas—Greek, Latin and Arabic are examples—and each of them has vanished in its turn. English seems more likely to survive, because those who speak it, either as native or as auxiliary, are more widely distributed than the speakers of any other tongue have ever been. Besides being the native speech of Britain, the United States, Australia, Canada, white South Africa, and many smaller places scattered over the globe, it is the second speech of millions of Europeans, Hindoos, Chinese, and others. It is more likely than were its predecessors to maintain its place because, for the first time in history, the same speech has been owned by two of the most powerful states in the world, and because facilities for mixing by travel and for communication—by books, newspapers, and broadcasting—greatly surpass mankind's past resources in these directions.

It is well qualified for such a position, in several ways. It is comparatively easy for a foreigner to acquire some command of English, because its grammatical structure is simple and does not require from him a great effort of memory before he can begin to express himself by means of it. In this respect it is easier than Spanish, and much easier than Russian, which are its chief possible competitors. Chinese is grammatically simpler than English, but is in other ways a very difficult tongue for foreigners to learn, and it is confined to one quarter of the globe.

That is one reason why English is well suited to be a universal auxiliary language. Another is that the English vocabulary is a mixed vocabulary, drawn from four principal sources, Old English, Latin, French, and Greek, and many minor sources, and can therefore be understood in part by a very large number of foreigners.

But there are objections, which must not be overlooked. The chief of these is that English spelling has no regular relation to the sounds of English words, so that a foreigner is unable to pronounce an English word at sight, and in learning English has to learn two languages, the spoken and the written, and he also has the trouble of associating the two by mere memory. This objection is valid, but it is not as serious as it appears, because a system of phonetic spelling could be devised for the use of foreigners if English were instituted as a universal second language; indeed, that would have to be done.

Another objection often raised is even less tenable. This is that the enormous English vocabulary is too big a meal for the ordinary memory and average perseverance, and the meal is made unnecessarily heavy by the immense number of partial synonyms that English possesses. This objection is not valid, because there is no obligation on the foreigner to learn the whole of the English vocabulary. Limited vocabularies of various sizes, consisting of the most frequent or the most useful words, are easily constructed, and would provide all that the foreign user of English as a second language would require.

There is one more observation to make on English as a universal second language. It is manifest that its adoption by a deliberate choice of the nations would powerfully stimulate the tendency, if there is such a tendency, of English to become the native speech of the whole world by displacing or absorbing other tongues. There are those who assert that this tendency is now unmistakeable.

The contemplation of such a prospect is enough to take one's breath away, for the native tongue of every human being is far from being a code of communicative signs. It has been described as the clothing of his thought. But it is more than that; it is the body of his thought. When heard, it is the manifestation of the man himself; and within him it is the man himself, as nearly as he can be captured. If English were to become the universal speech of the world it would modify the characters and minds of all who had abandoned other tongues, and would impart to them something of the English national character, and modes of thought, and way of life.

But nations cling to their traditions. It is certain, therefore, that the instinctive recognition of this inevitable effect would render it impossible to decree that all the rest of the human race should relinquish their own speeches and employ English or any other tongue, for that would be to instruct them to cease to be themselves as they now are; such an attempt would provoke either violent open resistance or stubborn evasion. Therefore, if the world is ever to enjoy a universal speech in this sense, the result will be brought about either by the gradual fusion of existing speeches, or by one of them insensibly ousting the others. For reasons that are too elaborate to be expounded in this short article, the second is the more probable alternative.

It is remarkable that the inhabitants of Britain seem to have had even in early times a belief that their influence would spread far beyond their island. As long ago as the commencement of the twelfth century a clever young monk, Geoffrey, wishing to play to King Henry I the part that Vergil played to the Emperor Augustus, wrote a poem (afterwards incorporated in his famous *History of the Kings of Britain*) in which he prophesied that Britons would rule in every land the wide world over; and the Elizabethans had glimmerings of the idea that English would become universal. The possibility, which was then immeasurably remote, can now be seriously entertained, both for the reasons already adduced in support of English as a second language, and because during the last hundred and fifty years the number of native English speakers has increased more rapidly than have those who speak any other tongue, till English is now the first language of one-tenth of the human race.

That is the picture viewed in a rosy light, which must be corrected by cold criticism. English has spread on account of the favoured political, commercial, and industrial position occupied by the English-speaking nations during the last century and a half quite as much as by the natural increase in their numbers. The birth-rate is already falling, and the industrial and commercial pre-eminence of the nineteenth century is being challenged, not because the British and

Americans are falling back, but because other nations are coming, and have come, forward.

However, let us behold, in imagination, the whole world speaking English. Our first impulse will be to picture all mankind speaking as we ourselves speak now. That is an illusive mirage. They will never do so; for to this consummation are attached conditions and implications which cannot be avoided. The first is that the vocabulary, already a synthesis, will have absorbed many more words from the tongues that English has superseded. The second is that the present native speech of each new speaker of English will have affected his English in a hundred other ways, and especially in pronunciation. The third is that English is not uniform throughout the world, and that the kind of English that will emerge as the dominant form may be expected to be the kind that is spoken by the largest group of English speakers; certainly their form will exercise a preponderant influence upon the final result. Now, two-thirds of the living speakers of English inhabit the continent of North America, so that the type of English that our imagination must envisage will be a descendant of American English, or, at the least, will resemble it more closely than it will resemble any other existing form of our tongue.

So much for the implications; now for the conditions. Every living language is in a state of gradual change; it contains within itself centrifugal and also integrating tendencies. When the members of a group are in contact, the latter tendencies keep the former in check, so that all the members advance imperceptibly and unconsciously in the same unknown direction. Contrariwise, isolated groups develop on their own lines, away from the main stream. A certain degree of contact must be maintained among the groups of those who speak the same tongue if it is not to split slowly into mutually incomprehensible dialects. That happened to Latin, when it became the world speech of Western Europe: it changed into Italian, French, Spanish, and Portuguese. It is true that the means of communication and of contact that the world now has are incalculably greater than they were in Western Europe in the early Middle Ages, but the area to be covered is also much greater. No one knows how intense world communication must be if a world speech is to be maintained in a sufficiently uniform state, but the intensity is certainly higher than the world has yet attained, even with all the resources it has recently acquired; so that if English were now to become suddenly the universal tongue it would at once begin to divide, as Latin did. The development of world speech and of world contact must go hand in hand.

BIBLIOGRAPHY

Little has been written exclusively on this subject. Readers desiring further information on its various aspects may, however, usefully consult :—

Pomona, or the Future of English. Basil de Sélincourt. (Kegan Paul).

Breaking Priscian's Head: or English as she will be spoke and wrote. J. Y. T. Greig. (Kegan Paul).

Debabelization. C. K. Ogden. (Kegan Paul).

The Extinction in Perpetuity of Armaments and War. A. W. Alderson. (P. S. King).

English in the Future. J. H. Jagger. (Nelson, 3s. 6d.).

Spoken English

BOOKS AND RECORDS FOR FOREIGN STUDENTS

GENERAL:

Our Spoken Language. A. Lloyd James. (Nelson, 3s.)

Talks on English Speech. A. Lloyd James. 5 records. (Linguaphone).

Spoken English and Broken English. G. Bernard Shaw. 2 records. (Linguaphone).

Phonetics of English. Ida C. Ward. (Heffer, 5s.)

Outline of English Phonetics. Daniel Jones. (Heffer, 12s. 6d.)

English Language Teaching. (British Council, 4s. 6d. per annum).

The Teaching of English as a Foreign Language. I. Morris. (Macmillan, 3s.).

Teaching of Oral English. H. E. Palmer. (Longmans, 2s.)

Grammar of Spoken English. H. E. Palmer. (Heffer, 12s. 6d.)

First Course in English Phonetics. H. E. Palmer. (Heffer, 3s. 6d.)

Colloquial English. H. E. Palmer. (Heffer, 3s. 6d.)

English Phonetics. Walter Ripman (Dent, 3s. 3d.)

Engelsk Fonetik. Otto Jespersen (Copenhagen).

English Speech for Asiatic Students. B. Lumsden Milne. (Heffer, 2s. 6d.)

Englische Phonetik. A. C. Dunstan (Berlin).

Introduction to English Phonetics. A. Trakhterov (Moscow).

Colloquial English. J. O. Kettridge. (Kegan Paul, 4s. 6d.)

Everyday English. C. E. Eckersley. (Longmans, 4s. 6d.)

Let's Talk English. Constance Ripman. (Dent, 2s.)

Say it in English. A. Musgrave Horner. (Nelson, 2s. 6d.)

Manual of English for Foreign Students. Marshal (Hatchette)

Let's Talk English. Onstance Ripman. (Dent, 2s. 6d.)

Hints on Learning English. Hyacinth Davies. 2 books. (Heffer, 6d. each)

Brush Up Your English. M. D. Hottinger and W. G. Hartog. (Dent, 3s. 6d.) Records for use with this (Linguaphone).

International English Course. H. E. Palmer (Evans Bros.)
English Talks for Foreign Schools (including children's voices). Prepared by P. A. D. MacCarthy. 5 records (Linguaphone).
English Conversation Course. 16 records (Linguaphone).
English Course. Walter Ripman. 12 records (H.M.V.)
Good Speech. Walter Ripman. 2 records (Columbia).
English Travel Course. A. Lloyd James and V. C. Clinton Baddeley. 15 records (Linguaphone).
English Spoken Here. 6 records of useful phrases. Daniel Jones and J. R. Firth (Heffer, out of stock).

PRONUNCIATION:

English Pronunciation. A Practical Handbook for the Foreign Learner. P. A. D. MacCarthy (Heffer, 5s.). 2 records to use with this. (Linguaphone).
Standard English Speech. G. E. Fuhrken. (Cambridge, 5s.)
English Speech Sounds. A. Lloyd James. 1 record (Linguaphone). Supplied to bone fide teachers only.
English Vowels and Consonants. Walter Ripman. 2 records (H.M.V.)
English Vowels and Diphthongs. Daniel Jones. 1 record (Heffer, out of stock).
English Speech Sounds (For Indian Students). H. S. Perera (Colombo).
The Sounds of English (For African Students). H. A. Harman (Longmans, 5s.)
English Pronouncing Dictionary. Daniel Jones. (Dent, 7s. 6d.)
English Pronouncing Vocabulary. P. A. D. MacCarthy. (Heffer, 3s. 6d.).
Certain Words of Doubtful Pronunciation. A. Lloyd James. (B.B.C., out of print). Record for use with this (Linguaphone).
Some English Place Names. A. Lloyd James. (B.B.C., 1s.)
Pronunciation of British Family Names. A. Lloyd James (B.B.C., 1s. 3d.)

INTONATION:

Handbook of English Intonation. Armstrong & Ward. (Heffer, 5s.) 3 records to use with this (Linguaphone).
Everyday Sentences in Spoken English. Palmer & Blandford (Heffer, 3s. 6d.) 5 records to use with this (Linguaphone).
English Intonation, with Systematic Exercises. H. E. Palmer. (Heffer, 5s.)
Intonation Curves. Daniel Jones (Leipzig).
The Role of Intonation in Spoken English. Maria Schubiger (Heffer, 6s.)

PHONETIC READERS:

English Phonetic Reader. Lilias Armstrong. (Univ. of London Press, 4s.)

Phonetic Transcriptions of English Prose. Daniel Jones. (Oxford, 2s. 6d.)

Phonetic Readings in English. Daniel Jones. (Heffer, out of print.) 7 records to use with this. (Heffer: Out of stock)

Specimens of English. Walter Ripman. (Dent, 2s. 6d.)

Passages of Standard Prose. Walter Ripman. (Dent, 1s. 6d.) 5 records to use with this (Heffer).

English Conversations in Simplified Phonetic Transcription. N. C. Scott. (Heffer, 2s.)

Some Specimens of English Phonetic Transcriptions. H. E. Palmer. (Heffer, 6d.)

English Humour in Phonetic Transcript. G. Noël-Armfield. (Heffer, 2s.)

Phonetic Reader for Foreign Learners of English. E. L. Tibbetts. (Heffer, 3s.)

For English Grammar, etc., see the book list, *The Teaching of English,* issued by the National Book League.

ENGLISH LITERATURE:

Literary Readings in English A. Lloyd James and Kenneth Barnes. 10 records (Linguaphone).

Passages of Standard Prose. Walter Ripman. (Dent, 1s. 6d.) 5 records to use with this (Heffer).

In Search of England. Passages read by Stuart Hibberd. 1 record (Columbia).

Bible Readings. See bibliography to "Use of Voice in Church," page 174.

Christmas Morning Sermon from *Murder in the Cathedral.* Spoken by Robert Speaight. (H.M.V.)

Literary Readings. Robert Speaight. 7 records. (Harvard Film Service, U.S.A.).

See also list of books and records to "Verse Speaking To-day" (pages 136 and 140), "Speech in Our Theatre" (page 154).

The British Council and its Work in Teaching English

The British Council is bound by its Charter of Incorporation to aim at promoting a wider knowledge of the United Kingdom and developing closer cultural relations with other countries, seeking not only to foster an understanding of Britain and the British, but to encourage with other nations a reciprocity of cultural exchanges which may well prove the rock on which future peace is built. A mutually intelligible means of communication is a major premise of international harmony, and it follows logically enough that the teaching of English is one of the Council's most important duties. The demand for instruction in English has shown a dramatic increase during the past four years.

In many countries overseas, the Council has set up British Institutes, where English lessons have been given from the elementary to the advanced stages, and where pupils if they wish may be prepared for the Cambridge Certificate of Proficiency in English. It is perhaps unnecessary to point out that while English is the most favoured subject, it is by no means the only one on the curriculum. Methods of teaching English vary according to the needs of the pupils, but the Council's teachers are intransigent in their insistence on the importance of the spoken language, and every effort is made to apply the findings of the most up-to-date research to modern methods of language teaching. Phonetics, charts, newly published text-books, films and other equipment are, when necessary, shipped from the United Kingdom, so that remoteness from the mechanics of civilisation is in no way synonymous with inefficiency or old-fashioned technique.

The Near and Middle East is the region where the Council's work has shown a remarkably rapid development. In some countries such as Turkey, where the Council has no Institutes of its own, instruction in English Language and other aspects of Britain is provided by Council teachers working within the framework of the Local Education Organisation. In some other countries, as for example in Latin-America, the Council's activities are centred in local Anglophil Societies, some being autonomous and born of local enterprise, others founded and administered by the Council. Apart from the Council's direct contribution to English teaching, financial assistance is given to schools abroad to encourage the study of English, and bursaries and scholarships are awarded to teachers and pupils. Summer Courses for overseas teachers of English are provided in Britain, as well as in some centres abroad. In countries where teachers are scarce, broadcast English lessons have proved both popular and successful.

During the war, a new problem for the teacher of English was presented in the large numbers of Allied Servicemen in this country. The British Council's teachers worked in the closest co-operation with the Services Education Authorities, and taught English to members of all the Allied European Brigades, to Allied Air Units and Naval Personnel.

In 1940 the teaching of English to many of the Allies who arrived in their thousands in the United Kingdom, became a matter of great urgency. For example, the Czechoslovak and Polish Airmen could not take part in operations until their knowledge of English was sufficient for them to understand British commands. Many of these airmen applied themselves with great energy to learning English, and the Council was privileged to provide the teachers. The airmen were thus able to take part in the Battle of Britain and play an outstanding part in that historical phase of the war.

Thousands of civilians who had been uprooted from their homes wished to continue to help in the war. Here again, they had to learn English before they could work side by side with British factory workers, and after several months many thousands of them were proficient enough in the language to play their full part.

Teachers of English helping the Services sometimes carried out their duties under strange circumstances. One teacher gave his classes for many months on board a Norwegian mine-sweeper off the North Coast of Scotland, fitting in his classes as best he could between the actual operations of mine-sweeping. Teachers with Allied Air Force units had to adapt themselves to the conditions on operational stations, but many of them made an important contribution in addition to the general morale of the Servicemen. On lonely stations they could provide educational activities and general advice which might otherwise have been completely lacking.

Other English classes have been organised at the Council's Allied Centres in Liverpool, Birmingham and Cardiff, where lessons have been given to Chinese, Belgians, Frenchmen, Dutchmen, Poles, Greeks, Norwegians, Soudanese, Yugoslavs and others. In many of the ports, members of the Mercantile Marine, particularly those who have had long periods ashore after losing their ships, or who needed rest, have taken English classes. The many pupils in the Mercantile Marine included a considerable number of officers and men of the Soviet Mercantile Marine and the Red Star Navy, although here the studies in port have been extremely brief, and the lessons have often been conducted by the Captain on board the ship when he has received the necessary books from Council officers in the ports.

In 1943, the Hull Education Authorities provided 4 teachers to give English lessons to Indian Merchant Seamen who put in to our ports. These teachers, selected on account of their knowledge of Indian dialects, took a special language-teaching course at the Allied Centre in Liverpool. Although Service requirements made a certain fluctuation in these classes inevitable, it was found that the men attend as long as possible and kept in touch with the Council after they left Great Britain. Letters and cards have been received from America, Africa, the Middle East, Iceland, Canada and even more remote addresses, so that continuity is maintained.

The majority of the Allied Governments then established in the United Kingdom were able to continue the education of their numerous school-children on the same lines as their own national education. Boarding Schools, Secondary Schools and Technical Schools were established in many parts of the country, and the Council in most cases provided a teacher of English at each of these schools. The Council collaborated with the English and Polish Ministries of Education and the Scottish Education Department in organising the Vacation Course for teachers of English intending to work in post-war Poland. Moreover, a specially valuable course for foreign students was organised on the Council's behalf by the Extra-Mural Delegacy of Oxford University, and many distinguished lecturers contributed to a programme of lectures on various aspects of English life and language and of British History.

It is perhaps worthy of record that many of the Allied pupils, whether Service or civilian, despite their very fully occupied lives, were able to sit for the various examinations in English arranged for foreigners by Cambridge University, and large numbers of them succeeded in obtaining certificates testifying to their proficiency.

The Work of The Orthological Institute

THE centre of interest in psychology has of recent years shifted considerably; and the symbolizing activities of the mind are more and more becoming its main concern. In some quarters there is actually a tendency to overestimate the importance of the language factor. Many who regard thinking as silent talking overlook the fact that one of the chief practical problems of psychology is to distinguish verbal from non-verbal thinkers. And even among verbalizers we must distinguish those who are at the mercy of their expressions from those who are not, a distinction of great practical importance in all discussion. There are some people, and those not the least eminent, who can only be persuaded to change their opinion when they are presented with a formal rearrangement of their own vocabulary, while others can grasp a point however it is put. In university and adult education generally this is of supreme importance, and the technique by which men can be delivered from the bondage of set phrases in earlier years is slowly being evolved. One of the first tasks of those who appreciate the bearing of this aspect of the psychology of thinking on human progress must be to make conscious the manifold strivings towards such a technique, which are found, for example, in grammatical reform movements, in the study of systems of notation, in new methods of language teaching, and even in simplified spelling. "Orthology"* is a convenient term by means of which these various converging tendencies may be focussed.

The Orthological Institute was founded in 1927, by Mr. C. K. Ogden (Editor of "The International Library of Psychology, Philosophy, and Scientific Method") as a private research organisation where this study might be carried out and research made into the influence of words and symbols on thought, argument and international affairs. It houses a library of some 50,000 volumes.

*The normative science of language. See also Karl Pearson, *The Grammar of Science* (Everyman's Library, p. 321)

From this general interest in language, Mr. Ogden's invention, Basic English, developed. The 850 words were first printed in 1928 after several years of experiment in finding a form which, in addition to its educational value, would serve as a quickly-acquired world language. With the help of Miss L. W. Lockhart and a group of able collaborators, more than a hundred different books in or about Basic were produced between 1930 and 1939—some of them textbooks for the teaching of Basic, others dealing with its economic, commercial, and scientific applications. In 1940 appeared *The New Testament in Basic* (as part of the *Basic Bible,* which was considered by many to be the most successful translation since the Authorised Version.

During this period, information about Basic English was being circulated in foreign languages, and as early as 1933, with the help of the Payne Fund of New York and the Rockefeller Foundation, a serious start was made in the Far East. Special attention was paid to the needs of educational authorities in China, where the Orthological Institute (Peking) was for some time under the direction of Professor R. D. Jameson of Tsing Hua University and Dr. I. A. Richards of Magdalene College, Cambridge. Parallel programmes in Japan directed by Mr. F. J. Daniels, and in India where Mr. Adolph Myers was co-operating with *The Times of India,* were also interrupted by the war. The value of Basic for international purposes in the Far East is very great—not only in trading with America, Australia, India, and Europe, but for science, invention, and general thought.

Research has continued in Britain since the war, and Basic has received the serious attention of scientists and students in every part of the world. But it was not until September 6th, 1943, that the world in general became familiar with the word. It was then that Mr. Winston Churchill spoke of it at Harvard University, and the newspaper public realised that Basic might have some important connection with their own lives :—

> "Some months ago I persuaded the British Cabinet to set up a Committee of Ministers to study and report upon Basic English. Here you have a plan. There are others, but here you have a very carefully-wrought plan for an international language capable of very wide transactions of practical business and interchange of ideas. The whole of it . . . can be written on one side of a single sheet of paper.
>
> What was my delight when, the other evening, quite unexpectedly I heard the President of the United States suddenly speak of the merits of Basic English. . . . It would certainly be a grand convenience for us all to be able to move freely about the world—as we shall be able to do more easily than ever known before as the science of the world develops—to be able to move freely about the world, and to be able to find everywhere a medium, albeit primitive, of intercourse and understanding. Might it not also be an advantage to

many races and an aid to the building of our new structure for preserving peace? . . .

Such plans offer far better prizes than taking away other people's provinces or land or grinding them down in exploitation. The Empires of the future are the empires of the mind."

Later it was announced by Mr. Churchill that the Government had decided to recommend the adoption of Basic as a world auxiliary language, and had established an Inter-Departmental Committee to enable support to be given to it by the British Council, the Colonial administration, the diplomatic service, and the B.B.C. (*White Paper Cmd.* 6511). It may take some for such a programme to be carried out, but it seems probable that the work of the Institute will be greatly increased as soon as the world settles down again.

(COMPILED FROM PRINTED SOURCES)

SOME BOOKS ON BASIC

PRO:

Basic English. C. K. Ogden. (Kegan Paul, 3s. 6d.)
The Basic Words. With French and German Equivalents. C. K. Ogden. (Kegan Paul, 3s. 6d.)
The ABC of Basic English. Translations in French, German, Spanish, Italian, and Dutch. (Basic English Publishing Co., 3s. 6d. each)
Basic Step by Step. Translations in French, German, Spanish, and Italian. (Basic English Publishing Co., 3s. 6d. each)
The General Basic English Dictionary. (Evans, 3s. 6d.)
Basic English Versus the Artificial Languages. C. K. Ogden. (Kegan Paul, 3s. 6d.)
The Sounds and Forms of Basic English. J. Rantz. (Kegan Paul, 3s. 6d.)
A Basic Phonetic Reader. A. Lloyd James. (Nelson, 3s. 6d.)
Basic English and Its Uses. I. A. Richards. (Kegan Paul, 3s. 6d.)
GRAMOPHONE RECORDS: Four records made by A. Lloyd James. The Sounds of Basic, and all the words. (*No longer available*)

CON:

Basic. G. M. Young. (Society for Pure English, 1s. 6d.)
A Critical Examination of Basic English. M. P. West and E. Swinson. (University of Toronto Press, 50 cents)
Basic English. (British Esperanto Association)
"Common Sense and Basic." George H. Ely. (*English,* Spring, 1944)
"Against Basic English." Rose Macaulay. (*Cornhill,* January, 1944)
"On Basic English: A Challenge to Innovators." A. Quiller-Couch. (*Times Lit. Sup.,* September 30th, 1944)

American English

As Dr. Jagger points out in his article on "English as a World Speech," the English most likely to be adopted as an auxiliary language will be a descendant of the type used to-day by the majority of English-speaking people—American English. This is itself subdivided into different types and dialects, but American English in one form or another is now spoken by more than 100 million people.

To discuss it would require a book in itself. Here there is room only to quote from a broadcast talk by the late Professor Lloyd James :—

> The popular opinion that American English is a debased form of standard English is an opinion that no intelligent man should hold for five seconds. Measure for measure there is as much bad English spoken in these islands as there is in America ; and there is one thing to be said for America —in their schools and their colleges and their universities they take the trouble to teach the spoken form of their language a little better than we do in these islands.
>
> A man's speech is but one facet of the man ; it is the reflection of his life—his cultural life—his mental and spiritual life. And the language of a nation is the same thing. It is the reflection of the whole of the nation's life—the whole of the nation's environment. Now when a language leaves the land of its birth, strange things happen to it. One thinks of great languages in the past, like Latin and Chinese and Arabic, which went on their cultural wanderings over large surfaces of the earth. And one thinks of English to-day, on the same mission. And when a language is adopted by 150 million people—people of different races, different origins, different stocks, different colours, different religions—then stranger things happen to that language. It develops amazingly. The more vigorous the nation is, the more vigorous is the language ; the more varied the social life, the more varied the language. . . . American English is a vigorous language. It is the language of—it is the reflection of—a varied and a vigorous nation."

The following are the chief books of reference :—

The Growth of American English. W. Craigie and J. R. Hulbert. (Oxford, 2s. 6d.)

The English Language in America. G. P. Krapp, 2 vols. (Oxford : out of print)

A Dictionary of American English. J. S. Kenyon and T. H. Knott. (Merriam, Springfield, Mass., $3.00)

A Dictionary of American English on Historical Principles. W. Craigie and J. R. Hulbert, 16 vols. (Milford, 17s. each)

American Dialect Dictionary. Harold Wentworth. (T. Crowell Co., New York, $6.00)

Report of the Conference on a Linguistic Atlas of the United States and Canada. (Linguistic Society of America).
A Dictionary of Modern American Usage. H. W. Horwill. (Oxford, 8s. 6d.)
The American Language. H. L. Mencken. (Kegan Paul, 25s.)
American Pronunciation. J. S. Kenyon. (Wahr, Ann Arbor, Michigan, $1.50)
The Pronunciation of Standard English in America. G. P. Krapp. (Oxford : out of print)
A Dictionary of English Pronunciation with American Variants. H. E. Palmer, J. V. Martin, F. G. Blandford. (Heffer, 5s.)
American Pronunciation. H. Kurath. (Society for Pure English)
The Intonation of American English. Kenneth Pike. (Oxford, 11s. 6d.).
Good American Speech. M. P. McLean. (Dutton, New York, $2.00)
American English. Conversation Course. W. Cabell Greet. 16 records. (Linguaphone Institute, New York).
Phonetic Transcriptions from American Speech. Edited by Jane Dorsey Zimmerman. (Oxford, 8s. 6d.).
American Speech. Edited by Cabell Greet. Quarterly. (Columbia University, $4.30 a year)
Quarterly Journal of Speech. (National Association of Teachers of Speech, Wayne University, Detroit, Michigan, $3.00 a year)

Foreign Speech

SOME BOOKS AND RECORDS FOR ENGLISH STUDENTS

GENERAL :

The Oral Method of Teaching Languages. H. E. Palmer. (Heffer, 5s.)
The Scientific Study and Teaching of Languages. H. E. Palmer. (Harrap, 12s. 6d.)
General Phonetics. G. Noël-Armfield. (Heffer, 5s.)
Learning to Speak a Foreign Language. Michael West. (Longmans Green, 2s. 6d.).
How to Teach a Foreign Language. Otto Jespersen. (Allen & Unwin, 4s. 6d.)
Reading and Speaking Foreign Languages. H. R. Huse. (Oxford, 12s.).
Modern Language Teaching and Learning with Gramophone and Radio. Thomas Beach. (Heffer, 3s. 6d.)
Modern Languages. Edited by A. H. Sleight. (Modern Language Association, 1s. 3d. every six months)

Modern Language Review. Edited by C. J. Sisson. (Cambridge University Press, 7s. quarterly)
Le Maître Phonétique. Edited by Daniel Jones. (International Phonetic Association, 3s.)

WELSH:

Welsh Phonetic Reader. Stephen Jones. (University of London Press, 4s. 6d.)

IRISH:

Irish Conversation Course. Thomas O'Maille, Michael Breathnach, Michael O'Maolain, Maire ni Ghuairim. 16 records. (Linguaphone)

FRENCH:

French Speech Sounds. E. M. Stéphan. 1 record. (H.M.V.)
Colloquial French Course. E. M. Stéphan and Daniel Jones. 15 records. (H.M.V.)
French Conversation Course. Paul Passy, H. E. Berthon, Daniel Michenot, Denis Saurat, J. Desseignet, H. Pernot, H. Coustenoble, E. M. Stéphan. 16 records. (Linguaphone)
Spoken French. K. Nyrop and Noël-Armfield. (Heffer, 7s. 6d.)
Colloquial French. W. R. Patterson. (Kegan Paul, 4s. 6d.)
Colloquial French. G. Bonnard. (Heffer, 4s. 6d.)
The Phonetics of French. Lilias Armstrong. (Bell, 5s.)
Introduction to French Phonetics. M. Nicholson. (Macmillan,
Handbook of French Pronunciation. André Classe. (Nelson, 2s. 6d.).
French Phonetic Reader. Paul Passy. (University of London Press, 2s. 6d.)
Lectures Françaises Phonétiques. Paul Passy. (Heffer, 1s. 6d.).
Dictionnaire Phonétique de la Langue Française. Michaelis and Passy. (Hachette)
Studies in French Intonation. Hélène Coustenoble and Lilias Armstrong. (Heffer, 10s. 6d.)
French Intonation Exercises. H. Klinghardt and M. Stéphan. (Heffer, 7s. 6d.) 5 records to use with this, spoken by M. Stéphan. (Linguaphone)
Brush Up Your French. Two series. W. G. Hartog. (Dent, 3s. 6d. each). 5 records to use with these. (Linguaphone)
Commercial French. A. C. Clark and M. Thiéry. (Dent, 3s. 6d.) 5 records to use with it. (Linguaphone)

GERMAN:

German Speech Sounds. Anton Winter. 1 record. (H.M.V.)
German Language Course. Otto Siepmann. Two parts: each 12 records. (H.M.V.)

German Conversation Course. Erich Drach, Theodor Siebs, Paul Menzerath, Carl Niessen, Walter Derlach, E. Herrnstadt-Oettingen. 16 records. (Linguaphone)
Colloquial German. W. R. Patterson. (Kegan Paul, 4s. 6d.)
Colloquial German. P. F. Doring. (Routledge, 4s. 6d.).
German Dialogues. Emil Otto. (Kegan Paul, 3s. 9d.)
German for Beginners. M. L. Barker. (Heffer, 6s.). 5 records to use with this. (Linguaphone)
News in German (from broadcast texts). D. H. Stott. (Harrap, 1s. 6d.)
German Phonetic Reader. Alfred Egan. (University of London Press, 4s. 6d.)
Handbook of German Intonation. M. L. Barker. (Heffer, 5s.)
Brush Up Your German. J. B. C. Grundy. (Dent, 3s. 6d.) 5 records to use with this. (Linguaphone)

DUTCH :

Dutch Conversation Course. E. Kruisinga, P. N. U. Harting, H. Michelson. 15 records. (Linguaphone)
Dutch Everyday Phrases. Pieter Geyl and Alan Howland. 2 records. (H.M.V.)
Dutch Phonetic Reader. Quick and Schilthius. (University of London Press, 3s. 6d.)

SPANISH :

Spanish Speech Sounds. S. Barragán. 1 record. (H.M.V.)
Spanish Sounds. Maria de Laguna. 1 record. (Linguaphone).
Spanish Conversation Course. Antonio Pastor, Pederico de Onis Jorge Guillen, Joaquin Casalduero, Allison Peers, Maria de Lara, Maria de Laguna. 16 records. (Linguaphone)
Spanish Language Course. E. Allison Peers. 12 records. (H.M.V.)
Everyday Spanish Phrases. S. Barragán and Rex Palmer. 1 record. (H.M.V.)
Outlines of Spanish Pronunciation and Intonation. Maria de Laguna. (Ginn, 1s. 6d.).
Spanish Conversation. C. E. Kany. 3 vols. (Harrap, 1s. 6d. each)
Colloquial Spanish. Patterson and MacAndrew. (Kegan Paul, 3s. 6d.)
The Pronunciation of Spanish. R. Stirling. (Cambridge : out of print)
Brush Up Your Spanish. L. de Baeza. (Dent, 3s. 6d.) 5 records to use with this. (Linguaphone)

PORTUGUESE :

Portuguese Conversation Course. A. A. Rodrigues, H. de Barros Gomes, Alberto d'Almeida, M. F. Paxeco, Paschoal Magno 16 records. (Linguaphone)

Everyday Portuguese Phrases. G. P. Cabral and Cyril Nash. 2 records. (H.M.V.)
Portuguese Conversation. 3 vols. (Harrap, 2s. each.).

GREEK:
Modern Greek Conversation Course. (Linguaphone: in preparation)
Ancient Greek. W. H. D. Rouse. (Linguaphone)

ITALIAN:
Italian Speech Sounds. T. Sambucetti. 1 record. (H.M.V.).
Italian Conversation Course. Riccardo Picozzi, Camillo Pellizzi, A. M. Bassani, Luigi Valazzi, Natalia Paresce. 16 records. (Linguaphone)
Rapid Italian Course. Walter Ripman. (Dent).
Colloquial Italian. A. L. Hayward. (Kegan Paul, 4s. 6d.)
Italian Phonetic Reader. Amerindo Camilli. (University of London Press, 4s. 6d.)
Brush Up Your Italian. Giovanna Tassinari. (Dent, 3s. 6d.) 5 records to use with this. (Linguaphone)

DANISH:
Danish Phonetic Reader. H. J. Uldall. (University of London Press, 3s.)
Everyday Danish Phrases. J. H. Helweg and Alan Howland. 2 records. (H.M.V.)

SWEDISH:
Swedish Conversation Course. Elias Wessen, Gösta Bergman, B. Willners, Brita Holmgren. 16 records. (Linguaphone)
Swedish Everyday Phrases. A. Wijk and Cyril Nash. 2 records. (H.M.V.)

NORWEGIAN:
Everyday Norwegian Phrases. I. C. Gröndahl and Alan Howland. 2 records. (H.M.V.)
Norwegian Conversation Course. D. A. Seip, Oscar Krogh, Harald Juell, Leif Thesen. 16 records. (Linguaphone)

FINNISH:
Finnish Conversation Course. 16 records. (Linguaphone)

CZECH:
Czech Phonetic Reader. A. Frinta. (University of London Press, 5s.)
Czech Conversation Course. 16 records. (Linguaphone)

HUNGARIAN:

Colloquial Hungarian. A. H. Whitney. (Kegan Paul, 7s. 6d.)
Hungarian Conversation Course. (Linguaphone: in preparation)

POLISH:

Polish Conversation Course. Tytus Benni, Konrad Gorski, Tadeusz Rochenski, K. Rychter. 16 records. (Linguaphone)
Polish Phonetic Reader. Z. M. Arend-Choinski. (University of London Press, 5s.)

SERBIAN:

Serb-Croat Phonetic Reader. Dennis Fry and Dorde Kostic (University of London Press, 5s.)

RUSSIAN:

Spoken Russian. S. C. Boyanus. (Sidgwick & Jackson, 42s.)
The Pronunciation of Russian. Trofimov and Jones. (Cambridge)
A Manual of Russian Pronunciation. S. C. Boyanus. (Sidgwick & Jackson).
Conversational Narratives in Russian. S. C. Boyanus. (Sidgwick & Jackson, 7s. 6d.).
Colloquial Russian. Mark Sieff. (Kegan Paul, 6s.)
Russian Conversation Course. Dimitri Svjatopolk-Mirskij, Basil Timothieff, Serge Ivanoff, I. Potiekhin. 16 records. (Linguaphone)
Russian Language Course. S. C. Boyanus and N. B. Jobson. 12 records. (H.M.V.)
Everyday Russian Phrases. A. M. Onou and Alan Howland. 2 records. (H.M.V.)

PERSIAN:

Colloquial Persian. L. P. Elwell-Sutton. (Kegan Paul, 4s. 6d.)
Iranian Conversation Course. Wolseley Haig and G. H. Darab Khan. 16 records. (Linguaphone)

TURKISH:

Turkish Conversation Course. (Linguaphone: in preparation)

ARABIC:

Arabic Conversation Course (Egyptian). J. Heyworth-Dunne, M. M. Goma'a, A. K. Sourour, O. I. El-Dessouky. 16 records. (Linguaphone)
The Phonetics of Arabic. J. Gairdner. (Oxford).
Colloquial Arabic. (Egypt, Syria, Irak). D. L. O'Leary. (Kegan Paul, 4s. 6d.)
Everyday Arabic. H. M. Nahmad and C. Rabin. (Dent, 5s.)
Handbook of Spoken Egyptian Arabic. J. S. Willmore. (Oxford).

HEBREW:

Modern Hebrew Conversation Course. 12 records. (Linguaphone)
Everyday Hebrew. Chaim Rabin. (Dent, 6s.)

AFRIKAANS:

Afrikaans Conversation Course. 15 records. (Linguaphone)
Brush Up Your Afrikaans. Jan Nieuwoudt Tromp. (Dent, 3s. 6d.)

AFRICAN LANGUAGES:

Phonetics for Students of African Languages. Westermann and Ward. (Oxford, 8s. 6d.).
Short Guide to Recording African Languages. (Oxford, 1s.).
Practical Suggestions for Learning an African Language in the Field. I. C. Ward. (Oxford, out of print).
Bulletin of the School of Oriental and African Studies (page 126)
Africa. Quarterly Journal of the International Institute of African Languages
The Phonetic Structure of Somali. Lilias Armstrong. (International Phonetic Association, page 64).
The Phonetic and Tonal Structure of Efik. I. C. Ward. (Heffer, 8s. 6d.) 2 records spoken by Akufo Addo and Afari Atta. (Linguaphone)
The Pronunciation of Twi. I. C. Ward. (Heffer, 2s. 6d.) 2 records to use with this. (Linguaphone)
Introduction to the Ibo Language. I. C. Ward. (Heffer, 6s.).
The Phonetics of the Hottentot Language. D. M. Beach. (Heffer, 21s.)
The Tones of Sechuana Nouns. Daniel Jones. (International Institute of African Languages)
Hausa Language Course. 2 records. (Linguaphone)
The Phonetic and Tonal Structure of Kikuyu. Lilias Armstrong. (Oxford, 12s. 6d.).
The Tones of Sechuana Nouns. Daniel Jones. (Oxford, 1s. 6d.).

INDIAN LANGUAGES:

Colloquial Bengali. W. Sutton Page. 5 records with text. (Linguaphone)
A Brief Sketch of Bengali Phonetics. S. K. Chatterji. (International Phonetic Association, 1s. 6d.)
Bengali Phonetic Reader. S. K. Chatterji. (University of London Press, 5s.)
Introduction to Colloquial Bengali. W. Sutton Page. (Heffer, 10s. 6d.)
Hindustani Conversation Course. T. Grahame Bailey, Narain Haksar, Mohibul Hasan. 16 records. (Linguaphone)
Colloquial Hindustani. A. H. Harley. (Kegan Paul, 4s. 6d.)

Punjabi Phonetic Reader, T. Grahame Bailey. (University of London Press, 2s.)
A Short Outline of Tamil Pronunciation. J. R. Firth. (International Phonetic Association)
Colloquial Sinhalese Reader. Daniel Jones and S. T. Plaatje. (Manchester University Press)

MALAYAN:

Malayan Conversation Course. 1 record and text. (Linguaphone)

BURMESE:

Burmese Phonetic Reader. Lilias Armstrong and Pe Maung Tin. (University of London Press, 4s. 6d.)
Burmese Conversation Course. (Linguaphone: in preparation)

CHINESE:

Chinese Conversation Course. J. Percy Bruce, E. Dora Edwards, Chien Chun Shu. 16 records. (Linguaphone)
Chinese National Language Reader. W. Simon and C. H. Lu (Lund Humphries, 15s.).
Chinese Speech Patterns. W. Simon. (Lund Humphreys, 6s.).
Chinese Conversations. Chao. (Lund, Humphries, 12s. 6d.).
Colloquial Chinese. A. N. J. Whymant. (Kegan Paul, 4s. 6d.)
Cantonese Phonetic Reader. Daniel Jones and Kwing Tong Woo. (University of London Press, 5s.)

JAPANESE:

Colloquial Japanese. W. M. McGovern. (Kegan Paul, 4s. 6d.)
Japanese Speech. Yoshitake. 1 record. (Linguaphone)

INTERNATIONAL LANGUAGE RECORDS:

Latin. W. H. D. Rouse. (Linguaphone)
Latin Records. Harvard Film Service, Cambridge, U.S.A.
Esperanto Conversation Course. Edmond Privat and M. C. Butler. 16 records. (Linguaphone)
Basic English. A. Lloyd James. 4 records. (Orthological Institute: out of stock.) (See page 185.)

Charts, Diagrams and Models

Phonetic Chart of the Sounds of English, French and German. F. E. Gauntlett and L. A. Triebel. (Heffer, 9d.)
English Phonetic Diagrams. J. V. Martin and H. E. Palmer. (Heffer, 7d.)
Sound Charts. F. Rausch and Daniel Jones. 9 charts showing tongue positions for important vowels. (Dent, 15s. the set)

Chart of the International Phonetic Alphabet. (International Phonetic Association, University College, London, 2d.)
English Speech Sounds. Wall chart. Daniel Jones. (Cambridge. 3s. 6d. or 7s. 6d.)
The Organs of Speech. Daniel Jones. (Cambridge, 3s. 6d. or 7s. 6d.)
New Method Pronunciation Chart. (Longmans Green, 1s. 3d.)
The Sounds of English. Walter Ripman. (Dent, 2s. or 5s.)
Throat, Pharynx and Larynx, illustrating vocal cords, etc. (H. K. Lewis & Co., 17s. 6d.)
Aiken Bone Props for jaw-opening and tongue training, $\frac{1}{2}$in., $\frac{3}{4}$in., $\frac{7}{8}$in. or 1in. (John Bell & Croydon, Wigmore Street, London, W.1., 1s. 3d. each, including postage.)

MODELS OF VOCAL APPARATUS :

Larynx, natural size, with muscles, thyroid gland, arteries and veins
Larynx with Tongue, divisible into 5 parts
Larynx, double size, the trachea represented up to the point of bifurcation
Larynx, two-and-a-half times enlarged, showing cartilages of the larynx. The adjusting cartilages with the vocal ligaments are movable. An excellent model for demonstrating voice production
Larynx with Tongue, double size, showing the oral and pharyngeal cavities. Larynx and tongue are removable.
Section through the nasal, pharyngeal and oral cavities, double natural size. The larynx is removable and divisible. A simple contrivance demonstrates the function of the epiglottis

All the above models are sold by Messrs. H. K. Lewis & Co. Ltd., 136 Gower Street, London, W.C.1

SPEECH THERAPY

Development and Training in Britain

By W. KINGDON-WARD

SPEECH therapy, the treatment of defects and disorders of speech and voice, has been practised in one form or another from far back in history, as is shown by the work of Hieronymus Mercurialis, who, writing in 1584, repeatedly quotes authorities from ancient times. It was not until recent times, however, that this practice became recognised as a separate and distinct profession, with a status of its own. This stabilisation was only achieved very gradually as it came by degrees to be seen that a clear distinction must be drawn between incorrect speech, adjustment of which is made through speech training, and abnormal speech, the treatment of which requires special knowledge in a number of other directions. The outstanding weakness of earlier methods of approach to the problem of abnormal speech lay in the failure to make this distinction, so that speech disabilities were treated as defects of utterance rather than as disturbance of function.

Apart from the attention paid to the elusive problem of stammering from early times onward, both by "quacks" and by more sincere students of the subject, and to that of aphasia by neurologists, on which subject there is probably an even greater amount of literature, there is little writing on speech disorders. We may perhaps take John Wyllie's book, *Disorders of Speech,* published in 1890, as the starting point of what was to become modern speech therapy in this country. While there is much in this which, in the light of later research, has been shown to be inaccurate, many of the therapeutic measures advocated being based on misconception of the nature of the speech disturbance, there is nevertheless a good deal that is of value, both from the neurological angle and from the historical point of view. It is worth noting, however, that this writer, whose graduation thesis was on the physiology of the larynx, makes no mention whatever of cleft palate speech, one of the commonest as well as one of the worst defects met with. This may be due to the belief, then generally held, that nothing could be done for these unfortunates other than the carrying out of such surgical treatment as was available at that period. The results of later surgical technique, combined with skilled speech therapy, show how far we have advanced since then.

In 1906 classes for stammerers in connection with their general education were instituted in Lancashire, on the lines advocated by Berquand. The first speech clinic to be established in this country was at St. Thomas's Hospital in 1913. Soon afterwards St. Bartholomew's started a speech clinic, and several other hospitals followed suit at varying intervals. Among the earlier speech clinics were those at the Children's Hospital, Great Ormond Street, the West End Hospital for Nervous Diseases, Guy's Hospital, Bethlem Royal Hospital, King's College Hospital, the West London Hospital, and the Maudsley Hospital.

From 1919 much work was done among ex-servicemen of the Great War of 1914-1918 in the treatment of speech and voice disorders, as a result of the activities of the Vocal Therapy Society, working under the Ministry of Pensions. Among other centres concerned was the Neurological Hospital at Mount Pleasant, Chepstow. Here and elsewhere seed was sown which was later to bear fruit in the founding of modern speech therapy. The 1914 war produced and exacerbated speech disturbances in great numbers, and fanned the flame of interest in the subject. Several of the hospital speech clinics owe their existence to this fact. Its most important outcome, however, was the directing of attention to the extremely common incidence of such disturbances quite apart from war conditions.

The need for the work done by speech therapists began gradually to be more widely realised. The ability to speak clearly, intelligibly and with ease is one of the most important of man's assets. The question of "accent" is of secondary importance. The factors which interfere with this function are disastrously common. It has been computed, for instance, that roughly 1 per cent. of the school population are stammerers, the percentage being higher in some countries; but this takes no account of the large number of children born with cleft palates, or the even larger number of those whose speech is interfered with by an apparently trivial disturbance, the effects of which may prove far from trivial. As a result of the work done in speech therapy, many conditions which would formerly have been considered hopeless are, if not completely normalised, at least greatly alleviated. Children growing up a-social, anti-social, maladjusted and miserable—are saved from such a fate by timely and adequate treatment of the speech conditions which bid fair to bring it about. In countless cases which have prevented or would prevent employment, or would relegate the sufferer to one of a nature for which he was temperamentally and constitutionally unfitted, the defect has been either overcome or so far ameliorated as to form no bar to suitable employment.

The work of speech therapy covers an enormously wide field of speech and voice disorders and defects, including, besides the well-known conditions of stammering, cleft palate speech, lalling and lisping, many less well-known, such as those due to operations on the larynx, tongue, etc., to inflammation or paralysis, to various cerebral conditions, including different forms of aphasia, and the effects of numerous types of nervous disease, as well as hysterical states.

Children are treated in the clinics from the age of three years, and adults up to sixty or sixty-five. In the case of children, the earlier they can be seen by the therapist the better; but many speech disorders do not manifest themselves until middle or late life—notably some of those brought about by the onset of nervous disease and vocal disorders caused by the misuse of the voice or by operations necessitated by disease. Some of these are treatable, others are not.

TRAINING

As work in speech therapy advanced, the necessity for training therapists in this field became apparent, and training schools were established, principally in London. These are: the Central School of Speech Training, the London Hospitals School of Speech Therapy, the National Hospital School of Speech Therapy, and the West End Hospital School of Speech Therapy. In Scotland also the importance of specialised training in speech therapy as distinct from general speech training has come to be recognised, and training schools are being developed in Glasgow and Edinburgh.

Candidates for this training are selected on the basis of cultural background, intellectual attainment, personality and general suitability. A reasonably high standard of health is a *sine qua non,* as the work is exacting. Neurotic subjects are unsuited for this work and would not be admitted as students. Training takes from two to three years, and covers a wide variety of subjects, including Anatomy and Physiology, Biology, Neurology, Psychology, Phonetics, Orthophonics (liberation, adjustment, control and use of the voice) and others. Fees for training are from approximately fifty to sixty guineas per annum.

While the work of speech therapy is entirely distinct from that of any other profession, it is closely related on the one hand to that of the medical profession and on the other to that of teaching. Close co-operation of speech therapists with physicians and teachers is, therefore, highly desirable and indeed essential if the best results are to be obtained.

Practice in speech therapy includes work in hospital speech clinics, in school speech clinics under local Education Authorities, and in private practice and research. By far the largest field of opening for the qualified speech therapist, however, is and will probably continue to be in school speech clinics.

THE COLLEGE OF SPEECH THERAPISTS

The governing body of the profession of speech therapy is The College of Speech Therapists, 68 Queen's Gardens, London, W.2, which was formed through the amalgamation of the British Society of Speech Therapists and the Association of Speech Therapists. The College is an examining, not a teaching, body and only those who hold the Diploma of the College are qualified to practise in speech therapy. It is also concerned with the general administration of the profession and constitutes a centre of information in this connection. It publishes a periodical, *Speech* (2s. 6d.).

In 1941 the Board of Registration of Medical Auxiliaries recognised speech therapy as a Medical Auxiliary Service, and elected to their Council two representatives of the College. The Board issues yearly a *National Register of Medical Auxiliaries* (*Speech Therapists Section*) in which the names of all qualified speech therapists are entered. The Register is available for the sum of one shilling on application to the Secretary of the Board of Registration of Medical Auxiliaries, B.M.A. House, Tavistock Square, W.C.1, and constitutes a safeguard for the public as regards the treatment of disorders of speech.

Much has already been accomplished, but the restrictions imposed by war conditions often held up or curtailed activity in many directions in which plans had been put forward. Now however, the College looks forward to a great expansion of activity in the field of speech therapy, and in particular to the development of research which shall materially increase our understanding of some of the many problems which confront us.

My thanks are due to Miss J. H. Van Thal, F.C.S.T., who kindly supplied some dates in connection with the inauguration of speech clinics in England, and to Miss Eileen MacLeod, F.C.S.T., Chairman of the Council of the College of Speech Therapists, who read the manuscript and contributed valuable comments and help.

A Hundred Years of British and Foreign Speech Therapy

By LEOPOLD STEIN

UNTIL the third decade of the last century the historian can hardly speak of Speech Therapy as a coherent remedial speciality. Before that time not even the two main classes of speech disorders, viz., stammering and disorders of articulate speech had been clearly separated.

A first advance in this direction was made by the British physician MacCormack (1828). Similar contributions by workers in Switzerland, France, England, and Germany, followed (Schulthess, 1830; Serre d'Allais, 1829; Colombat, 1830; Arnott, 1830; Schmalz). The knowledge that aphasia (the loss or impairment of the faculty of transforming mental states into conventional communicative audible signs) is due to lesions of certain brain areas we owe to the investigations of French workers such as Bouillaud (1825), M. Dax (1836), and Broca (1861), and of British neurologists such as William Ogle (1867), Gairdner,

Broadbent and Jackson. The German-Jewish philologist Steinhal in 1871 separated the impaired faculty of grammatical construction (akataphasia, agrammatism) from the disturbances of word finding and word formation. Neurologists and speech therapists, particularly in Great Britain, France, Germany, Austria and Switzerland, have contributed to the elucidation of the anatomical and psychological conditions entailed in aphasic disorders (Bastian, 1898; Jackson, Head, 1926; Déjérine, 1907; Marie, Moutier, 1908; Liepmann, 1909; Wernicke, 1906; Froeschels, Stein; Monakow, and others). Worcester-Drought (1930) in this country has established the syndrome of congenital auditory imperception, characterized chiefly by the failure to appreciate the meaning of words heard and to distinguish between less specialized sounds than those of spoken language. The inability is manifest in a distorted and individual form of conventional language. Valuable suggestions as to the remedial approach have been made by the same worker.

The factors causing either excessive or diminished nasal resonance have been thoroughly examined by German, Austrian, American and French speech therapists (Gutzmann, Froeschels, O. Russell, Tarneaud, Husson, and others). Especially cleft palate speech has presented speech therapists with many baffling problems. Compared with early efforts in Germany and Austria (Langenbeck, Wolff, Billroth), the technique of surgical repair of congenital clefts has reached a high standard in France and Great Britain (Veau, Kilner, Ritchie, Oldfield and others). Functional treatment (Trélat and others in France, Gutzmann in Germany, Froeschels in Austria) has been highly evolved in this country (J. Van Thal).

About the middle of the nineteenth century the growth of speech therapy culminated in the works of such workers as Lee (1841), Poett (1842), Hunt (1859) in Great Britain, Lichtinger (1844), Rosenthal (1861) in Germany, Violette (1862), Chervin (1869) in France. Since then a vast storehouse of facts has been built up in all countries. So much so that in these pages only a few of the builders can be mentioned to guide us on our way.

Kussmaul's *Disorders of Speech* marked the birth of Speech Therapy as a coherent and systematized body of knowledge. Availing himself of Darwin's evolutionary doctrine, the author, a German physician, realized that the systematic study of the science of language must be based upon a knowledge of "man's rudest means of conversing by gestures and cries" and upon the recognition of the "higher devices of articulate speech" as "improvements on such lower levels" (E. B. Taylor). The infant's lalling with its clicking, spitting, gnarling and sputtering sounds mirror—according to Kussmaul—mankind's primordial sounds.

An account of the development of speech has since then served as an introduction to the theory of speech disorders in most textbooks. Continental authors, however, seem to have failed to realize the value of the evolutionary viewpoint (H. Spencer,

Jackson, Freud and their followers) in establishing a comprehensive and unified theory of speech and its disorders. Recent advances in this direction are mainly due to British specialists such as Seth and Guthrie (1935), and M. M. Lewis (1936), together with their forerunners, the French psychologist Egger (1886) and his German follower Ament (1899).

Continental speech therapists are, however, to be credited with the determination to comply with two of the main principles of science: exact observation and correct description. This procedure was adopted by H. Gutzmann. He conceived speech as a physiological rather than a psychological event, although he was aware of the psychological background. On the interrelation between physiological and psychological phenomena he expressed no clear-cut opinion. In his bias towards physiological comprehension he analyzed speech into physical units such as sounds, phonation, respiration and so on, but disregarded the temporal (evolutionary or developmental) setting. He adhered to the still widely held doctrine which regards "spasticity" as the morbid principle of stammering (Nadoleczny, 1926, Kingdon-Ward, 1940, and others).

The analysis of speech as a psycho-somatic phenomenon following evolutionary principles, led to different results. Hoepfner in Germany (1911) and Froeschels in Austria (1913) subjected all symptoms of stammering to a minute examination and arranged them on a temporal scale. It appeared that the various types of stammering were to be regarded as successive stages of the same disorder. The outward symptoms revealed themselves to be prompted by conscious experiences erroneously interpreted. This recognition (propounded in this country by J. Van Thal) opened the gate for a systematic psychological treatment. Yet Froeschels, repudiating the idea of an unconscious self, based his therapy mainly on diversion of attention and persuasion with a tinge of metaphysics.

As Speech Therapist to the Tavistock Clinic (The Institute of Medical Psychology) in London, the present writer has in recent years subjected the bio-psychological make-up of patients with disordered speech or voice to a detailed analysis. The application of the theory that disordered behaviour brings earlier stages of evolution to the fore (H. Spencer's and J. H. Jackson's doctrine of dissolution; Freud's psycho-analysis) has revealed that in stammering standard speech first regresses to the next lower level of speech which comprises the various stages of babbling, as, for instance, in "clocloclock" (Stein, 1924, 1941). Severer stages recapitulate movements and postures characterized by tension. These represent the primordial "freezing" attitude symbolic of fear. Co-movements such as grinding the teeth, drawing the corners of the mouth and the like symbolize primordial aggressive emotions conjured up by unconscious reminiscences. In some cases the primitive "clicks," *i.e.*, sounds accompanying sucking movements, re-appear as the dramatization of, for instance, the patient's unconscious urge to re-establish the infantile relationship between himself and his mother or mother-substitute. It may be remarked in passing that the technical language of phonetics would describe the erotic activity of kissing as a labial click.

If the examination of Dyslalia, *i.e.,* the production of sounds different from those used in the language of the community (commonly known as lisping or baby-talk) is guided by the rules of comparative philology it appears that it is by no means a chaotic "sound-salad." The comparision of such dyslalic utterances as *t* for *k* and *sh* for *ch* ("lo*ch*") as in *tishe* for German "Kirche"; *sh* for *ch* in the pronunciation of the English "cheek"; *ts* for *k* in the pronunciation of "cat," etc., with historical sound-changes as in the development of Latin "coelum" (letter "c" equals *k*) into Rumanian "ceriu" and Italian "cielo" (*ch*), etc., reveals that both in dyslalia and in the evolution of standard languages the same natural tendencies of sound change are at work. The difference between dyslalia and normal language consists in that in the former the inherent tendencies towards sound change surge forward unbridled and at an excessive speed, whilst in the latter these same tendencies are to a greater or lesser extent checked by tendencies of social adjustment (Stein, 1925, 1940, 1942).

The therapy worked out at the Tavistock Clinic is based on the analysis of the natural patterns which in their faulty integration constitute a given disorder. Having isolated the behavioural sets of reactions the therapist traverses with the patient the levels which in their harmonious integration serve standard communication. Such speech movements start and terminate in postures characterized by an optimum of tension without which no movement is possible. The technique elaborated by British speech therapists (Richardson, Boome, Baines, Harris, and others) aims at "relaxation" in rest rather than in action.

In so far as the speaker's Body-Mind communicates with others, speech can be styled a dramatization of socio-psychological occurrences. Once the patient has realized the bio-psychological significance of the expressive levels to which he has regressed and which are faultily linked up, he can be enabled to re-dramatize them and so bring them into coherence and harmony. It is in this effort that Speech Therapy gets a touch of art, and this in its turn enhances the chances of the "scientific" approach. The artistic attitude has been stressed by Fogerty, Thurburn and others in England.

The speech therapist in this country "doth not" (to use Francis Bacon's words) "change his country manners for those of foreign parts, but only prick in some flowers of that he hath learned abroad into the customs of his country." Thus he can claim to be leading (Boome, Baines and Harris, 1940) in Speech Therapy, especially in its organization. British Speech Therapy has weighed the findings of foreign workers and integrated them with

British ideas in such a way as to arrive at first principles, and to weave the facts into a systematic fabric of knowledge.

BOOKS ON SPEECH THERAPY

Students wishing to consult books on the subject are referred to the section, "Speech Therapy" in the book list *Speech,* obtainable from the Speech Fellowship, 9 Fitzroy Square, London, W.1, price 7d. by post.

List of addresses on page 212.

DIRECTORY

Speech Societies

ASSOCIATION PHONÉTIQUE INTERNATIONALE: see International Phonetic Association

ENGLISH ASSOCIATION, 3 Cromwell Place, S.W.7

BRITISH COUNCIL, 3 Hanover Street, W.1

ELOCUTION & DRAMA DIPLOMA TEACHERS' ASSOCIATION, 9 Palace Mansions, Addison Bridge, W.14

ENGLISH DIALECT SOCIETY (dissolved)

FOLK-LORE SOCIETY, 21 Bedford Square, W.C.1

INCORPORATED ASSOCIATION OF TEACHERS OF SPEECH AND DRAMA, "Oakhurst," Steep, Petersfield, Hampshire

INTERNATIONAL PHONETIC ASSOCIATION, c/o University College, Gower Street, W.C.1

LAMDA TEACHERS' ASSOCIATION, Tower House, Cromwell Road, S.W.5

MODERN LANGUAGE ASSOCIATION, 5 Stone Buildings, Lincoln's Inn, W.C.1.

NATIONAL ASSOCIATION OF TEACHERS OF SPEECH AND DRAMA (see Speech Association of America).

ORTHOLOGICAL INSTITUTE, 45 Gordon Square, W.C.1

PHILOLOGICAL SOCIETY, c/o University College, Gower Street, W.C.1

SCOTTISH DIALECT SOCIETY, William Grant, Training Centre, Aberdeen

SOCIETY FOR PURE ENGLISH, c/o Clarendon Press, High Street, Oxford

SPEECH ASSOCIATION OF AMERICA, University of Missouri, Columbia, Missouri, U.S.A.

SPEECH FELLOWSHIP, 9 Fitzroy Square, W.1

WELSH LANGUAGE SOCIETY, 14 Mackintosh Road, Pontypridd, Glamorganshire

YORKSHIRE DIALECT SOCIETY, Stanley Umpleby, Derry Lodge, Darlington, Yorkshire

Periodicals

AMERICAN SPEECH. Quarterly. (Columbia University Press, 2960 Broadway, New York City, $4.30 a year, including postage)

ANNUAL BIBLIOGRAPHY OF ENGLISH LANGUAGE AND LITERATURE. Edited by Angus Macdonald. (Cambridge University Press)

BULLETIN, Incorporated Association of Teachers of Speech and Drama, "Oakhurst," Steep, Petersfield, Hampshire. (To members only, periodically)

BULLETIN, London School of Oriental and African Studies, University of London, W.C.1 (15s., occasionally)

ENGLISH. 3 Cromwell Road, S.W.7

ENGLISH LANGUAGE TEACHING, 3 Hanover Street, W.1

GOOD SPEECH. Quarterly, suspended: see Speech Fellowship *News Letter*

LAMDA PAMPHLETS. London Academy of Dramatic Art, Tower House, Cromwell Road, S.W.5 3 per year

MODERN LANGUAGE REVIEW, Cambridge University Press, Euston Road, N.W.1. (7s. quarterly)

MODERN LANGUAGES, 23 Lawn Road, Hampstead, N.W.3. (Twice yearly, 1s. 3d.)

MODERN PHILOLOGY, University of Chicago Press, 5750 Ellis Avenue, Chicago, Illinois, U.S.A.

MAITRE PHONÉTIQUE. Quarterly to members of the International Phonetic Association, University College, Gower Street, W.C.1

NEWS LETTER, Speech Fellowship, 9 Fitzroy Square, W.1. (Bimonthly, included in 10s. yearly subscription)

QUARTERLY JOURNAL OF SPEECH, University of Missouri, Columbia, Missouri, U.S.A.. $3.00 a year, including postage

PSYCHE, Orthological Institute, 45 Gordon Square, W.C.1. (10s. annually)

SPEECH MONOGRAPHS, Wayne University, Detroit, Michigan, U.S.A.

STUDIES IN EXPERIMENTAL PHONETICS, University of Iowa, U.S.A.

YEAR'S WORK IN ENGLISH STUDIES, English Association, 3 Cromwell Road, S.W.7

Occasional articles in *Teachers' World, Child Education, New Era, Schoolmaster, Journal of Education, The Listener,* and *Times Educational Supplement*

Schools and Academies

ASSOCIATED BOARD OF THE ROYAL SCHOOLS OF MUSIC, 14/15 Bedford Square, W.C.1

BIRMINGHAM SCHOOL OF SPEECH TRAINING, Queen's College Chambers, Paradise Street, Birmingham

CENTRAL SCHOOL OF SPEECH TRAINING AND DRAMA, Royal Albert Hall, Kensington Gore, S.W.7

GUILDHALL SCHOOL OF MUSIC AND DRAMA, John Carpenter Street, Embankment, E.C.4

GLOVER, TURNER - ROBERTSON SCHOOL OF SPEECH, 90 George Street, Edinburgh

LONDON COLLEGE OF MUSIC, Great Marlborough Street, W.1

LONDON ACADEMY OF MUSIC AND DRAMATIC ART, Tower House, Cromwell Road, S.W.5

MANCHESTER SCHOOL OF MUSIC, 16 Albert Square, Manchester

NEW ERA ACADEMY, Cavendish Square, W.1

ROYAL ACADEMY OF MUSIC (Speech and Drama Dept.), York Gate, Marylebone Road, N.W.1

ROYAL COLLEGE OF MUSIC, Prince Consort Road, S.W.7.

ROYAL IRISH ACADEMY OF MUSIC, Westland Row, Dublin, Eire

ROYAL MANCHESTER COLLEGE OF MUSIC, Ducie Street, Oxford Road, Manchester, 15

ROYAL SCOTTISH ACADEMY OF MUSIC, St. George's Place, Glasgow, C.2

SCHOOL OF ORIENTAL AND AFRICAN STUDIES, Senate House, W.C.1

SCHOOL OF SLAVONIC AND EAST EUROPEAN STUDIES, W.C.1

TRINITY COLLEGE OF MUSIC, Mandeville Place, W.1

UNIVERSITY COLLEGE (Phonetics Dept.), Gower Street, W.C.1

UNIVERSITY COLLEGE (Dept. of Spoken Language), Nottingham

Vacation Schools

The following usually have short courses in speech during the Christmas, Easter or Summer holidays:

ABERDEEN TRAINING CENTRE, St. Andrew Street, Aberdeen

BINGLEY TRAINING COLLEGE, Bingley, Yorkshire

CENTRAL SCHOOL OF SPEECH TRAINING, Royal Albert Hall, S.W.7

DEPARTMENT OF PHONETICS, University College, Gower Street, W.C.1

INCORPORATED ASSOCIATION OF TEACHERS OF SPEECH AND DRAMA, Miss Carey-Field, Bedales School, Petersfield, Hants.

JORDANHILL TRAINING COLLEGE, Glasgow

LONDON ACADEMY OF MUSIC AND DRAMATIC ART, Tower House, Cromwell Road, S.W.5

London University, Extension Lectures, Senate House, W.C.1. (English language, phonetics, etc., for foreign students).
Moray House Training College, Edinburgh
Polytechnic, Regent Street, London, W.1
Speech Fellowship, 9 Fitzroy Square, London, W.1

An annual list of all vacation courses in Great Britain is issued by the Registrar, Selly Oak Colleges, Selly Oak, Birmingham. The Ministry of Education also publishes a "Programme of Short Courses" (H.M.S.O., 9d.)

Verse-Speaking Organisations

English Verse-Speaking Association (Disbanded)
Here and Now Society, 26 Willow Road, N.W.3
Incorporated Association of Teachers of Speech and Drama, "Oakhurst," Steep, Petersfield, Hants.
International Arts Centre, 3 Orme Square, W.2
"Poetry in Pubs," Room 167, St. Stephen's House, S.W.1
Poetry Lovers' Fellowship, 24 Denby Road, Loscoe, Derby
Poetry Society, 33 Portman Square, W.1
Poets' Theatre Guild, 2 Ladbroke Road, W.11
Progressive League, Alec Craig, 140 Holland Road, W.14
Speech Fellowship, 9 Fitzroy Square, W.1
Verse-Speaking Fellowship, (Now Speech Fellowship)

Speech Festivals

English Festival of Spoken Poetry; Miss V. Birnie, 2 Park Avenue, London, N.W.11
London Speech Festival; Speech Fellowship, 9 Fitzroy Square, W.1
National Federation of Musical Festivals, 106 Gloucester Place, W.1
Oxford Festival of Spoken Poetry (Now "English Festival of Spoken Poetry.")
Oxford Recitations (Discontinued)
Verse - Speaking Contests, Incorporated Association of Teachers of Speech and Drama; Miss Mabel Gulick, Roedean School, Brighton, Sussex
(See also speech sections of musical festivals in *Musical Festivals Yearbook*

Discussion Group Organisations

Army Bureau of Current Affairs: see Bureau of Current Affairs
Association for Education in Citizenship, 51 Tothill Street, S.W.1
B.B.C. Discussion Groups: see Central Council for Group Listening
British Institute of Adult Education, 29 Tavistock Square, W.C.1
Bureau of Current Affairs, 117 Piccadilly, W.1
Central Council for Group Listening, 55 Portland Place, W.1. *Other Offices*: 282 Broad Street, Birmingham; Broadcasting House, Woodhouse Lane, Leeds; Broadcasting House, Piccadilly, Manchester; 39 York Place, Cardiff; 23 Whiteladies Road, Clifton, Bristol; Broadcasting House, Ormeau, Belfast
Industrial Discussion Groups Experiment, 51 Tothill Street, S.W.1

LONDON CO-OPERATIVE SOCIETY, Education Dept., 37 Tavistock Square, W.C.1

NATIONAL ADULT SCHOOL UNION, 30 Bloomsbury Street, W.C.1

NATIONAL FEDERATION OF GRAMOPHONE SOCIETIES, 25 Museum Street, W.1

NATIONAL FEDERATION OF WOMEN'S INSTITUTES, 39 Eccleston Street, S.W.1

NATIONAL UNION OF TOWNSWOMEN'S GUILDS, 2 Cromwell Place, S.W.7

P.E.N. ASSOCIATION, 45 Belgrave Square, S.W.1

ROTARY INTERNATIONAL OF GREAT BRITAIN, Tavistock House, W.C.1

SCOTTISH AREA COUNCIL FOR GROUP LISTENING, 5 Queen Street, Edinburgh

WORKERS EDUCATIONAL ASSOCIATION, 38a, St. George's Drive, S.W.1

Speech Recording

BRITISH DRAMA LEAGUE (Dialect records), 9 Fitzroy Square, W.1.

COLUMBIA GRAPHAPHONE COMPANY, Hayes, Middlesex

DAGNALL, H., 168 Briggate, Leeds

DECCA RECORD CO., 1 Brixton Road, S.W.9

ERPI PICTURE CONSULTANTS, 250 West 57th Street, New York City, U.S.A.

GRAMOPHONE COMPANY, Hayes, Middlesex

GRAMOPHONE SHOP, 18 East 48th Street, New York City, U.S.A.

HARVARD FILM SERVICE (Poets' recordings), Biological Laboratories, Cambridge, Massachusetts, U.S.A.

HEFFER & SONS (Phonetic records), 3 Petty Cury, Cambridge, England

H.M.V., 363 Oxford Street, W.1

LINGUAPHONE INSTITUTE, 207 Regent Street, W.1

LINGUAPHONE INSTITUTE, 18 R.C.A. Building, Rockefeller Centre, New York City, U.S.A.

NATIONAL COUNCIL OF TEACHERS OF ENGLISH, 211 West 68th Street, Chicago, Illinois, U.S.A.

ORTHOLOGICAL INSTITUTE (Basic English Records), 45 Gordon Square, W.C.1

RECORDED SOUND LTD., 6a Whitehorse Street, Piccadilly, W.1

VOX RECORDISTS (Poetry Records) Sylvanlake, Fairholme Gardens Finchley, N.3

Recording Apparatus:

"MIRROPHONE" PLAY-BACK GRAMOPHONE: see Western-Electric

PHONO-DISC LTD., 65 Bolsover Street, W.1

WESTERN - ELECTRIC COMPANY Filmicity House, St. Martin's Lane, W.C.2

Broadcasting

British Broadcasting Corporation:

Head Office: Broadcasting House, Portland Place, W.1

Other Offices: Beechgrove Terrace, Aberdeen; Merion Road, Bangor; Ormeau Avenue, Belfast; 282 Broad Street, Birmingham; 21-25 Whiteladies Road, Bristol; 11 Sharia Ahmed Pasha, Cairo; 38 Park Place, Cardiff; Queen Street, Carmarthen; 5-6 Queen Street Edinburgh; Queen Margaret Drive, Glasgow; Woodhouse Lane, Leeds; 54 New Bridge Street, Newcastle; 630 Fifth Avenue, New York; Seymour Road, Plymouth

ADVISORY COMMITTEE ON SPOKEN ENGLISH (Suspended), Broadcasting House, Portland Place, W.1

CENTRAL COUNCIL FOR SCHOOL BROADCASTING, 55 Portland Place, W.1

CENTRAL COMMITTEE FOR GROUP LISTENING, 55 Portland Place, W.1

DEPARTMENT OF SCHOOL BROADCASTING, Broadcasting House, Portland Place, W.1

DRAMA DEPARTMENT, Broadcasting House, Portland Place, W.1

PUBLICATIONS DEPARTMENT, Grammar School, Scarle Road, Wembley, Middlesex

TALKS DEPARTMENT, Broadcasting House, Portland Place, W.1

SCOTTISH COUNCIL FOR SCHOOL BROADCASTING, 5 Queen Street, Edinburgh

Periodicals

LISTENER, Broadcasting House, London, W.1. (3d. weekly)

LONDON CALLING, Broadcasting House, W.1

PROGRAMME OF SCHOOL BROADCASTS, Department of School Broadcasting, Portland Place, W.1. (1d.)

RADIO TIMES, Broadcasting House, W.1. (2d. weekly)

VOICE OF THE WORLD (Vox Mundi Ltd., 1s. 6d. quarterly)

WIRELESS WORLD, Dorset House, Stamford Street, S.E.1. (1s. monthly)

Speech Therapy

Organisations:

BRITISH SOCIETY OF SPEECH THERAPISTS: see College of Speech Therapists)

COLLEGE OF SPEECH THERAPISTS, 68 Queen's Gardens, W.2

INSTITUTE OF MEDICAL PSYCHOLOGY, 2 Beaumont Street, W.1

NATIONAL REGISTER OF MEDICAL AUXILIARIES (Qualified Speech Therapists), B.M.A. Building, Tavistock Square, W.C.1

TAVISTOCK CLINIC: see Institute of Medical Psychology

WEST-END HOSPITAL FOR NERVOUS DISEASES, 73 Welbeck Street, W.1

Recognised Training Centres:

CENTRAL SCHOOL OF SPEECH TRAINING AND DRAMATIC ART, Therapy Training Section, Royal Albert Hall, S.W.7

LONDON HOSPITALS SCHOOL OF SPEECH THERAPY, 17 Cavendish Square, W.1

NATIONAL HOSPITAL FOR DISEASES OF THE NERVOUS SYSTEM, Queen Square, W.C.1

ROYAL HOSPITAL FOR SICK CHILDREN, Speech Therapy Department, Glasgow

Periodicals:

JOURNAL OF SPEECH DISORDERS, State University of Iowa, Iowa City, U.S.A.

SPEECH, College of Speech Therapists, 68 Queen's Gardens, W.2 (Pitman & Sons).

QUARTERLY JOURNAL OF SPEECH, Wayne University, Detroit, Michigan, U.S.A.

Occasional articles in "The Lancet" "British Medical Journal" and "British Journal of Medical Psychology"

Education of the Deaf:

DEPARTMENT OF EDUCATION OF THE DEAF, Manchester University, Manchester, 13

NATIONAL INSTITUTE FOR THE DEAF, 103 Gower Street, W.C.1

OTOLOGICAL RESEARCH UNIT, National Hospital, Queen's Square, W.C.1

Drama Organisations

AGENTS' ASSOCIATION, 26, Charing Cross Road, W.C.2.

ARTS COUNCIL OF GREAT BRITAIN, 9 Belgrave Square, S.W.1

*ARTS THEATRE CLUB, 6 Great Newport Street, W.C.2

ASSOCIATION OF TOURING AND PRODUCING MANAGERS, 18 Charing Cross Road, W.C.2

BRITISH ACTORS' EQUITY ASSOCIATION, 56 Kingsway, W.C 2

BRITISH DRAMA LEAGUE, 9 Fitzroy Square, W.1

---

*Membership Societies with Sunday performances

C.E.M.A. (Council for the Encouragement of Music and the Arts): see Arts Council

CONCERT ARTISTES ASSOCIATION, 20 Cranbourn Street, W.C.2

*CHANTICLEER THEATRE CLUB, Clareville Street, S.W.7.

CRITICS' CIRCLE, 2-4 Tudor Street, E.C.4

ENGLISH THEATRE GUILD, 24 Whitcomb Street, W.C.2

ENTERTAINMENTS PROTECTION ASSOCIATION, Cranbourne Mansions, Cranbourn Street, W.C.2

*GATE THEATRE. (Temporarily closed)

*GATEWAY THEATRE, 18 Chepstow Villas, W.11

*GROUP THEATRE. (Temporarily closed. Enquiries to Miss Aitchison, 213 Makepeace Mansions, N.6)

INCORPORATED SOCIETY OF AUTHORS, PLAYWRIGHTS AND COMPOSERS, 84 Drayton Gardens, S.W.10

INCORPORATED STAGE SOCIETY, 77 Edith Road, W.14

INTERNATIONAL ONE-ACT PLAY THEATRE, 20 Galesbury Road, S.W.18

JOINT COMMITTEE FOR MUSIC AND DRAMA, Carnegie Trust, 26 Bedford Square, W.C.1

LEAGUE OF BRITISH DRAMATISTS, 84 Drayton Gardens, S.W.10

LONDON THEATRE COUNCIL, 8-10 Charing Cross Road, W.C.2

NATIONAL ASSOCIATION OF THEATRICAL EMPLOYEES, 71 South End Road, N.W.3

NATIONAL OPERATIC & DRAMATIC ASSOCIATION, Emanwye House, Bernard Street, W.C.1

NATIONAL THEATRE COMMITTEE, 9 Fitzroy Square, W.1

PERFORMING RIGHT SOCIETY, 33 Margaret Street, W.1

PLAY ENCOURAGEMENT COMMITTEE, 9 Fitzroy Square, W.1

PLAYERS' THEATRE, 13 Albemarle Street, W.1

PLAYWRIGHTS' CLUB, 11 West End Avenue, Pinner, Middlesex

POETS' THEATRE GUILD, 2 Ladbroke Road, W.11

PROVINCIAL ENTERTAINMENTS PROPRIETORS AND MANAGERS ASSOCIATION, 18 Charing Cross Road, W.C.2

PROVINCIAL THEATRE COUNCIL, 8-10 Charing Cross Road, W.C.2

RELIGIOUS DRAMA SOCIETY, S.P.C.K. House, Northumberland Avenue, W.C.2

SCOTTISH COMMUNITY DRAMA ASSOCIATION, 3 Frederick Street, Edinburgh 2

SHAW SOCIETY, 7 Harrington Square, N.W.1

SOCIETY OF WEST END THEATRE MANAGERS, 8-10 Charing Cross Road, W.C.2

STAGE AND ALLIED ARTS LEAGUE, 8-10 Charing Cross Road, W.C.2

THEATRE LADIES' GUILD, 50 Great Russell Street, W.C.1

THEATRICAL MANAGERS' ASSOCIATION, 8-10 Charing Cross Road, W.C.2

*TORCH THEATRE CLUB, 37 Wilton Street, Knightsbridge, S.W.7

*UNITY THEATRE SOCIETY, 9 Gt. Newport Street, W.C.2

VILLAGE DRAMA SOCIETY — see British Drama League

Stage Papers

AMATEUR THEATRE (suspended)

ARTS COUNCIL BULLETIN, 9 Belgrave Square, S.W.1

CHRISTIAN DRAMA, S.P.C.K. House, Northumberland Avenue, W.C.2

DRAMA, 9 Fitzroy Square, W.1

N. O. D. A. BULLETIN, National Operatic and Dramatic Association

PERFORMER, 18 Charing Cross Road, W.C.2

SPOTLIGHT, 43 Cranbourn Street, W.C.2

STAGE, 19-21 Tavistock Street, Covent Garden, W.C.2

STAGE GUIDE, 19 Tavistock Street, W.C.2

THEATRE, Bradford Playhouse, Chapel Street, Bradford

THEATRE ARTS MONTHLY, 2 Ladbroke Road, W.11

THEATRE CRAFT (suspended). Enquiries to 16 Central Chambers, Stratford-on-Avon

---

* Membership Societies with Sunday performances.

THEATRE IN EDUCATION, 77 Dean Street, W.1
THEATRE NEWS-LETTER, 77 Dean Street, W.1
THEATRE TO-DAY, 28 Southampton Street, Strand, W.C.2
THEATRE MANAGERS' JOURNAL, 8-10 Charing Cross Road, W.C.2
THEATRE WORLD, 1 Dorset Buildings, Dorset Rise, Salisbury Square, E.C.4

London Theatrical Clubs

ARTS THEATRE CLUB, 6 Great Newport Street, W.C.2
AUTHORS' CLUB, 2 Whitehall Court, S.W.1
ECCENTRIC CLUB, 9 Ryder Street, S.W.1
GALLERY FIRST-NIGHTERS' CLUB, "Duke of Argyll," Great Windmill Street, W.1
GARRICK CLUB, 13 Garrick Street, W.C.2
GREEN ROOM CLUB, 62 Whitcomb Street, W.C.2
GRAND ORDER OF WATER RATS, 9 Ryder Street, S.W.1
INTERVAL CLUB, 23 Dean Street, W.1
MAYFAIR CLUB, opposite Streatham Hill Theatre, S.W.
PLAYERS' THEATRE CLUB, 1 Carlton House Terrace, S.W.1
SAVAGE CLUB, 1 Carlton House Terrace, S.W.1
THEATRE CLUB, 111 Charing Cross Road, W.C.2
THREE ARTS CLUB, 76 Gloucester Place, W.1

Drama Schools

*BRITISH DRAMA LEAGUE, 9 Fitzroy Square, W.1
CENTRAL SCHOOL OF SPEECH TRAINING AND DRAMA, Royal Albert Hall, London, S.W.7
*CITIZEN HOUSE, Bath
CONTI SCHOOL (Children), Tavistock Little Theatre, Tavistock Place, W.C.1
GINNER MAWER SCHOOL OF DANCE AND DRAMA, Boscastle, Cornwall
GLOVER TURNER-ROBERTSON SCHOOL, George St., Edinburgh
GUILDHALL SCHOOL OF MUSIC AND DRAMA, John Carpenter Street, E.C.4
LAMDA DRAMA SCHOOL, London Academy of Music and Dramatic Art, Tower House, Cromwell Road, S.W.5
*MORLEY COLLEGE, 61 Westminster Bridge Road, S.E.1
NEW VIC SCHOOL (see Old Vic)
OLD VIC DRAMA SCHOOL, Waterloo Road, S.E.1
RADA, ROYAL ACADEMY OF DRAMATIC ART, 62 Gower Street, W.C.1
PRADA (Preparatory Section of the RADA)
*TOYNBEE HALL, 29 Commercial Street, E.1
WEBBER-DOUGLAS SCHOOL OF ACTING, 34 Clareville Street, S.W.7
"YOUNG VIC" (Children), Lyric Theatre, Hammersmith, W.6

*Part-time and Vacation Courses

Puppetry

BRITISH PUPPET GUILD, 82 Sherringham Avenue, Southgate, N.14
CLASSES IN PUPPETRY, City Literary Institute, Stukeley Street, W.C.2, and Eltham Hill School, S.E.9
EDUCATIONAL PUPPETRY ASSOCIATION, Minett Lodge, Heath Drive, Theydon Bois, Essex
LANCHESTER MARIONETTE THEATRE, Mr. Waldo Lanchester, Malvern
PUPPETEERS OF AMERICA, 600 Merchants Laclede Building, St. Louis, Missouri, U.S.A.
ROEL SCHOOL OF PUPPETRY, Roel Farm, Guiting Power, near Cheltenham, Glos.
VIENNESE GLOVE PUPPET THEATRE, 26 Albert Road, Withington, Manchester 20
YEAR-BOOK OF PUPPETRY, 12 Eversley Way, Shirley, Croydon

Films

Organisations:

British Film Institute, 4 Great Russell Street, W.C.1
British Instructional Films, 11 Wardour Street, W.1
Central Film Library, Imperial Institute, S.W.7
Central Information Bureau for Educational Films, Kingsway House, Kingsway, W.C.2
Crown Film Unit, Pinewood Studios, Fulmer Road, Ivor Heath, Bucks.
Ealing Studios, Ealing Common, W.5
Film Appreciation Classes, City Literary Institute, Stukeley St., Drury Lane, W.C.2
Films of Fact, 21 Soho Square, W.1
Film Centre, 34 Soho Square, W.1
Film Producers Guild, Guild House, Upper St. Martin's Lane, W.C.2
Film Rights Agency, 24 Whitcomb Street, W.C.2
Film Society, 31 Poland Street, W.1
Film Writers' Club, 64 Adelaide Road, N.W.3
G-B Instructional Films, 142 Wardour Street, W.1
London Scientific Film Society, 165 Oxford Street, W.1
National Film Library, 4 Great Russell Street, W.C.1
Rotha Productions, 21 Soho Sq., W.1
Scientific Films Committee, Association of Scientific Workers, 73 High Holborn, W.C.1
Sound Film Music Bureau, 9a Sackville Street, W.1

Periodicals:

Sight and Sound, 4 Great Russell Street, W.C.1
Documentary News Letter, 34 Soho Square, W.1
Penguin Film Review (Penguin Books, 1s.)

Other Educational Addresses

Youth Organisations:

Co-Operative Youth Clubs, Pioneer House, Gray's Inn Road, W.C.2
International Youth Centre, 30 Pont Street, S.W.1
International Youth Council, 18 Grosvenor Place, S.W.1
London Association of Mixed Clubs, 35 Great Russell Street, W.C.1
London Federation of Boys' Clubs, 222 Blackfriars Road, S.E.1
London Union of Girls' Clubs, 35 Great Russell Street, W.C.1
National Association of Boys' Clubs, 17 Bedford Square, W.C.1
National Association of Girls' and Mixed Clubs, Hamilton House, Bidborough St., W.C.1
National Council of Youth Service Officers, 10 Bruce Grove, N.17
Standing Conference on Juvenile Organisations, 26 Bedford Square, W.C.1
World Youth Council, 123 Grand Buildings, Trafalgar Square, W.C.2
Youth Advisory Council, c/o Ministry of Education, Belgrave Square, S.W.1
Youth House, 250 Camden Road, N.W.1
Youth Leaders' Association, 60 Thornhill Road, N.1
Young People's Section, National Adult School Union, 30 Bloomsbury Street, W.C.1
Youth Service Volunteers, 19 Cowley Street, S.W.1
Y.M.C.A., Central Offices, Great Russell Street, W.C.1
Y.W.C.A., Central Club, Great Russell Street, W.C.1

Teachers' Associations:

ASSOCIATION OF HEAD MISTRESSES, 29 Gordon Square, W.C.1
LONDON HEAD TEACHERS' ASSOCIATION, 224 Colchester Road, Leyton, E.10
LONDON TEACHERS' ASSOCIATION, 185 Aldersgate Street, E.C.1
NATIONAL ASSOCIATION OF HEAD TEACHERS, Charter House, Claremont Road, Surbiton
NATIONAL ASSOCIATION OF SCHOOLMASTERS, 59 Gordon Square, W.C.1
NATIONAL UNION OF STUDENTS, 3 Endsleigh Street, W.C.1
NATIONAL UNION OF TEACHERS, Hamilton House, Mabledon Place, W.C.1
NATIONAL UNION OF WOMEN TEACHERS, 41 Cromwell Road, S.W.7
ROYAL SOCIETY OF TEACHERS, 29 Gordon Square. W.C.1

Other Educational Bodies:

BUREAU OF SPECIAL ENQUIRIES, Ministry of Education, Belgrave Square, S.W.1
CARNEGIE COMMITTEE FOR MUSIC AND DRAMA, 106 Gloucester Place, W.1
CHILD GUIDANCE COUNCIL, 39 Queen Anne Street, W.1
EDUCATIONAL INSTITUTE OF SCOTLAND, 46 Moray Place, Edinburgh 1
ENGLISH-SPEAKING UNION, 37 Charles Street, Berkeley Square, W.1
FROEBEL INSTITUTE, Ebstock Place, Roehampton, S.W.15
MINISTRY OF EDUCATION, Belgrave Square, S.W.1
MONTESSORI SOCIETY, Mapledrakes, Ewhurst, Surrey
NATIONAL FROEBEL FOUNDATION, 2 Manchester Square, W.1
NUFFIELD COLLEGE, 17 Banbury Road, Oxford
NEW EDUCATION FELLOWSHIP, 1 Park Crescent, N.W.1
NURSERY SCHOOLS ASSOCIATION, 1 Park Crescent, N.W.1
PARENTS' NATIONAL EDUCATION UNION, 171 Victoria Street, S.W.1
U.N.E.S.C.O., 19 Avenue Kleber, Paris, 16
WORKERS' MUSIC ASSOCIATION, 9 Great Newport Street, W.C.2

Books and Libraries

Chief Reference Libraries:

BRITISH MUSEUM, Bloomsbury, London, W.C.1
BODLEIAN LIBRARY, Oxford
UNIVERSITY LIBRARY, Cambridge
NATIONAL LIBRARY OF SCOTLAND, Edinburgh
TRINITY COLLEGE LIBRARY, Dublin, Eire
NATIONAL LIBRARY OF WALES, Aberystwyth

Chief Lending Libraries:

BOOTS LIBRARY SERVICE, Stamford Street, S.E.1
COUNTY LIBRARIES, Centres throughout England
HARRODS LTD., Brompton Road, S.W.1
LONDON LIBRARY, St. James's Square, S.W.1
NATIONAL CENTRAL LIBRARY, Books obtainable through County Libraries
W. H. SMITH & SONS, Strand House, Portugal Street, W.C.2
TIMES BOOK CLUB, 42 Wigmore Street, W.1

British Books Abroad:

BRITISH COUNCIL, 3 Hanover St., W.1

Educational Books:

MINISTRY OF EDUCATION LIBRARY, 9 Belgrave Square, S.W.1

LONDON COUNTY COUNCIL LIBRARY, County Hall, S.E.1

Foreign Books:

BOOKS-ACROSS-THE-SEA (American Outpost in Great Britain), 13 Old Square, Lincoln's Inn, W.C.2, and 16 South Charlotte Street, Edinburgh

LIBRARY, LONDON SCHOOL OF ORIENTAL AND AFRICAN STUDIES, University of London, W.C.1

LIBRARY, LONDON SCHOOL OF EAST EUROPEAN AND SLAVONIC STUDIES, 12 Cavendish Place, W.1

ORTHOLOGICAL INSTITUTE, 45 Gordon Square, W.C.1

General Book Enquiries:

ASSOCIATION OF SPECIAL LIBRARIES AND INFORMATION BUREAUX, 52 Bloomsbury Street, W.C.1

LIBRARY ASSOCIATION, Chaucer House, Malet Place, W.C.1

NATIONAL BOOK LEAGUE, 7 Albemarle Street, W.1

NATIONAL CENTRAL LIBRARY (Students' Enquiries), Malet Place, W.C.1

Speech Books:

H. K. LEWIS & CO., 136 Gower Street, W.C.1 (Scientific)

SPEECH FELLOWSHIP BOOK SERVICE, 9 Fitzroy Square, W.1 (General)

Who's Who Among the Contributors

ALLAN, DOUGLAS. Taught English and history in Scottish secondary schools for ten years. Started broadcasting (plays, feature programmes, poetry readings, etc.) in 1932. Joined the School Broadcasting Department of the B.B.C. in 1936. Since then has been writing, producing and taking part in programmes for that department. Chairman of the evening series for young people, "To Start You Talking."

ARNOTT, MARGARET. Assistant Hon. Secretary, Incorporated Association of Teachers of Speech and Drama. Has taught in day schools since 1936, mostly under the Middlesex County Council. Taught in private schools in Potters Bar and Enfield; as visiting teacher in Notre Dame Convent, Clapham; Gumley House Preparatory and Secondary Schools, Isleworth; and in the day Departments of Commerce at Chiswick Polytechnic, Kilburn Polytechnic, Hendon Technical College, City Literary Institute, and at the G.P.O. under their Further Education scheme. Has adjudicated for the Stewart Headlam Festivals, and done a great deal of verse-speaking for the Oxford Festivals of Spoken Poetry, and for John Masefield's "Oxford Diversions," and has given many recitals for schools.

BARNES, SIR KENNETH, M.A. Principal of the Royal Academy of Dramatic Art since 1900. Educated Westminster and Christ Church, Oxford. Knighted 1938. Journalist and dramatic critic, 1903-9. Served India, Mesopotamia, Siberia, 1914-19; Captain 1/9 Hant. Regt., Despatches. Plays: *Glass House,* produced Globe Theatre, 1909; *Undercurrent,* produced R.A.D.A. Players, 1922; *The Letter of the Law,* produced Grand Theatre, Fulham, 1924, and in the provinces.

BENNETT, RODNEY, M.A. (London). Formerly lecturer in Speech Training at University College, Reading; Goldsmiths' College; and Borough Road Training College. Adjudicator and Lecturer at refresher courses, etc. Author of many books, especially on speech and dramatic work, including *Let's Do a Play!*, *Classroom Dramatics, Playway of Speech, The First Steps in Speech Training, Adventures in Words,* and *Practical Speech Training for Schools.*

BOWIE, DULCIE, F.R.A.M., L.R.A.M. (Eloc), M.R.S.T., M.I.A.T.S.D. Trained Royal Academy of Music under Mrs. Tobias Matthay. Studied production and stage-craft at the Royal Academy of Dramatic Art. Has taught at Sevenoaks Grammar School, Francis Holland School for Girls, Roedean, etc. Has given recitals of poetry all over Britain. Adjudicator at major festivals. Founded the "Troubadours" verse-speaking company, 1941. C.E.M.A. tour, 1944. Hon. Sec. of the English Verse-Speaking Association, 1929-36. Prize-winner at John Masefield's early Oxford Recitations, and spoke and acted for him in the poems and plays at Boar's Hill, and later for Laurence Binyon and Gordon Bottomley in their Festivals of Spoken Poetry, 1937-39. At present on staff of R.A.D.A.

BROWNE, E. MARTIN. Produced all T. S. Eliot's plays in London; also Gordon Bottomley's *Acts of St. Peter.* Was the first Director of Religious Drama (Chichester Diocese, 1930), and is now Director of the Religious Drama Society. Founded the Pilgrim Players at the outbreak of war, and has directed them since then. Broadcast a series of talks on play production and many readings of poetry and prose. Author of *The Production of Religious Plays,* and editor of Sheldon Plays and others.

CARROLL, DIANA. Y.W.C.A. National Drama Advisor since 1940. Has demonstrated and adjudicated at clubs and youth drama festivals in many parts of the country. Has spoken and given demonstrations (often in co-operation with Jennifer Greenwood) at courses held by the British Drama League, Ministry of Education, Speech Fellowship, British Council of Churches, local education authorities, etc. Professional experience in Northampton and Croydon Repertory Theatres. Publications: *To Meet the Occasion* (with Jennifer Greenwood), *Drama and Youth* (with Anthony Thomas) and collection of poems, *These Growing Years.*

CHURCH, RICHARD. Poet, novelist and critic. Author of *The Porch, The Stronghold, Green Tide, Twentieth Century Psalter, The Solitary Man, Twelve Noon, Eight for Immortality,* etc. One of the Directors of the English Festival of Spoken Poetry

COMPTON, JOHN, M.A. Director of Education for Ealing. Chairman of the Incorporated Association of Teachers of Speech and Drama. Chairman of the University of London Advisory Committee on the Diploma in Dramatic Art. Publications include *Spoken English* (a symposium), *Open Sesame, Magic Sesame, The Curtain Rises, Beginners Please* and *The Queen's Treasury of Verse.*

CRAWFORD, ARCHIBALD, K.C. Member of the Scottish Bar. Called in 1906, and practised until 1927 when he was invited by the Heavy Industries to become the leading platform exponent of private enterprise. Later became industrial administrator and advocate, and independent chairman, also giving advice and tuition in public speaking. Author of *Guilty as Libelled* (a criminal defence reminiscence), *Public Speaking,* and *Mind Training for Speech Making.* At present engaged on what might be called a "crusade" to interest industrialists and others as to the value of training in the spoken word.

CRUMP, GEOFFREY, M.A. (Camb.), L.R.A.M. Honorary Secretary of the Incorporated Association of Teachers of Speech and Drama. Professor of Speech and Drama at the Royal Academy of Music, and at the Central School of Speech Training and Dramatic Art. Member of the Examining Board for L.R.A.M. Lecturer in English to various Institutions, including the Staff Colleges of the Army and R.A.F. Director of the Steep Shakespeare Players and the English Amateur Players. Senior English Master, Bedales School, 1919-1945. Author of books of poetry, drama, literary and dramatic history and criticism, and of *A Manual of English Speech.*

EWING, IRENE R., O.B.E., M.Sc. Mistress in charge of the Henry Worrall School for Deaf Children, Old Trafford, Manchester, from 1912-1919—the first infant school for deaf children in Great Britain. 1919 onwards, Ellis Llwyd Jones Reader in the Education of the Deaf, University of Manchester, the only department of its kind in a European University. The first hearing-aid clinic for the deaf was established in the department in 1934. Publications: *Lipreading,* 1930; *The Handicap of Deafness,* 1938 (with A. W. G. Ewing); *Lipreading and Hearing Aids,* 1944; "Deafness in Infancy and Early Childhood," *Journal of Laryngology and Otology,* 1943. 58-4. "The Psychological Aspects of Deafness," *Proceedings of the Royal Society of Medicine,* April 1941. Norman Gamble Prize, Royal Society of Medicine, 1942; Actonian Prize, Royal Institution, 1943—both with A. W. G. Ewing.

FOULIS, WILFRID. Governing Director of the London Academy of Music and Dramatic Art. Educated at Cargilfield School, Edinburgh, and at Trinity College, Glenalmond. Has wide mechanical and civil engineering knowledge. Pioneer aviator, and served in the Great War. Studied dramatic art and music at the Royal College of Music and elsewhere. Has been responsible for the great extension of the work of L.A.M.D.A. since 1935.

FRY, DENNIS., Ph.D. (Lond.). Studied phonetics, Phonetics Department of University College, London, under Professor Daniel Jones. Was appointed to the staff of the Department in 1934, and three years later was placed in charge of the University College Phonetics Laboratory. Since 1939 has been occupied in research for the Royal Air Force into problems connected with the transmission and reception of speech signals.

GULLAN, MARJORIE. Joint Founder and President of the Speech Fellowship. Principal of the Speech Department, London Polytechnic, Regent Street, 1925-32. Lecturer in Speech Training at the Institute of Education, University of London, 1926-34, and from 1944 onwards. University of California, Summer Session, 1933. Teachers' College, Columbia University, New York City, 1935. National Council of Education for Canada, 1936. Founder of the Choral Speaking Movement in Great Britain. Author of *Poetry Speaking for Children* (with P. Gurrey), *The Poet Speaks* (with Clive Sansom), *Spoken Poetry in the Schools, Speech Training in the School, Choral Speaking* and *The Speech Choir*.

HOLLINGWORTH, CATHERINE, A.R.A.M., L.C.S.T. Superintendent of Speech Training and Speech Therapy, Aberdeen Education Committee. Speech Therapist to the Royal Aberdeen Hospital for Sick Children. Trained at the Royal Academy of Music, London, and at King's College Hospital, London. Has had experience in the production of plays, lecturing, adjudicating and Speech Therapy in various parts of the country.

JAGGER, J. HUBERT, M.A., D.Litt. London County Council Divisional Inspector of Schools. Author of *Modern English, Poetry in School, The Sentence Method of Teaching Reading, English in the Future,* etc.

KERBY, GERTRUDE. Joint Founder and Honorary Secretary of the Speech Fellowship. Has always been deeply interested in psychology and education, and since 1921 has co-operated with Marjorie Gullan in helping self-expression among school children in very poor districts. Since 1940 has also been engaged in work with Youth Clubs, and social service work generally, with the W.V.S. and L.C.C. Children's Care Committees.

KINGDON-WARD, WINIFRED. Founder Fellow of the College of Speech Therapists. Director of Speech Therapy, West London Hospital. Director of the Speech Department, Maida Vale Hospital for Nervous Diseases. Principal, London Hospitals School of Speech Therapy. Consulting Speech Therapist, West End Hospital for Nervous Diseases. Lecturer in Speech Therapy, 1933-6, to the Fellowship of Medicine (Post Graduate Section). Founder and late Director of the Speech Therapy Training School, West End Hospital for Nervous Diseases, and late Director of Speech Therapy at the same. Formerly Speech Therapist to Bethlem Royal Hospital, and to the Infants' Hospital, and at the Neurological Hospital, Chepstow, under the Ministry of Pensions. Lecturer to the National Union of Teachers, etc. Author of *Stammering: A Contribution to the Study of its Problems and Treatment.* Has contributed to *The Lancet, The Practitioner, The British Journal of Dental Science, The Nursing Mirror,* etc.

KYLE, WILLIAM GALLOWAY. Journalist, lecturer and publisher. Formerly on editorial staff of *North Star, Newcastle Leader* and *Yorkshire Post*. Founder, with Mr. Harold Pease, of the *Northern Counties Magazine* (subsequently the *County Monthly*), *Vision;* and the *Poetry Review*. Founder of the Poetry Recital Society, now the Poetry Society (Incorporated). Many years Honorary Director, organiser of and examiner in verse-speaking for a third of a century. Derives greatest pleasure from reading poetry aloud, and hearing it read. He is a Knight of the Order of the Redeemer (Greece).

LEONA, MARGARET. Professional actress, working in Paris and London, at the Festival Theatre, Cambridge (with Joseph Macleod), at the Gate Theatre, the Grafton, Westminster, Perth Repertory, and the ordinary commercial theatre. Has done a considerable amount of teaching, for the Co-operative movement, Labour Stage, Unity Theatre, Speech Institute, Old Vic, and London Theatre Studio. When war started was appointed C.E.M.A. Adviser of Drama to the National Union of Townswomen's Guilds, and toured all over Britain. Now working at Admiralty; adviser to the N.U.T.G. Teaching and producing at Toynbee Drama School, and wrote *The Wheels Go Round* for production with the students.

LEWIS, M. M., M.A., Ph.D. Vice-Principal, Goldsmiths' College, University of London. Formerly Senior Lecturer in Education, University College, Nottingham. Fellow of the British Psychological Society. Hon. Fellow of the College of Speech Therapists. Member of Council, Incorporated Association of Teachers of Speech and Drama. Author of *Infant Speech* and *Language in School.*

MANVELL, ROGER, M.A., Ph.D. Has spent the larger part of his working life in the British adult education movement, as tutor in literature, drama and the film. He is a graduate and doctor of philosophy of London University, writing his thesis on the poetry and critical works of W. B. Yeats. He had a wide experience in dramatic production with amateurs. Other experience includes broadcasting and radio script-writing, and during the war he was an organiser in the distribution of documentary films. Has lectured on the cinema in many parts of the country, and is the author of the Pelican book, *Film.*

McCONNEL, GORDON. General Instructor in the B.B.C. Staff Training Department. From 1925 (when he joined the B.B.C.) until 1942, was producer and writer of radio material; produced plays, feature programmes, variety, operetta and grand opera. Specialised in studio and microphone technique, concentrating upon the training and coaching of players, speakers and singers in studio work. Began to study voice production and acting in Paris before the last war, went through a two-year general course of training for the stage in London, but his career as an actor had only just begun when he joined up in 1914.

PARROTT, LEONARD GURNEY. Hon. F.R.A.M.. Served in R.A.F. 1919-24. Instructor in Aerial Photography, R.A.F. School of Photography, Farnborough. Joined administrative staff of the Royal Academy of Music, May 1924; appointed Private Secretary to the Principal, 1925; Assistant Secretary, 1926; Assistant to the Principal, 1929; Secretary, 1933; Hon. Fellow, 1944.

PEAR, T. H., M.A., B.Sc. Professor of Psychology, University of Manchester. Author of *Remembering and Forgetting, Fitness for Work, The Art of Study, Skill in Work and Play, Religion and Contemporary Psychology, Voice and Personality, The Psychology of Effective Speaking, The Matured Mind,* and *The Psychology of Conversation.*

PERTWEE, E. GUY, A.R.A.M., F.G.S.M. Chairman of the Poetry Society, Joint Chairman of Elocution and Drama Teacher's Certificate (E.D., D.T.A.). Author of *The Reciter's Treasury,* etc. Adjudicator at principal Festivals. Hon. Speech Director to Staff Association of the G.W.R. Examiner in Speech and Drama for the Guildhall School of Music and Drama.

RATCLIFF, A. J. J., M.A.(Durham). Taught in secondary and public schools; lecturer in a Training College, part-time W.E.A. lecturer. Since 1940, Editor at Nelson's. First book published 1923, *A History of Dreams* (translated by Prof. Otto Francke in Germany). Edited a number of school textbooks, notably *Prose of Our Time,* 1930. Became interested in broadcast discussion groups, 1930. Tutor at B.B.C. Summer Schools; led one of the largest groups in the country. During the war helped with officers' discussion group training schools, Scottish Command. Put forward suggestion that led to the publication of Nelson's Discussion Books under joint editorship with Dr. Richard Wilson. Contributed to the series *The Adult Class* and *The Nature of Dreams.*

REES, ALEXANDER T., Hon. T.C.L. Joined the administrative staff of Trinity College of Music, London, in 1911, and with the exception of military service overseas, 1915-19 (when he was attached to Headquarters Staff of General Officer commanding 16th Corps Heavy Artillery) his association with the College has been continuous since that time In the year 1936 he was appointed Assistant Secretary to the College, and in 1938 to the office of Secretary in succession to the late Mr. C. N. H. Rodwell. In January, 1944, Mr. Rees was elected by the Board to Honorary Membership of the College.

ROWLEY, JOHN DE LA MARE. General Editor, National Institute for the Blind (Braille and Moon Books; Braille Panda Series; 23 newspapers and magazines in Braille and Moon types; Talking Books); Editor of *The New Beacon,* a periodical devoted to the welfare of the blind. Author of *The Passage in Park Lane,* short stories and articles.

ROYDEN, A. MAUDE, C.H., D.D., LL.D. Educated at Cheltenham Ladies' College and Lady Margaret Hall, Oxford. Worked in Liverpool at the Victoria Women's Settlement for some years, and then became lecturer in English literature to the Oxford University Extensions Delegacy. Joined National Union of Women's Suffrage Society (non-militant) in 1908 and was editor of their paper, *The Common Cause,* until 1914. During the first world war was a pacifist, and spent her time in writing and speaking in the cause of pacifism. Became pulpit assistant at the City Temple, London, in 1917; and in 1920, with the late Dr. Percy Dearmer, founded the Fellowship Services at Kensington Town Hall—later transferred to The Guildhouse, Eccleston Square, which with Dr. Royden as its minister carried out a unique work. During 1928 Dr. Royden travelled round the world, visiting the United States, New Zealand, Australia, China, Japan, Singapore, Ceylon and India, speaking and preaching. Made a Companion of Honour in 1930, and received honorary degree of Doctor of Divinity from the University of Glasgow in 1932—an honour only once before given to a woman. In 1936 was made an honorary Doctor of Law by the University of Liverpool. Her books include *Prayer as a Force, The Friendship of God, Political Christianity, Life's Little Pitfalls, Beauty in Religion, Christ Triumphant, I Believe in God, Here—and Hereafter,* and *Sex and Commonsense.*

SANSOM, CLIVE. Teacher's Diploma in English Phonetics, University College, London. First Place, Oxford Festival of Spoken Poetry, 1934. Formerly lecturer in Speech Training at Borough Road Training College, Isleworth. Has also lectured at the Speech Institute, evening schools, and teachers' refresher courses. Festival adjudicator. Examiner in elocution, London Academy of Music and Dramatic Art. Editor of *Good Speech* and the Speech Fellowship *News Letter.* Author of *The Poet Speaks* (with Marjorie Gullan), *Adventures in Words* (with Rodney Bennett), and *Speech Rhymes.* A collection of his poems, *The Unfailing Spring,* was published in 1943, with an introduction by Walter de la Mare

STEIN, LEOPOLD, M.D., F.C.S.T., Physician in Charge of Speech Therapy, Tavistock Clinic, London (Institute of Medical Psychology). Examiner to the Central School of Speech Training and Dramatic Art. Founder Fellow and Member of Council, College of Speech Therapists. Fellow of the Royal Anthropological Institute. Formerly Director of the Speech Departments of the Policlinic and the Institute of Children's Diseases in Vienna. Author of *Speech and Voice; Their Evolution, Pathology and Therapy,* 1942. "The Scope of Speech Pathology," *British Journal of Medical Psychology,* Vol. XIX, 1943; "The Growth and Present State of Speech Therapy," *Medical Press and Circular,* 1942, Nos. 5389 and 5390; "A New Method of Treating Stammering." *The Lancet,* 1941, p. 831. "On Disorders of Articulate Speech," *British Medical Journal,* 1940, Vol. I, pp. 902 ff.

STONE, KATHLEEN, L.R.A.M.(Eloc.), L.G.S.M.(Eloc.), Teachers' Diploma in English Phonetics, University College, London. Has lectured on verse speaking, mime and drama at the Speech Institute, London . Adudicated at Hastings, Exeter, Bristol, Swansea, Dungannon, Ballymena, Gainsborough and other festivals; South Wales Boys and Girls Club Eistedfodd, etc. On examining board of London Academy of Music and Dramatic Art. Formerly on the faculty of Maryville College of the St. Louis University, St. Louis, U.S.A. Conducted class for young Gibraltese women for two years during the war.

THURBURN, GWYNNETH. Principal of the Central School of Speech Training and Dramatic Art. Member of the Advisory Committee of the Diploma in Dramatic Art of London University. Member of the Council of the Incorporated Association of Teachers of Speech and Drama. Has lectured at teachers' courses arranged by the Ministry of Education, and for various education authorities. Author of *Voice and Speech.* Contributor to *Spoken English.* etc.

THOMAS, W. JENKYN, M.A. Councillor of the English Association. Ex-Headmaster of Hackney Downs School. Ex-President of the Incorporated Association of Headmasters. Member of the Middlesex Education Committee.

WHITWORTH, GEOFFREY. On leaving New College, Oxford, he joined the staff of the Burlington Magazine, and a year later was appointed Art Editor to the publishers, Messrs. Chatto & Windus. In 1919 he founded the British Drama League, and later became full-time Director of that organisation. He has published several books on the theatre—notably *The Theatre of My Heart,* a plea for a National Theatre—and is the author of two plays which have been produced not only in this country, but abroad—*Father Noah* and *Haunted Houses.* He is also Honorary Secretary of the Shakespeare Memorial National Theatre Committee, and a Governor of the Shakespeare Memorial Theatre at Stratford-on-Avon.

SUBJECT INDEX

(Where there are several references to the same subject, the main page-numbers are in italics)